MORE FOR YOUR MONEY!

Richard J. Stillman, Ph.D., Syracuse University, is Professor of Management, University of New Orleans. He has taught personal finance and investments at Ohio University, West Point, The George Washington University, Monterey Peninsula College, and in the Armed Forces Educational Program.

Dr. Stillman, a well-respected author in the field of personal finance, has among his most recent books *Guide to Personal Finance: A Lifetime Program of Money Management* (third edition), *Moneywise: The Prentice-Hall Book of Personal Money Management, Personal Finance Guide and Workbook: A Managerial Approach to Successful Household Recordkeeping,* and *Your Personal Financial Planner* (Fall, 1980).

RICHARD J. STILLMAN
MORE FOR YOUR MONEY!

PERSONAL FINANCE TECHNIQUES TO COPE WITH INFLATION & THE ENERGY SHORTAGE

A SPECTRUM BOOK

Prentice-Hall, Inc., Englewood Cliffs, New Jersey 07632

Library of Congress Cataloging in Publication Data

Stillman, Richard Joseph   (date).
  More for your money!

   (A Spectrum Book)
   Published in 1979 under title: Guide to
  personal finance.
   Includes bibliographical references and index.
   1. Finance, personal.   I. Title.
HG179.S84   1980   332.024'02   80-13547
ISBN 0-13-601005-9
ISBN 0-13-600999-9 (pbk.)

1   2   3   4   5   6   7   8   9   10

*Editorial/production supervision
and interior design by Eric Newman
Manufacturing buyer: Barbara A. Frick*

Prentice-Hall International, Inc., *London*
Prentice-Hall of Australia Pty. Limited, *Sydney*
Prentice-Hall of Canada, Ltd., *Toronto*
Prentice-Hall of India Private Limited, *New Delhi*
Prentice-Hall of Japan, Inc., *Tokyo*
Prentice-Hall of Southeast Asia Pte. Ltd., *Singapore*
Whitehall Books Limited, *Wellington, New Zealand*

For my family:

Darlene Ellen
Richard Joseph, II
Kathleen McKinley
Thomas Slater
Ellen Darlene
Helen Fisher
Roy Fisher
Grace Joseph
Philip Joseph
Shannon Marie

CONTENTS

Banks, Savings and Loan Associations,
Credit Unions, Money Market, *183*

Bonds, *202*

The Stock Market, *218*

Real Estate, *238*

Income Tax, *251*

Retirement, Wills, and Trusts, *273*

Index, *297*

PREFACE

The energy shortage and inflation require all of us to take a fresh approach in order to manage our money successfully. The primary purpose of this book is to provide readers with new concepts in order to make sound personal financial decisions.

This book has been derived from my text *Guide to Personal Finance: A Lifetime Program of Money Management. Guide* has been adopted by more than 250 colleges and universities in 46 states and was also a book-club selection. This abbreviated version has been updated and new material included to reflect the impact of inflation and the energy crisis. Each chapter points out actions that readers can take to cope with these two serious problems.[1]

The managerial concept used in this book portrays the reader as a business manager, responsible for all of his or her financial affairs — a systems approach that permeates the entire writing. The view taken is that personal finance is an integrated entity and can best be examined from this perspective. By using this systems approach, each

[1] As a further help, you may wish to obtain my book titled *Your Personal Financial Planner* (Prentice-Hall, Inc., 1980). It includes numerous tables that permit you to see what inflation has done to your dollars in past years, and space is available to plot what you believe will happen in the years ahead. These projections can assist you in arriving at appropriate solutions.

chapter enables the reader to carry forward the main points of previous chapters as part of an integrated whole. The application of this general-systems theory to personal finance is presented in nonquantitative terms. Such an approach provides the reader with realistic information with which to build a sound lifetime program.

This book can be helpful to anyone who wishes to do a better job in handling money. It can also be used as a textbook in schools teaching personal finance or consumer economics and in all classes in which teachers desire to disseminate current information on money management.

ACKNOWLEDGMENTS

I would like to thank a number of organizations and their specialists in the field of personal finance for their assistance — including banks, savings and loan associations, credit unions, insurance companies, real estate firms, brokerage houses, consumer agencies, and departments of the federal government.

I also want to express special appreciation to my family. My wife, Darlene, contributed valuable administrative assistance. Tom and Ellen provided an insight to students' financial interests and problems. Richard, our eldest son, an author and professor at California State, Bakersfield, reviewed the manuscript and offered helpful suggestions.

To Helen and Roy Fisher, I express appreciation for their many years of wise counsel in the financial-management area. Their delightful apartment provided an atmosphere for creative writing.

My associates at the University of New Orleans were most helpful, particularly Dr. John E. Altazan, dean of the College of Business Administration; Dr. Olof Lundberg, chairman of the Management and Marketing Department; and Dr. Walton T. Wilford, chairman of the Economics and Finance Department. Becky Copley has been my indispensable assistant for the past year, and without her this book would have been delayed.

John Hunger, my editor; Eric Newman, my production editor; and Elaine Luthy, my copy editor, also deserve a note of appreciation and thanks for their splendid cooperation.

Finally, in the event that there are errors or shortcomings in this work, the responsibility is mine. Please inform me of needed revisions or modifications for future editions.

MORE
FOR YOUR
MONEY!

The manager has the task of creating a true whole that is larger than the sum of its parts, a productive entity that turns out more than the sum of the resources put into it.

— PETER F. DRUCKER

HOW TO DEVELOP YOUR PERSONAL FINANCE PROGRAM

What is personal finance? In my view, it is the development and implementation of a sound money management program tailored to meet your objectives. Achievement of these objectives requires an understanding of all investment resources and their interrelationships. It also calls for a knowledge of a sound spending program, since 95 percent or more of today's average budget goes toward the purchasing of goods and services.

The know-how needed for effective financial planning can best be acquired by using a management approach. The old approaches to personal finance may be challenged in view of the current dynamic changes in our society — social, political, military, economic, and technological.

IMPACT OF INFLATION

During the depression of the 1930s a prominent advertisement spoke of "How to Retire on $100 a Month." In the intervening years this sum increased to $200, $300, and now $900 per month. What might it be in the year 2000?

The obvious point is that inflation is eroding the value of the dollar, so that each year it takes more to buy the same items. In the

1

winter of 1979-80, the erosion amounted to more than 16 percent a year. People who placed the bulk of their savings in insurance annuities during the period 1930-1979 found that their dollars had shrunk in value by as much as 78 percent. And it does little good to invest the majority of your earnings in a savings institution at 5¼ percent because, without even taking taxes into consideration, the current rate of erosion means that your savings are actually decreasing in value by about 8 percent each year.

The marked loss in the purchasing power of the dollar is apparent from a look at the Consumer Price Index (CPI) for the period 1951-1979 (Figure 1-1). This index, prepared by the U.S. Department of Labor, can be helpful in keeping track of inflation. The CPI is defined as a statistical measure of change, over time, in the prices

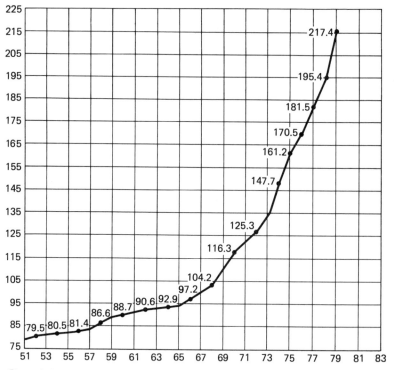

Figure 1-1. The Rise in the Cost of Living from 1951 to 1979. Note the sharp rise since 1967 in contrast to earlier years. From 1951 to 1967 the CPI rose 22.2 percent, but between 1967 and 1979 it rose 117.4 percent. The yearly CPI used in this chart is based on the average for each year and not the year-end CPI. (Source: *Monthly Labor Review*, U.S. Department of Labor, Bureau of Labor Statistics.)

Table 1-1. Consumer Price Index, All Items, 1951-1979.

Year	Index	Percent Change
1951	77.8	7.9
1952	79.5	2.2
1953	80.1	.8
1954	80.5	.5
1955	80.2	-.4
1956	81.4	1.5
1957	84.3	3.6
1958	86.6	2.7
1959	87.3	.8
1960	88.7	1.6
1961	89.6	1.0
1962	90.6	1.1
1963	91.7	1.2
1964	92.9	1.3
1965	94.5	1.7
1966	97.2	2.9
1967	100.0	2.9
1968	104.2	4.2
1969	109.8	5.4
1970	116.3	5.9
1971	121.3	4.3
1972	125.3	3.3
1973	133.1	6.2
1974	147.7	11.0
1975	161.2	9.1
1976	170.5	5.8
1977	181.5	6.5
1978	195.4	7.7
1979	217.4	11.3

Source: *Monthly Labor Review*, U.S. Department of Labor, Bureau of Labor Statistics.

of goods and services in major expenditure groups — such as food, housing, apparel, transportation, and health and recreation — typically purchased by urban consumers.[1] Each of the major groups of goods and services will be examined in the course of this book with emphasis on how to get the most from every dollar spent in these areas.

In 1979, the CPI was 11.3 percent higher than in 1978. This was a larger increase than that for the 1974-1975 period and very sizable if compared with other years since 1951 (see Table 1-1). The first

[1] U.S. Department of Labor, U.S. Government Printing Office, Washington, D.C., *The Consumer Price Index*, rev. ed. (1978), p. 1. The CPI was revised effective with the January 1978 index to reflect substantial changes in what Americans buy and the way they live. The Bureau of Labor Statistics (BLS), Department of Labor, now publishes (1) a revised *CPI for Urban Wage Earners and Clerical Workers*, and (2) a new *CPI for All Urban Consumers*.

3

months of 1980 found very substantial consumer price increases. This was apparent from the fact that the CPI shot up an annual rate of over 16 percent for this period.

During World War II, many people bought 25-year U.S. Treasury bonds at 2½ percent interest per annum. These people took a terrible beating in terms of low interest received over the years; and if the bonds were sold prior to maturity, they often suffered considerable loss of principal. Yet, in terms of so-called safety, Treasury bonds had been given the highest rating. This book will question the old standards. It will suggest new means to keep pace with our fast-changing society.

THE ENERGY SHORTAGE

The need for effective money management is greater than ever today due to the eroding effects of inflation and the energy crisis. As William Simon said on national television during his term as Federal Energy Administrator, "We must learn to change our life-style." He went on to point out that the energy shortage facing the United States will have an impact on the lives of all Americans in the coming decade. Furthermore, President Carter recently informed the nation that the energy shortage "is the greatest challenge that our country will face during our lifetime."

The energy shortage has already taken its toll on our tempers and pocketbooks. We can all remember the rising cost and frustration involved in obtaining gas in 1974, when the Arabs reduced their supplies and increased prices fourfold. Since that date, oil prices have continued to rise markedly. The overthrow of the Shah of Iran in 1978 and unsettled conditions in the Middle East have pushed gas prices to over $1.50 per gallon. The result has been a change in our transportation habits. Consumers have turned to smaller cars that provide better mileage. Manufacturers, too, are looking at means of further increasing mileage, as well as at alternative forms of power, such as electricity, diesel, and steam. The U.S. government reduced the speed limit to 55 miles per hour and increased its efforts to improve mass transportation, while encouraging citizens to form driver pools and make greater use of presently available public transportation. The federal government is also providing the public with helpful information in the conservation field. An example of this trend is the Environmental Protection Agency's annual reports on gas mileage for a variety of cars.

We clearly need new guidelines to help us keep pace with these and other changes. It is essential to remember, for example, that most of your money should be placed where it has the potential to increase at a rate faster than the loss in the purchasing power of the dollar. This means investing a good share of your funds in areas in which your principal has a chance to grow — areas such as owning your home, and investing in stocks, land, and housing. To acquire adequate funds for this purpose, it is wise to use successful money-management concepts.

Successful money management requires a certain amount of work. There is no magic formula for turning your income into a sizable nest egg while you lie in a hammock. Of course, there is always the element of luck — but it pays to court the lady.

PERSONAL FINANCE MODEL

For an overview of the approach presented in this book, let us discuss the personal finance model shown in Figure 1-2. Visualize yourself as a manager responsible for all of your personal financial affairs. As your own money manager, you must consider five major components of the model: objective, personal finance topics, resources or educational tools, functions to be performed, and the decision-making process.

Objective

You must establish your own long-range personal finance goal. Perhaps it is to become a millionaire and enjoy "good living" in the process. This has been a popular objective in my classes, and Figure 1-3 indicates how time can work to the advantage of the young in achieving this nest egg of over $1 million.

How would you go about accumulating that amount? One approach would be to invest the sums in Table 1-2 at a return of 10 percent compounded annually.

In this concept you would set aside $1,000 in each of the first five years. This amount would be increased by $500 in each succeeding five-year increment. Thus, in the second five years (6–10) you would put aside $1,500 annually, and in the final years (41–43) you would be setting aside $5,000 annually.

The assumption in this program is that the higher your salary through the years, the more you will save. Another assumption is that you can obtain a 10 percent annual return. The *super* magic of 10 percent compounded interest, increasing savings, and the impor-

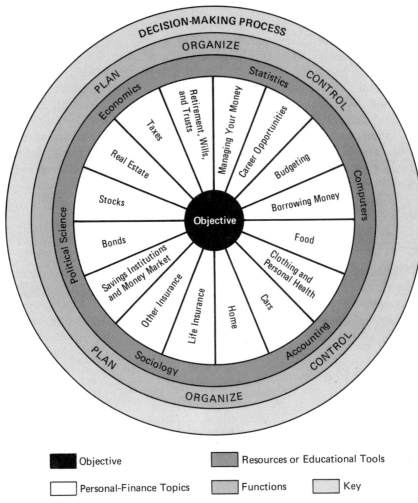

Figure 1-2. A Graphic Overview of the Five Major Components of Personal Finance from a Managerial Perspective.

tance of time in obtaining a sizable retirement nest egg of over $1 million is portrayed in Figure 1-3.

On the other hand, in contrast to making a sizable fortune, you may wish to set a modest financial goal and devote your life to public service. Perhaps you desire only enough savings to educate your children and leave a charitable contribution. In such a situation, it is equally important to determine your objective and decide how best to achieve it. Otherwise, you may spend much unnecessary time on your personal money problems.

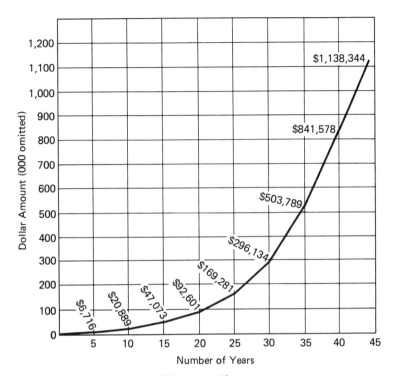

Figure 1-3. How to Become a Millionaire in 43 years.

Table 1-2. Investment Program.

Years	Dollars Invested Each Year[a]	Cumulative Dollars Invested Each 5-Year Period[b]
1-5	$1,000	$ 5,000
6-10	1,500	7,500
11-15	2,000	10,000
16-20	2,500	12,500
21-25	3,000	15,000
26-30	3,500	17,500
31-35	4,000	20,000
36-40	4,500	22,500
41-43	5,000	15,000
Grand Total		$125,000

[a]It is assumed that all dividends and interest are reinvested and payment of income taxes is made from other earnings.
[b]Only three years included in the 41-43 period in this program.

Personal Finance Topics

Once your personal finance goal is established, it is necessary to determine what areas of endeavor are available to help you achieve it. Those listed in the model (Figure 1-2) may be classified into the 16 topics discussed in this book: managing your money; career opportunities; budgeting; borrowing money; food; clothing and personal health; cars; home; life insurance; other insurance; savings institutions and money market; bonds; stocks; real estate; taxes; retirement, wills and trusts. An understanding of each of these topics will help you to make sound decisions in regard to earnings, spending, saving, investing, protecting, and — alas — leaving your money.

Educational Experience

Now that we have established our objective and listed the personal finance topics, let us turn to the third ring portrayed in Figure 1-2. The field of personal finance draws upon your educational experience. As a manager taking responsibility for your personal finances, you must use your educational tools in order to meet your objective. Significant areas that can be of much value include political science, economics, statistics, sociology, accounting, and computer technology.

The turbulence in our world today and the prospect for the greater turbulence tomorrow play a significant role in relation to your personal finance program. Undoubtedly, an understanding of the political and social ramifications will be helpful in arriving at your financial decisions.

Computers, too, will play an ever increasing role in money management. One class utilized the university computer in developing a "New Orleans Industrial Average" derived from local issues. This facility, because of its speed and accuracy, permitted our analyzing a far greater amount of statistical data than would otherwise have been possible. You may find it helpful in the world of tomorrow to have a low-cost minicomputer assist you in your own program. Time is money, and the less time you devote to personal finance, the more you will have available for other activities.

Accounting and statistics can be of assistance in analyzing various investment media and in preparation of that yearly income tax return.

Functions

Managing your personal finances effectively requires the performance of functions comparable to those in the managing of any other

8

activity — be it a small business, a school, or a large government agency. As presented in Figure 1-2, the three major functions are (1) plan what you are going to do, (2) do what you plan, and (3) check what you have done.

Decision-Making Process

The final ring portrayed in Figure 1-2 is the decision-making process. This is the key to successful money management. In arriving at your major personal finance decisions, keep these questions in mind:

1. What is your objective?
2. Do you have the necessary facts to make a sound decision?
3. What are the alternatives?
4. Have you chosen the most profitable alternative?

The personal finance model can assist you in arriving at your decision. For example, assume that your objective is to buy the cheapest form of transportation — a reliable vehicle for school, travel, and your first job after graduation. You should give appropriate attention to prepurchase planning about such items as costs, service, condition, compact or standard, foreign or domestic, where to buy, testing, and impact of inflation and the energy crisis. This planning effort will require the use of certain educational tools — economic considerations, compiling of statistical data, and basic accounting. The result of the analysis should be the selection of adequate transportation at a fair price. (See Chapter 7 for a detailed discussion on cars.)

GUIDELINES

You may also wish to give consideration to the following guidelines in arriving at your personal finance decisions. These points are highlighted throughout the book.

1. Time is a valuable commodity; employ it to your advantage. Figure 1-3 illustrates one aspect of its importance. A management approach to personal finance also minimizes time spent on money matters.

2. Be flexible and imaginative. In our dynamic society, have a program attuned to the times. Do not sacrifice vision and bold decisions for the rigidity often characteristic of an "organization man."

3. Within this climate of flexibility, develop a long-term plan, imple-

ment the plan, and check to see that it is being accomplished. Have a cradle-to-grave approach, with adequate provisions for after your departure.

4. Make your personal finance program a family affair. It is usually the husband who provides and the wife who survives; in any case, both should understand the program.

5. Go first class. If the higher-priced item is of better quality, it will cost less in the long run and give greater satisfaction.

6. Get out of debt and stay out of debt — with few exceptions. Why pay credit charges of 18 to 42 percent or higher? You can normally earn only 5 to 15 percent on your money, so why make the other person rich by paying such a high return?

7. Minimize your costs and maximize your returns. Eliminate the middleman wherever possible. If you can buy through a reputable discount house at 20 to 40 percent off list prices, why not take advantage of it?

8. Deal only with reputable people who have a good track record of achievement. There are many honorable firms that have been successful. Patronize those companies that stand behind their products.

9. Keep your money working for you at all times; you work hard for it. Keep in mind how banks employ their money; ask a bank manager what happens if she fails to invest her excess funds daily.

10. Place the majority of your funds in growth situations. Growth opportunities may present themselves in strange packages. For example, 9 to 13 percent bond offerings in 1979 provided both a high yield and capital gains potential. Gold could have been purchased in 1979 for resale a few weeks later at a sizable profit.

11. Develop a profitable hobby. It provides a delightful way to spend your leisure time — particularly if you make it a family affair.

12. Capitalize on your experience. It worked for people like Billie Jean King, Mark Spitz, Bill Russell, Bobby Riggs, John Glenn, Joe Namath, and Bruce Jenner. They turned to writing books, going into politics or business, and so on. You may not achieve their prominence, but you can capitalize on your own personal knowledge. Even professors capitalize by publishing texts, acting as consultants, and conducting finance and management programs. As you go through life, there will be ample opportunity to acquire expertise — don't be afraid to take advantage of it.

13. Maximize after-tax dollars in your pocket. If you are in the 40 percent federal tax bracket, it may be better for you to buy a 5½

percent prime municipal bond in lieu of a comparably rated 13 percent corporate bond. A $1,000 municipal, for example, would provide an annual return of $70, whereas the corporate bond would leave you with only $65 after payment of your federal income tax.

14. Timing is important. It applies to such areas as grocery store shopping, buying and selling securities, and purchasing an automobile. For example, buy food when there are weekend specials, cars when sizable discounts are offered, and stocks in periods of recession.

15. It helps to be in good physical and mental condition. Taking care of yourself permits better management and greater enjoyment from the monetary rewards. Furthermore, replacements for parts are difficult to come by.

16. The energy shortage will increase in the years ahead. Prior to making an important financial decision, you should have the necessary facts on energy costs and future projections. For example, before building a new home you should estimate costs for heating and cooling with gas, electricity, and solar energy.

17. Inflation must be carefully weighed in arriving at all important personal finance decisions. For example, in selecting a job you should find out if annual cost-of-living increases are provided and if retirement benefits have an escalation clause.

18. An understanding of the American way of life is a cornerstone of the personal finance program. The democratic environment with a free enterprise system provides a fertile climate for financial success, and this is the framework within which you will be working.

19. *Have faith in yourself!* Be willing to work your way to financial success. The American way of life provides the opportunity but *you* must supply the determination. This determination is expressed well in the following anonymous poem I read as a young man:

IT'S ALL IN THE STATE OF MIND

If you think you are beaten, you are,
If you think you dare not, you don't;
If you like to win, but you think you can't
It's almost a cinch you won't.
If you think you'll lose, you've lost,
For out in the world you find
Success begins with a fellow's will;
It's all in the state of mind.
Full many a race is lost
Ere ever a step is run;

And many a coward fails
Ere ever his work's begun.
Think big and your deeds will grow,
Think small and you'll fall behind,
Think that you can and you will;
It's all in the state of mind.
If you think you're outclassed, you are;
You've got to think high to rise;
You've got to be sure of yourself before
You can ever win a prize.
Life's battles don't always go
To the stronger or faster man,
But sooner or later the man who wins
IS THE FELLOW WHO THINKS HE CAN.

ORGANIZATION

How do you organize to manage your money effectively? One approach, as I have said, is to consider yourself a business manager responsible for your personal finance matters. We have portrayed this in a chart (Figure 1-4). Let us look at the various blocks in the organization, beginning with the one at the top.

If you are a bachelor or a single woman, there is not any question of who is the boss. But marriage may present a different story. I indicated that one of the guidelines is to make personal finance a family affair. Accordingly, you may wish to have co-presidents rather than the arrangement in the chart. You and your spouse will have to make this decision first, and I wish you luck.

Let us assume that you either remain single or have resolved the leadership problem and can turn your attention to what you have to manage in regard to personal finances. For most college students, it is precious little — so this is the ideal time to develop your organizational system as portrayed in Figure 1-4. Let me stress that such an approach should be flexible. To begin with, you should have a workable filing system. This can be very helpful as you face up to the annual income tax demands from the state and federal governments. Monthly bills also appear all too frequently, and late payments mean an unhealthy penalty charge.

In the chart the filing section is shown enclosed in a solid line to indicate it is open for business — bills and other financial records are an immediate responsibility. In this hypothetical organization chart,

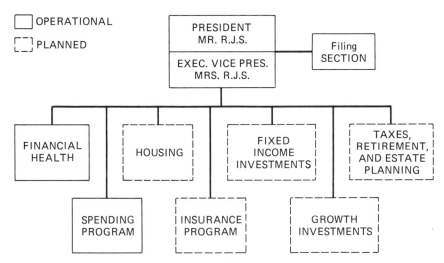

Figure 1-4. A Hypothetical Organization to Manage a Personal-Finance Program.

broken lines indicate those functions that can be activated as you need them. The figure portrays seven major divisions. The first, financial health, is shown within solid lines, because it provides a solid foundation for other personal finance activities (Chapters 1-4). The second, spending program, is also shown within solid lines, as it too is an immediate responsibility. It would include such expenditures as food, cars, clothing, and personal health (Chapters 5-7). The five other major elements in the organization—housing (Chapter 8), insurance (Chapters 9-10), fixed income investments (Chapters 11-12), growth investments (Chapters 13-14), and taxes, retirement, and estate planning (Chapters 15-16)—can be activated as required.

You might begin your personal finance enterprise with little more than the clothes on your back and a fair-sized debt as you receive your degree. Perhaps your parents have lent you a family car and paid the insurance. Or your first job may permit you to buy that dream sports car, and this means you will need insurance protection. Also, an apartment of your own can become a necessity. So at this point, you could activate two other divisions—housing and insurance. After the first year, you might be debt free and ready to look at the investment areas. There is also the annual mid-April federal income tax responsibility, and perhaps the investment fever beckons you to look at the stock market. Thus your personal finance organization could be completely operational within one year. In succeeding chapters we shall discuss each area.

13

ACTIONS YOU CAN TAKE TO COPE WITH INFLATION AND THE ENERGY SHORTAGE

1. Support political leaders who favor measures to conserve energy and reduce inflation. These measures should include massive cuts in wasteful local, state, and federal spending with a goal of achieving balanced budgets. After all, individuals (or families) can be superb money managers and still have their lifetime savings melt away as a result of unsound financial management by government officials. Actions to reduce the high inflation rate and excessive energy usage should apply in both their official duties and personal habits. President Carter, in a 1979 press briefing,[2] was asked, "What steps have you taken to conserve energy?" He replied, "We are regulating our thermostat to conserve in both the winter and summer; cars for the executives have been reduced in size; solar heat is being installed in the White House; and we plan to travel less."

2. Think small. Whatever you plan to buy, you might consider the slogan "smaller is better." If you plan to buy a house, minimize the square footage and maximize the available living space. If you plan to buy a car, the smaller size may be the wiser purchase. Cadillac, for example, reduced the weight of its Eldorado model for 1979 by 1,000 pounds to provide better gas mileage. What will the resale value of gas guzzlers be in the years ahead?

3. Review the four questions in the decision-making process in arriving at every major money-management decision.

4. Use appropriate management guidelines. Give particular attention to items 16 and 17.

5. Keep the inflation chart (Figure 1-1) current and plot your own efforts to keep pace with inflation, using information in the later chapters.

6. List the energy-conservation measures you plan to take next month and in the years ahead.

SUMMARY

How do you successfully manage your money in this era of inflation and the energy shortage? The basic theme of this book is that to be most successful in managing your money you should consider all

---

[2] White House, April 10, 1979, New York Times, April 11, 1979, p. 4.

legitimate sources of *investing* in order to arrive at the best program for yourself and your family. This concept also requires that you establish and maintain a sound *spending* program. After all, a major part of the average budget consists of expendable items such as food, rent, recreation, taxes, medical bills, interest on loans, and vacations. In some cases over 95 percent of the budget is spent on items that have a short dollar life with less than 15 percent going to acquiring capital. Therefore, important expenditures, as well as important sources of savings, will be discussed in future chapters. In addition to spending and investing money wisely, it is important to be familiar with the topics of *earning* (job opportunities), *protecting* (insuring), and *leaving* (estate planning) money.

This total approach to your personal finances can best be achieved by utilizing sound management principles. Chapter 1 has presented my concept of money management. Each succeeding chapter will look at a specific aspect of personal finance and point out its place (interrelationship) in the complete money management program. In this manner, every aspect of personal finance is given appropriate consideration. You should refer to the personal finance model (Figure 1-2) as you read each chapter, for it portrays this total money management approach.

In order that people may be happy in their work, these three things are needed: They must be fit for it. They must not do too much of it. And they must have a sense of success in it.

—JOHN RUSKIN

CAREER OPPORTUNITIES: HOW TO ACQUIRE MONEY

Today's college graduate can expect to earn between $800,000 and $2 million in his or her lifetime. That is a lot of money. This chapter will provide background information that may be helpful in selecting the job best suited to your values and goals. I would like to emphasize the interrelationship of this chapter on earning a livelihood to the other topics in the book. Earnings, for example, appears in the budget. The salary from your job also determines your spending patterns as well as housing, insurance needs, investment program, taxes, retirement, and estate planning. In addition, an understanding of the management concept and borrowing can assist you in using your earnings to your best advantage. Thus, in making a decision on matters relating to earnings you should take into consideration the other areas of personal finance.

HOW TO OBTAIN MONEY

There are a number of legitimate ways to acquire money. As pointed out in the money flow chart (Figure 2-1), it can be obtained by jobs, gifts, loans, payments from wills and trusts, insurance benefits, unemployment compensation, retirement pensions, Social Security,

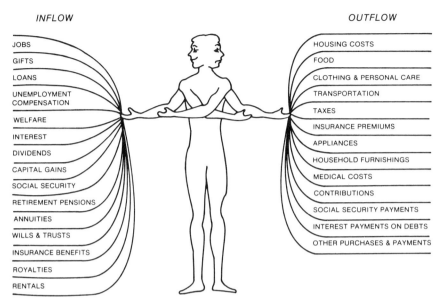

INFLOW	OUTFLOW
JOBS	HOUSING COSTS
GIFTS	FOOD
LOANS	CLOTHING & PERSONAL CARE
UNEMPLOYMENT COMPENSATION	TRANSPORTATION
WELFARE	TAXES
INTEREST	INSURANCE PREMIUMS
DIVIDENDS	APPLIANCES
CAPITAL GAINS	HOUSEHOLD FURNISHINGS
SOCIAL SECURITY	MEDICAL COSTS
RETIREMENT PENSIONS	CONTRIBUTIONS
ANNUITIES	SOCIAL SECURITY PAYMENTS
WILLS & TRUSTS	INTEREST PAYMENTS ON DEBTS
INSURANCE BENEFITS	OTHER PURCHASES & PAYMENTS
ROYALTIES	
RENTALS	

Figure 2-1. Money Flow Chart.

welfare, interest, dividends, royalties, annuities, rentals, and capital gains. However, the most important way most people get money is via a job. Such benefits as Social Security, retirement pensions, and unemployment compensation are paid based upon having had a job.

MANAGEMENT APPROACH

As emphasized throughout this book, it is helpful to take a management approach in order to obtain the best available job for you. This requires adequate planning, implementing your plan, and checking to see that the job considered meets your expectations.

The initial step in the decision-making process would be to list your objective as discussed in Chapter 1. Next you should obtain adequate information (facts) on the job market. (Some of this material will be discussed in this chapter.) Once you obtain the facts, you can proceed to examine the alternatives. And from the alternatives you can make a sound decision. This concept applies to both part-time jobs and your permanent position. Very often your college placement office can provide helpful information on how to get a job. Help might include information on how to prepare a résumé, where to obtain background on various firms, and how to take advantage of campus visits by organizations seeking to interview prospective employees.

FACTORS INFLUENCING EARNINGS

Education, skills, desire, whom one knows, location, sex, color, number of working years, and timing all affect the amount of money a person will earn in a lifetime. In succeeding sections we shall examine how to utilize properly the large amount of money received from working and other sources. Our concern here is with the factors that influence getting a job.

Education

A basic premise of this text is that it is relatively easy to be moderately successful today, thanks to our abundant society in the United States. By "moderately successful," I mean that a person who is a college graduate can generally obtain a position that will pay the going rate for the field he or she enters, with promotions to follow, commensurate with the average progress of one's classmates. The dollar value of education is apparent from Table 2-1. Income for males with twelve years of schooling amounts to $13,299, against only $8,829 for males with less than an eighth-grade education. However, by spending five or more years in college the male salaries increased 55 percent to $20,582. Although females with more education likewise received higher salaries, the dollar amount is far less than that for men. Recent federal legislation, unions, and women's consciousness movements have improved the situation. These continuing efforts, coupled with the work of such women as Billie Jean King,

Table 2-1. Average Annual Income of Full-Time Workers in the United States Age 25 and Over (as of March 1975).

Years of Schooling Completed	Income	
	Males	*Females*
Less than 8	$ 8,829	5,048
8	10,334	5,915
9–11	11,751	6,373
12	13,299	7,399
13–15	15,134	8,460
16	18,011	9,975
17 or more	20,582	11,962

Source: U.S. Department of Commerce, Bureau of the Census, *Current Population Reports,* 1976, Series P-60, No. 101, pp. 116, 120.

Barbara Jordan, and Barbara Walters, will seek to reduce this inequity in the future. In some areas today — the military, government civil service, and professional entertainment — opportunities for men and women are relatively equal.

Occupational Pay Scales

When considering how you should earn your living and what job field to enter, you should investigate the pay offered in various occupations. Table 2-2 points out that self-employed male physicians and surgeons rank at the top of the list of earners with a $41,116 annual income. In contrast, female private household workers receive $3,017. Other high incomes are earned by self-employed men (other than physicians and surgeons), $22,548; male salaried engineers, $17,821; male managers, $17,280; and male craftsmen $14,995.

It is apparent from a study of Table 2-2 that a college education is required in all but two areas — the crafts and the self-employed. So, if you do not intend to graduate from college, you might consider, from a money point of view, becoming a craftsperson or going into business for yourself. There are risks however, in going into business for yourself; 30 percent or more of all small businesses fail each year. And to achieve a skill in a craft normally requires technical training and on-the-job apprenticeship.

Although education has generally been the path to higher earnings, we are seeing changes in its dollar rewards. The virtue of a relatively free enterprise system in the United States results in people being paid based upon the demand for their services. Superathletes and movie and TV stars, for example, command high salaries because it is they who attract the buyers and thus make money for their sponsors or owners. Likewise, if the vast majority of Americans have a college education and seek white-collar jobs, the market for such jobs will be flooded; in contrast, there will be a shortage of people to do the so-called blue-collar work, and this work then will command higher wages in order to attract the necessary number of people.

A study in one community revealed the following facts regarding annual salaries of individuals of 21 to 25 years of age:

Position	Salary
Management position for a college graduate with a large retail department store	$ 9,400
Salesman trainee, a college graduate, for a drug firm	9,900
Bus driver	11,300
Garbage collector	12,900
Plumber	13,500
Carpenter	15,700

Table 2-2. Pay of Various Full-Time Workers in the United States (as of March 1975).

Occupation	Male	Female
Professional, technical, and kindred workers, total	16,679	9,739
Self-employed, total	25,537	a
Physicians and surgeons	41,116	a
Other self-employed	22,548	a
Salaried, total	15,908	9,805
Engineers, technical	17,821	a
Physicians and surgeons	28,215	a
Teachers, primary and secondary schools	12,559	9,656
Other salaried workers	15,620	9,841
Farmers and farm managers	7,809	a
Managers and administrators, Excluding Farm, total	17,280	8,843
Self-employed, total	13,674	5,631
In retail trade	12,792	5,897
Other self-employed	14,676	a
Salaried	18,062	9,470
Clerical and kindred workers, total	11,397	6,968
Secretaries, stenos, and typists	a	7,034
Other clerical and kindred workers	11,395	6,925
Sales workers, total	13,942	6,158
In retail trade	10,381	5,380
Other sales workers	15,532	8,425
Craft and kindred workers, total	11,995	6,824
Blue-collar workers, supervisors	13,718	7,573
Craft workers	11,697	6,489
In construction	12,092	a
Other craft workers	11,597	6,388
Operatives, including transport, total	10,153	5,892
Manufacturing, total	10,115	6,066
Durable	10,280	6,572
Nondurable	9,744	5,616
Other operatives and kindred workers	10,200	4,910
Private household workers	a	3,017
Service workers, excluding private household	9,136	5,081
Farm laborers and supervisors	5,559	a
Laborers, excluding farm	8,312	6,295

[a]Base less than 75,000.

Source: U.S. Department of Commerce, Bureau of the Census, *Current Population Reports*, January 1976, Series P-60, No. 101, pp. 131–133.

In addition to the shift in payments based upon education, there has been a reduction in the money spread between different levels of responsibility. For example, in the civilian sector of the federal government there have been marked increases at the lower levels, whereas the top grades are not comparable to salaries in major corpor-

Table 2-3. Pay of Officers in the U.S. Armed Forces as of October 1, 1978.

Pay Grade	Title	Years													
		Under 2	2	3	4	6	8	10	12	14	16	18	20	22	26
	Commissioned Officers														
O-10	General (Admiral)												4364	—	4635
O-9	Lt. General (Vice Admiral)												3817	—	4090
O-8	Major General (Rear Admiral)										3272	3414	3545	3687	—
O-7	Brig. General (Commodore[a])									2727	3000	3206	—	—	—
O-6	Colonel (Captain)									1973	2286	2403	2455	2598	2817
O-5	Lt. Colonel (Commander)							1687	1777	1896	2039	2156	2221	2298	—
O-4	Major (Lt. Commander)	1100	1338	1428	—	1454	1519	1622	1714	1792	1870	1922			
O-3	Captain (Lieutenant)	1022	1142	1221	1351	1415	1467	1545	1622	1662	—	—			
O-2	1st Lieut. (Lieut. J.G.)	891	973	1169	1208	1233	—	—							
O-1	2nd Lieut. (Ensign)	773	805	973	—	—									
	Commissioned Officers With More Than 4 Years of Active Service as Enlisted Persons														
O-3					1351	1415	1467	1545	1622	1687					
O-2					1208	1233	1272	1338	1390	1428					
O-1					973	1039	1078	1117	1158	1208					

[a]A wartime rank only. In peacetime the Navy equivalent paywise to Brig. General is a Rear Admiral (lower half).

Source: U.S. Department of Defense release, Washington, D.C., November, 1978.

Table 2-4. Starting Salaries for Selected Classes, Harvard Business School, 1929–1979.

Class	Median Starting Salary
1929	$ 1,820
1932	1,400
1939	1,800
1942	2,950
1949	3,602
1952	4,416
1957	6,300
1959	6,600
1962	8,000
1964	9,000
1968	12,500
1969	14,000
1973	17,000
1977	22,000
1978	24,000
1979	28,000

Source: Harvard Business School.

ations. In 1942, a college graduate might have started as a GS-5 and received $2,000 per annum. Currently a GS-5 is paid over $10,000.

In the U.S. Armed Forces there have been sizable pay increases in the lower ranks in order to obtain the required number of men and women in the all-volunteer Army, Navy, Air Force, and Marine Corps (and also to keep pace with inflation). An individual with a college degree can enter service as a second lieutenant and receive an annual salary of $10,276. (See Table 2-3 for the salary and other allowances of all commissioned officers).

In 1942 a newly commissioned second lieutenant received $150 per month in contrast to the present $773 — a 515 percent increase. What will the young officer receive upon graduation in 2014? A colonel with over 30 years service in 1942 received $500 a month. In 1978 he or she received $2,817. What will a colonel's base pay be in 2014?

The sizable increases in salaries in all areas over the years is also apparent from a look at Table 2-4. Starting salaries of Harvard Business School graduates have increased from $2,950 in 1942 to $28,000 in 1979. This is a 949 percent rise.

Financial Benefits Other Than Salary

Pay, however, is only one of the financial factors to consider in job selection. Early retirement may be important to you. A young man

Table 2-5. Salary and Other Benefits of Companies as of ＿＿＿＿ 19 ＿＿.

	A	B	C	D	E
Annual salary					
Bonus (cash and/or stock)					
Car					
Club membership					
Cost-of-living increases					
Credit union					
Discount buying facilities					
Educational payments					
Expense account					
Home purchase and/or sales assistance					
Incentive awards					
Insurance, accident					
Insurance, dental					
Insurance, family					
Insurance, life					
Insurance, medical					
Insurance, unemployment					
Loans from company					
Maternity leave					
Military leave					
Moving expenses					
Overtime pay					
Pension					
Personal financial and estate counseling					
Profit sharing					
Savings program — employer contributes					
Sick leave					
Social Security					
Stock purchase					
Travel allowance					
Union coverage					
Vacations, paid					
Other					
Total Salary	$ ＿＿＿＿				
Total Other Benefits	$ ＿＿＿＿				
Total Compensation	$ ＿＿＿＿				

or woman, for example, may enter the military as a commissioned officer at 21 years of age and receive 50 percent of base pay at the end of 20 years. This would amount to $14,730 annually for a colonel who retires today. In addition, this person would receive for life other privileges, such as free medical care, use of officer clubs, and shopping at commissaries and exchanges at savings of 20 to 30 percent on food, clothing, appliances, and similar purchases.

As for benefits other than salary and early retirement, there are a sizable list of "goodies" being offered by various firms to prospective employees. Prior to accepting a position with a company, you should learn what benefits it offers. To evaluate these in money terms, you may wish to use the format of Table 2-5. By placing a dollar value on each of the various other benefits, you can arrive at the total compensation offered by each company. The benefits may include a bonus, car, club membership, expense account, incentive awards, insurance, and maternity leave. A former student commented how helpful it was to select a company with a fine health protection program: "I was married while in college. Shortly after I went to work my wife had to have a major operation. Fortunately, my company paid all expenses. Otherwise, it would have cost me over $24,000."[1] You must decide what forms of compensation are important to you, and then select the job that will best provide these — presuming, of course, that all other aspects of the jobs you are considering are equal.

JOB OPPORTUNITIES

The most complete information about job opportunities can be found in the current edition of *Occupational Outlook Handbook* prepared by the Bureau of Labor Statistics (BLS). It is usually available in school and community libraries. It is a good reference to own, and it can be purchased from the Superintendent of Documents, U.S. Government Printing Office, Washington, D.C., 20402. The 1978–1979 edition costs $8.00 (paper cover). The *Handbook* provides data on 35 industries in several hundred occupations.

The BLS also publishes a valuable magazine every three months entitled *Occupational Outlook Quarterly*. It has many helpful articles for those seeking employment.

Another valuable source of information is the *College Placement Annual.* The 1978 edition included occupational needs anticipated by approximately 1,300 corporate and governmental employers who normally recruit college graduates. The current *Annual* also provides excellent advice on such topics as: Studying Yourself; Collecting Information; Preparing Strategy; Conducting Interviews; Graduate School?; Off to a Good Start; Look Before You Leap; Are You Ready for Separation?; The Principles and Practices of College Career

---

[1] Information on the value of health insurance coverage will be presented in Chapter 9.

Planning, Placement, and Recruitment. The importance of doing a good research job is emphasized in the *Annual*. A splendid checklist is included that is titled "Job Search Barometer."

A third source of information on jobs available is newspapers and professional journals. The Sunday edition of *The New York Times* has pages of job offerings as do all other large city Sunday newspapers.

Jobs can also be obtained through placement agencies. Their advertisements appear in newspapers. All private organizations charge a fee for their services — either paid by the employee or the employer. State employment offices, however, provide their services free.

Whatever sources you use, don't forget that some of the most valuable information about job opportunities can be obtained from individuals who are currently working in occupations that may interest you. For example, I spoke recently with two highly respected New Orleans dermatologists about what advice they would give a student considering a career in medicine with specialization in dermatology. Their comments were as follows:

You should first determine if your values and goals indicate a strong preference for becoming a physician. It may be helpful to take an aptitude test to support your position. Likewise, your scholastic and financial capabilities must be considered — do you have the mental capacity and money to make it?

Perhaps this is a field that you are considering. In arriving at your decision, you should realize the time required to become a dermatologist is normally an arduous twelve years: four years of undergraduate schooling, in which it is essential to make good grades;[2] four years in medical school; one year of general training; and three years of specialized training in dermatology in order to be eligible to take qualifying board examinations. On passing the oral and written exams, you are eligible to receive your certification from the American Board of Dermatology.[3] A practicing successful dermatologist made the following statement to an aspiring dermatologist:

I must emphasize, that to become a dermatologist you must sacrifice many good times in your twenties in order to make it.

---

[2] In 1978, over 42,000 students applied for the 16,100 openings in medical schools.

[3] There is one other requirement to receive your certification. In addition to passing the exams you must have a total of five years of specialty practice or experience. The three-year specialty training counts toward this total.

After all, you will be about 30 years old before you can practice your specialty. Furthermore, you only earn money so long as you work. Unlike a successful business, you cannot pass your practice to your heirs and have them receive an income from it. Besides there is much less schooling involved going into business. In spite of these negative factors I am satisfied with my life's work. It is a dignified career and the income is good.

Beginning salaries for board certified dermatologists in 1979 approximate the following in the New Orleans metropolitan area:

1. About $42,000 if you work for an existing partnership. After three to five years you may become a partner and income could rise to $50,000 or more.
2. From $30,000 to $50,000 if you join a foundation or government organization like the Veterans Administration or the U.S. Armed Forces.
3. From $38,000 to $60,000 if you work for a drug firm in research.
4. From $35,000 to $48,000 if you open your own office. However, your start-up costs would require the expenditure of this amount or more.[4] You would be lucky to break even during your first year.

Nationwide job opportunities in dermatology are published by a private firm. Income is based in some measure on need for your services in a particular locality.

The cost of a medical education is expensive — $52,000 to $78,000. You only start to earn money upon becoming an intern — about $9,000 the first year. The succeeding three years your income may vary from $10,000 to $18,000.

TWO-CAREER FAMILIES

There are abundant opportunities today for both husband and wife to have full-time careers. The financial rewards of two college graduates may initially double the gross income from only one worker. It is helpful, however, to determine net income (see Chapter 16 on income taxes) after deducting the additional taxes, clothing, transportation, household help, child care, and related expenses, in order to arrive at the true monetary gain from two-career marriages.

---

[4] There are major expenses required for equipment, office help, rental space, and professional liability insurance. The present cost for insurance is $4,000 to $6,000 annually. And inflation results in costs rising 5 to 10 percent each year.

I indicated above that gross income may initially double. Most families however, eventually have one or more children. Thus, income and promotion possibilities for the partner who assumes primary responsibility for the children — still usually the wife — may be hurt in the long run. Another important question to ask is whether both partners can have successful and fulfilling careers. A recent law graduate in a formal address commented:

Last year, at my fifth reunion, the problem on everyone's mind was that of career versus family. Could one have a loving husband, children, and *two* successful and fulfilling careers? This question must be considered in view of the kind of man a Radcliffe woman is likely to marry — a man who has been and expects to continue to be "successful," who intends to enjoy his work, work hard at it, and derive his ego satisfactions from it. Such a man — a doctor or lawyer, for example — does not work a forty-hour week.

I stand before you today, law degree practically in hand, mother of two glorious children, and I bring you bad news: It will be a long time before the needs of family and career will be comfortably wed.

Child raising is important work. It has its moments of unequalled joy. It is also difficult and time-consuming. Yet, child raising is not a respected profession. If it were, men as well as women would want to do it. The corollary of this is that by taking a few years out to raise your children you will inevitably hurt your career. Having those years on your résumé, explicitly or by omission, will put you at a competitive disadvantage with anyone who has been "working," studying, or traveling during those years. That you are a mother may also hurt because of the stereotype to which, I think, we are all susceptible — that "mommies" are dumb.[5]

My recommendation in regard to potentially two-career families is that husband and wife should take a management approach in arriving at their decision. The material presented in Chapter 1 on values, goals, and the decision-making process can be helpful in deciding on the appropriate course of action.

[5] An address delivered by Marylyn Siegal Smith at the Harvard commencement ceremonies, June 17, 1976 and appearing in *Harvard Today*, Summer 1976, p. 8.

OBSERVATION OF THE JOB MARKET
IN THE YEARS AHEAD

It will be important to take your time prior to selecting a company to work for upon graduation. You may wish to use the format shown in Table 2-6 to help determine which job is best for you. Keep in mind that competition in the job market will increase in the years ahead. Young adults will comprise over 50 percent of the work force by 1985. Furthermore, more people are receiving specialized training; thus there will be more applicants for the specialized openings. Likewise, blacks, females, Native Americans, Chicanos, and other minority groups will be given greater opportunities to receive a quality education. They also are benefiting from active affirmative-action employment programs. This increase in competition was pointed out by Harvard's President Derek C. Bok in his commencement address:

Women, minority students, and other disadvantaged groups have begun to enter careers that were once very difficult to enter. Although we must applaud their progress, it adds undeniably to the competition. And competition is clearly present in the very careers that have long been most attractive to Harvard students. In the last fifteen years, the number of applicants to law school has risen fivefold while applications to medical school have trebled.

The outlook for jobs also leaves something to be desired. Opportunities in teaching have sharply declined. Other fields, such as journalism and architecture, are badly oversupplied.[6]

The Bureau of Labor Statistics presents a more optimistic picture. Its *Occupational Outlook Handbook* has valuable statistical information on job opportunities in the United States in the years ahead. The chapter entitled "Tomorrow's Jobs," in its 1978-1979 edition, points out that employment growth will vary widely by industry through the mid-1980s (see Figure 2-2). As shown in the figure, agricultural opportunities are expected to diminish by over 30 percent. All others will increase, however, and services will be the fastest growing industry. The *Handbook* states:

Most of the Nation's workers are employed in industries that provide services, such as education, health care, trade, repair and

[6] *Harvard Today*, Summer 1976, p. 9.

28

Table 2-6. Format to Help Determine Which Job is Best for You.

	Job A	Job B	Job C
How well does the job appear to meet my values and goals in life?	Outstanding ___ Good ___ Fair ___ Poor ___	Outstanding ___ Good ___ Fair ___ Poor ___	Outstanding ___ Good ___ Fair ___ Poor ___
What about starting salary?	Outstanding ___ Good ___ Fair ___ Poor ___	Outstanding ___ Good ___ Fair ___ Poor ___	Outstanding ___ Good ___ Fair ___ Poor ___
What about other benefits that appeal to me such as security; cars; travel; education; insurance; etc. Does the medical and dental protection include my family?	Outstanding ___ Good ___ Fair ___ Poor ___	Outstanding ___ Good ___ Fair ___ Poor ___	Outstanding ___ Good ___ Fair ___ Poor ___
How are promotion possibilities? Will the career program permit me to reach my full potential?	Outstanding ___ Good ___ Fair ___ Poor ___	Outstanding ___ Good ___ Fair ___ Poor ___	Outstanding ___ Good ___ Fair ___ Poor ___
What about the integrity, reputation and future of the company?	Outstanding ___ Good ___ Fair ___ Poor ___	Outstanding ___ Good ___ Fair ___ Poor ___	Outstanding ___ Good ___ Fair ___ Poor ___
How are working conditions?	Outstanding ___ Good ___ Fair ___ Poor ___	Outstanding ___ Good ___ Fair ___ Poor ___	Outstanding ___ Good ___ Fair ___ Poor ___
Is it convenient to my residence?	Outstanding ___ Good ___ Fair ___ Poor ___	Outstanding ___ Good ___ Fair ___ Poor ___	Outstanding ___ Good ___ Fair ___ Poor ___
How good is the retirement program?	Outstanding ___ Good ___ Fair ___ Poor ___	Outstanding ___ Good ___ Fair ___ Poor ___	Outstanding ___ Good ___ Fair ___ Poor ___
How congenial are my fellow workers?	Outstanding ___ Good ___ Fair ___ Poor ___	Outstanding ___ Good ___ Fair ___ Poor ___	Outstanding ___ Good ___ Fair ___ Poor ___
Other considerations	Outstanding ___ Good ___ Fair ___ Poor ___	Outstanding ___ Good ___ Fair ___ Poor ___	Outstanding ___ Good ___ Fair ___ Poor ___
Total[a]			

[a]Total points based on the following scale: Outstanding = 4; Good = 3; Fair = 2; Poor = 1.

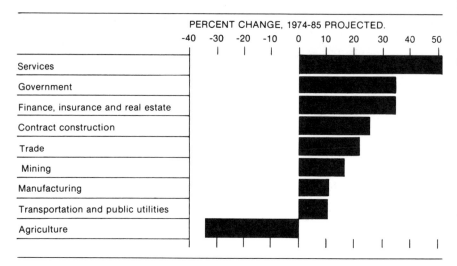

PERCENT CHANGE, 1974-85 PROJECTED.

Services
Government
Finance, insurance and real estate
Contract construction
Trade
Mining
Manufacturing
Transportation and public utilities
Agriculture

Figure 2-2. Employment Growth. (Source: U.S. Department of Labor, Bureau of Labor Statistics, *Occupational Outlook Handbook, 1978-1979 Edition* [Washington, D.C.; U.S. Government Printing Office, 1978], p. 21.)

maintenance, government, transportation, banking, and insurance . . . employment in the goods-producing industries has remained relatively constant since World War II, whereas the service-producing industries have expanded rapidly. Among the factors contributing to this rapid growth were the migration from rural to urban areas and the accompanying need for more local government services, and rising incomes and living standards that resulted in a demand for improved health and education services. These factors are expected to continue to cause the demand for services to grow.[7]

"Tomorrow's Jobs" concludes with this advice:

College can provide many valuable opportunities for personal growth and self-discovery, as well as the chance to increase one's knowledge of particular subject areas. Attending college for personal reasons alone can be worthwhile, but a student solely interested in career preparation may find alternative types of education and training programs more appropriate — either as an addition to or as a substitute for college attendance.

[7] U.S. Department of Labor, Bureau of Labor Statistics, *Occupational Outlook Handbook,* 1978-1979 ed. (Washington, D.C.: U.S. Government Printing Office, 1978), p. 22.

30

Whatever one's goals and aspirations, beginning the planning process early allows students time to consider all the choices that are available for preparing for tomorrow's jobs.[8]

ACTIONS YOU CAN TAKE TO COPE WITH INFLATION AND THE ENERGY SHORTAGE

1. Although earnings in general have kept pace with inflation in recent years, you are interested in your ability to keep abreast of or exceed the rise in inflation in the years ahead. In order to make a valid comparison with the Consumer Price Index (Chapter 1), it will be necessary for you to convert your earnings to a percentage basis. This can be accomplished yearly as follows: Determine the difference between your annual earnings in the previous year and in the current year; then divide the difference by your earnings in the previous year:

$$\frac{\text{Earning in current year} - \text{Earning in previous year}}{\text{Earnings in previous year}} = \begin{array}{l}\text{Percentage}\\\text{increase or}\\\text{decrease}\\\text{from the}\\\text{previous}\\\text{year}\end{array}$$

For example, assume that earnings for 1978 were $20,000 and for 1979 were $22,000.

$$\frac{\$22,000 - 20,000}{\$20,000} = \frac{\$2,000}{\$20,000} = 10 \text{ percent increase}$$

2. Consider such energy-conservation measures as living closer to work, using public transportation, and car pooling.

SUMMARY

College graduates can expect to earn a sizable fortune in their lifetimes. The amount will vary based upon each individual's values and goals. Therefore, prior to selecting a job it is helpful to take a manage-

[8] Ibid., p. 27.

ment approach in order to obtain a position that best meets your needs. This requires adequate *planning, implementing* your plan, and *checking* to see that the job meets your expectations. In order to arrive at a sound decision you should list your objective; obtain adequate information (facts) on the job market; examine the alternatives (choices); and from the alternatives select the position most appropriate for you.

It is desirable to learn the financial benefits available, other than salary, before deciding on a job. With the high cost of medical care, for example, you should examine this aspect very carefully. What medical coverage is provided by the company? Does it include my family? What costs, if any, must I pay? You may want to ask questions of this type in regard to benefits that are of concern to you. By putting a dollar value on each of the other benefits, in addition to salary, you can arrive at your total compensation.

The most complete information on job opportunities can be found in the current edition of *Occupational Outlook Handbook* prepared by the Bureau of Labor Statistics. In addition to current data it includes valuable information on job opportunities in the years ahead.

Light purse, heavy heart.
— BENJAMIN FRANKLIN

THE BUDGET PROCESS: A PLAN TO ACHIEVE YOUR GOALS

The problem today is not so much how to make money as how to manage it, once it is acquired, to serve your needs best. The slick Madison Avenue types have their hands in your pockets before you realize it. Sophisticated marketing techniques make it difficult to say no. And the clever pitches by loan companies make them sound as if they are your best pals:

"We have you in mind."

"Money in minutes."

"Let us eliminate your financial worries by consolidating all your loans."

"We are not a loan company, but a money management service established to help you."

Because of "kindhearted" businesses willing to give you merchandise with nothing down and loan companies that make it all so simple, there are a lot of people in dire financial straits. These people are found at all income levels, but the symptoms are the same in each case — too many bills and too little cash. The effect of these business and financial forces is often to drain off dollars faster than one can replenish them. One solution is to join those companies — if they are

33

so profitable, it may be desirable to invest money here or to enter the field yourself.

We shall take up the subject of investments later. Now let us consider how to establish a sound personal finance program.

FINANCIAL HEALTH

Three years ago, a young man told me that he was in debt to 20 different firms. He owed them a total of more than $5,000. The burden of these bills was causing him great strain and preventing him from doing satisfactory work. He indicated that he had had no training in financial management, and that having a job that paid $19,000 a year made it too easy to borrow funds. Contrary to the advertisements, he had found that instant store credit and "happiness" loans had given him a bucketful of headaches.

Eighteen months later, he was out of debt, thanks to a logical plan. He had discovered that by getting out of current debt, he had more "goodies" for all the tomorrows. After all, spending is delayed saving, and saving is delayed spending. And if you do not think loan companies expect you to save to meet your payments, try skipping a payment and watch their incomparable harassment technique. Furthermore, by saving today, you have a lot more to spend tomorrow.

What is the object of having a logical plan to acquire and conserve capital? The need for saving a portion of earnings for tomorrow instead of spending it all (and more) today is based upon a combination of several requirements. First, you may want a special vacation, a new sports car, a European honeymoon, a nest egg to buy that boat or meet an emergency, an education reserve for the children, and/or a home of your own.

Second, you may wish to provide funds to augment your retirement income. Retirement seems a thousand years away at graduation, but remember what a short time ago your high school graduation took place. Look around at some of the people of your grandparents' generation trying to live off meager Social Security. It is a tough deal, and do not expect a utopian government to provide a cornucopia in the twenty-first century for all its senior citizens.

Third, money is power; throughout life you can use it to help achieve your goals — political, social, or otherwise. There may also be the satisfaction of giving or leaving a sizable sum to what you deem to be a worthy cause; there will always be plenty of those around, even if pollution, race problems, the energy shortage, war, and urban ills are eliminated.

Finally, peace of mind is difficult to come by these days. Freedom from financial worry saves a lot of headaches. My colleague put it well: "When I got out of debt, it was great to be able to tell my creditors where to go!"

Each individual must be the judge of his or her own personal finance needs. In determining what should be set aside for these needs, bear in mind constantly that the long-term trend has been inflationary; therefore, ample amounts should be projected to meet each requirement. For example, in the last 20 years the cost of attending college has tripled, and in a number of areas housing has quadrupled in value. Most of you can expect a retirement income after having worked for a corporation or government agency, and Social Security will follow soon after. However, those having commitments, such as children requiring a college education after their parents' retirement, will normally need a large amount of additional funds. And, of course, professional and self-employed people will have to set up adequate long-range savings programs.

BUDGET PROCESS

In this chapter and the next we shall look at the means of achieving financial health. The first consideration is to find out what you have today and what you desire for tomorrow. After reviewing this budgetary process, we shall examine the resources available to achieve your objectives. An effective program can be of invaluable assistance either to get out of debt or to stay out of debt—or both. This concept— the budget process—may be divided into five phases:

1. Determine where you stand today (net worth).
2. Estimate income and expenses for the current year.
3. Develop a long-range plan based upon your primary objective and intermediate goals.
4. Maintain records indicating actual income and expenditures.
5. Compare your plan with actuality, and modify your estimates where appropriate.

Net Worth

Acquiring and conserving capital in order to reach your objectives involves saving a percentage of income and using dollars effectively. This is so simple to state—and yet so difficult to achieve. In order to save a percentage of what you earn, it is helpful to know what you are worth and what you will receive (income) in relation to expenses for the current year. A good way to begin the budget process is to find out where you stand today (see Table 3-1). This process doesn't require that you major in accounting. People who try to itemize every minute expenditure soon give up because of the time and effort required.

It is necessary, however, for you to determine what you own (assets) and estimate their current value. List such items as cash, bonds, furniture, car, value of home, and cash value of life insurance. Prices should be based on the current market value of these items if they were to be converted into dollars. Against these assets, list all the amounts owed (liabilities). They may include installment purchases, funds borrowed from banks, and money due on home and car, as well as outstanding obligations to hospital, doctors, or dentists. The amount owed is then subtracted from that owned, and the result indicates your dollar ownership (net worth) as of that date. ·

This terminology of *assets, liabilities,* and *net worth* is common parlance in the accounting field, and your listing of them may be referred to as a balance sheet, or statement of financial condition. Assets minus liabilities equals net worth. Knowing your net worth,

Table 3-1. Where I Stand Today, December 31, 1979.

My worldly possessions (assets):		
Cash on hand	$ 20	
Cash in checking account	300	
Cash in savings account	100	
Cash in S&L association	100	
U.S. savings bonds	100	
U.S. Treasury note	1,000	
Corporate stocks:		
One share, ABC Co.	400	
Five shares, DEF Co.	300	
Car	1,000	
Furniture	500	
Clothing	180	
Mobile home	8,000	
		$12,000
My debts (liabilities):		
Notes payable	$1,600	
Car payments	750	
Furniture payments	150	
Mobile-home mortgage	6,500	
		$ 9,000
My true worth		$ 3,000

you can establish a course of action. In some cases, you may be chagrined to find that you are deeply in debt. Conversely, you may be pleasantly surprised to find that you even *have* a net worth. Table 3-1 indicates that "I" have $12,000 in assets and $9,000 in liabilities, for a net worth of $3,000, on December 31, 1979.

Income and Expenses

The second aspect of the budget process is to estimate your income and expenses for the year. Table 3-2 points out that "I" would have an income of $15,100 and expenses of $12,800, with the tidy sum of $2,300 saved, by December 31, 1980.

The preparation of your annual income-and-expense statement requires keeping adequate records. The income portion would include salary paid by your employer, plus moonlighting work or extra funds earned by your mate and other sources of income, such as bonds, bank interest, gifts, and so forth. Against this income, all expenses for the year should be itemized. These should include the repetitive expenses, like food and clothing, and such budgeted costs as insurance, automobile payments, and mortgage, as well as a myriad of other possible outlays. Subtracting expenses from income gives you the savings or dissavings estimated for the one-year period.

It is essential that income exceed expenditures, or it will be impossible to pay up debts or save funds for investment purposes. If the expenses of a married couple, for example, exceed income, hus-

Table 3-2. My Estimated Income and Expenses, January 1–December 31, 1980.

Income:		
Earnings (salary)	$15,000	
Interest	90	
Dividends	10	
		$15,100
Expenses:		
Home	$ 3,600	
Food	3,000	
Car	1,200	
Clothing	700	
Vacation and recreation	700	
Medical	400	
Insurance premiums	60	
Taxes	3,140	
		$12,800
Savings		$ 2,300

Table 3-3. Intermediate Budgets for Four-Person Families, Autumn 1976 (Percentage Basis).

	Urban United States	Anchorage, Alaska	Nonmetropolitan South
Food	24	20	25
Housing	24	28	22
Transportation	9	8	10
Clothing	7	6	8
Personal care	2	2	2
Medical care	5	6	6
Other family consumption	5	4	5
Other items	4	4	5
Social Security and disability payments	6	4	6
Personal income taxes	14	18	11
Total	100	100	100

Source: U.S. Department of Labor, Bureau of Labor Statistics, *News*, May 5, 1977.

band and wife had better sit down together and determine how expenses can be reduced or income increased. An additional source of revenue may be achieved by having both partners work, or the present wage-earner take on added employment. If this is not feasible, then certain expenses must be reduced or eliminated in order to improve their financial condition.

It may also be helpful to look at Table 3-3 in estimating your expenditures. This table lists the amount on a percentage basis allocated by a family of four for food, housing, transportation, clothing and personal care, other family consumption, Social Security and disability payments, personal income taxes, and other costs. The expenses for these items vary in different regions of the country. For example, a four-member family in Anchorage, Alaska, spends 28 percent on housing in contrast to 20 percent for a family in nonmetropolitan areas in the South.

In order to see how you are doing from month to month, you will have to take your annual income and expenditures and break them down into monthly increments. For example, if $250 of the monthly income is to be spent on food, you must stay within this budget. The same approach can be applied to rental costs, entertainment, clothing, and furniture. The important point to remember is the necessity to *remain* within the guidelines established, yet to stay away from minute details. Each month a review can be made of how effective the planning has been to date.

Long-Range Plan

The third phase of the budget process is to develop a long-range plan based upon your primary objective. Let us assume that your objective is a million dollars, with a retirement date of 2008. Table 3-4 presents a format for recording the necessary data.

Such a concept begins with the current year and makes an initial estimate for one year ahead. This format proceeds forward in time, to 5, 15, and 29 years ahead. These projections are obviously only "guesstimates"; but such an approach forces you to come to grips

Table 3-4. A Long-Range Financial-Health Program (Prepared December 31, 1979).

	Dec. 31, 1979	Dec. 31, 1980	Dec. 31, 1984	Dec. 31, 1994	Dec. 31, 2008
My worldly possessions:					
Cash					
Notes and bonds					
Stocks					
Automobile					
Furniture and household equipment					
Clothing					
Home					
My debts:					
Notes payable					
Automobile payments					
Installments due on furniture					
Mobile-home mortgage					
My true worth					
My estate:					
Insurance protection (term)					
Total estate					
My income for the year:					
Earnings (salary)					
Interest					
Dividends					
My expenses for the year:					
Home					
Food					
Car					
Clothing					
Vacation and recreation					
Medical					
Insurance premiums					
Taxes					
My savings for the year					

Table 3-5. Actual Daily Expenses, January 1–31, 19 —.

Date	Food	Housing	Transpor-tation	Personal Care	Medical Care	Other Family Consump-tion	Other Items	Social Security and Disability Payments	Personal Income Taxes
1/1									
1/2									
1/3									
1/4									
1/5									
. . .									
1/31									
Total									

with answers to the questions "Where am I today? Where do I want to be tomorrow?" By revising your long-range plan annually, you may be pleasantly surprised at how effective this document can be in assisting you to reach your ultimate objective and various goals en route.

In order for your plans to be successful, it will be necessary for you to complete the fourth and fifth phases in the budget process. The fourth step requires you to record your actual income and expenditures. You may wish to make a daily record utilizing the format shown in Table 3-5. Each month, these expenditures should be totaled and posted to a monthly income-and-expense statement (see Table 3-6 for a sample format).

The final phase of the budget process involves comparing your planned income and expenses with what actually happens. This should be done on a monthly basis. For example, if you find at the end of February that your actual expenses have exceeded the estimate by 10 percent, you must take steps to reduce expenditures during the next 10 months to make up for this overspending, or perhaps secure additional income. In addition to the monthly analysis, it is essential to review your long-range plan yearly. You should review your goals and make corrections where appropriate. Likewise, more current information on your future salary projections could change

Table 3-6. Monthly Income and Expenses, January 1–December 31, 19 __.

	Jan.	Feb.	Mar.	...	Dec.	Year's Total
Income:						
Salary						
Interest						
Dividends						
Total						
Expenses:						
Food						
Housing						
Transportation						
Clothing						
Personal care						
Medical care						
Other family consumption						
Other items						
Social Security and disability payments						
Personal income taxes						
Total						
Savings						

your estimates. It is important to make these corrections in order for your long-range program to be of real assistance to you.

In the case that follows, a long-range plan is presented that utilizes the format found in Table 3-4.

CASE: NATALIE AND NARCO NAMLLITS

To illustrate how to develop a budget, let us see how one college couple — Mr. and Mrs. Namllits — went about developing their first budget.

"Ever since my college career began," says Natalie, "I have had to live on limited means. Out of the money I made each summer, I have had to pay for my tuition, sorority dues, clothes, contact lenses, insurance, and miscellaneous expenses. My parents have had to be thrifty, having a family of five girls, two of college age. Accordingly, everyone in the family has had much firsthand experience with keeping a budget. I kept my own from freshman days; it was a necessity. My total net worth on December 31, 1978, was a meager $258.25 (Table 3-7). My income and expenses for 1978 permitted net savings of $66.00 (Table 3-8)."

Table 3-7. Natalie's Balance Sheet, December 31, 1978.

Assets:		
Cash	$ 25.00	
Notes and bonds	—	
Stock	—	
Car	—	
Furniture	—	
Clothing	300.00	
Home	—	
		$325.00
Liabilities:		
Charge accounts	$ 66.75	
Notes payable	—	
Car payments	—	
Furniture installments	—	
Home mortgage	—	
		$ 66.75
Net worth		$258.25

Table 3-8. Natalie's Income and Expenses, January 1–December 31, 1978.

Income:		
Earnings (salary)	$1,200	
Interest	2	
Dividends	—	
Money from my parents	390	
		$1,592
Expenses:		
Rent ($900 less $870 scholarship)	$ 30	
Tuition ($1,100 less $900 scholarship)	200	
Food ($1,200 paid direct from parents)		
Sorority dues	235	
Laundry	30	
Insurance	15	
Taxes	36	
Vacation	240	
Medical expenses		
Spending money	390	
Clothing	250	
Gifts	100	
		$1,526
Savings		$ 66

"Since I married Narco last month, it is about time to plan a budget for two and then for a family. Narco is too busy with his football and photography interests to take care of a budget; at least, that's his story. But we did work out our long-range objective, as well as the intermediate goals (Table 3-9). We want that million dollars, but we have objectives along the way that are more important. Being together, being able to sleep peacefully — that's what we equate happiness with. Of course, that may *take* a million dollars by the year 2008, if inflation gets much worse.

"My husband is doing his graduate work in finance. He has received an assistantship for his remaining year in graduate school. I now have a part-time job to help out while I am earning my degree. I will obtain a part-time teaching position after I graduate, in January 1980. Most of our expenses will be related to graduate school and living expenses, independent of parental help. Narco thinks I am fudging a bit on expenses when I list only $600 for recreation — he doesn't plan to miss a pro football game this fall. Perhaps I can convince him that those seats behind the goal line aren't so bad.

"As for income, in 1979 both of us will work during the school year. Narco has received a job offer from an accounting firm for

Table 3-9. Natalie and Narco's Objectives, January 1, 1979–December 31, 2008.

Second year:
  Pay off all debts
  Save money for furniture
  Start investment portfolio
  Start a family
Fourth year:
  Start purchasing antique furniture
  Build up investment portfolio
  Purchase a second car
  Have a second child
Sixth year:
  Build our own home
  Natalie starts part-time teaching again
Eighth year:
  Purchase two cars (one subcompact used car and one compact new sedan)
    and trade in every three years
  Increase size of investment portfolio
  Reduce debt on home
Twelfth year:
  Purchase boat and trailer
Sixteenth year:
  Install swimming pool
  Trade in boat
Twentieth year:
  Pay off debt on home
  Finance children in college
  Save for retirement
  Travel to Europe
  Have net worth of $480,000
  Trade in boat
Twenty-fifth year:
  Terminate our payment of children's education
  Take extended vacation
  Trade in boat
  Natalie stops teaching in order to devote more time to her art hobby
Longest term (30 years):
  A million-dollar retirement nest egg for children and charity

Table 3-10. Natalie and Narco's Estimated Income and Expenses, January 1–December 31, 1979.

Our income:		
Narco's earnings	$5,700	
Natalie's earnings	2,000	
Interest	15	
		$7,715
Our expenses:		
Home and insurance	$2,400	
Food	1,500	
Car	800	
Recreation and vacation	600	
Clothing	600	
Medical	200	
Insurance premiums	60	
School	550	
Furniture	0	
Taxes	955	
		$7,665
Savings		$ 50

the summer, with a starting salary of $900 per month. I will work for a law firm where I am paid $4.00 per hour. Our income estimate for 1979 amounts to $7,115 and will, we hope, permit us to live within our anticipated expenses (Table 3-10). To permit a frequent comparison of actual income and expenses against our estimate, we prepared a monthly statement for the period January 1–December 31, 1979 (Table 3-11).

"We have figured that things will be tight for a while, at least until I am a regular teacher. Even then, we will not be able to really get on our feet until Narco finishes graduate school. After that, it should be pretty smooth sailing! Narco is ambitious and quite intelligent. He plans on advancing rapidly in an accounting firm, and hopes to be a partner some day in such a firm, or a treasurer or controller in a corporation. As for myself, I will probably stop working for a few years to have children, but I plan to teach thereafter. My art hobby is fascinating and may eventually contribute to our income. A final review of our long-range plan (Table 3-12) convinces us that we can reach our objectives. At least we have expectations.

"Now all I hope is that it turns out as well as we both think it will."

Table 3-11. Natalie and Narco's Estimated Monthly Income and Expenses, January 1–December 31, 1978.

	Jan.	Feb.	Mar.	Apr.	May	June	July	Aug.	Sept.	Oct.	Nov.	Dec.	Year's Total
Our income:													
Narco's earnings	$333	$333	$333	$333	$333	$ 900	$ 900	$ 900	$333	$334	$334	$334	$5,700
Natalie's earnings	167	167	167	167	167	165	165	170	167	166	166	166	2,000
Interest	—	—	—	—	—	—	—	—	—	—	—	15	15
Dividends	—	—	—	—	—	—	—	—	—	—	—	—	0
Total	$500	$500	$500	$500	$500	$1,065	$1,065	$1,070	$500	$500	$500	$515	$7,715
Our expenses:													
Home and insurance	$200	$200	$200	$200	$200	$ 200	$ 200	$ 200	$200	$200	$200	$200	$2,400
Food	125	125	125	125	125	125	125	125	125	125	125	125	1,500
Car	66	66	66	66	67	67	67	67	67	67	67	67	800
Clothing	10		50	40		180	130	40		50		150	600
Vacation and recreation	40	10		20	30	20	40	300	10	20	10	50	600
Medical	20	20	20	10	20	10	20	20	20	10	10	20	200
Insurance premiums	15			15			15			15			60
School	275								275				550
Furniture	—	—	—	—	—	—	—	—	—	—	—	—	—
Taxes	70	70	70	70	70	110	105	110	70	70	70	70	955
Total	$821	$491	$531	$546	$512	$ 712	$ 702	$ 862	$767	$557	$482	$682	$7,665
Savings													$ 50

Table 3-12. The Namllitses' Long-Range Financial-Health Program, as of December 31 Each Year.

	1979	1980	1982	1984	1986	1990	1994	1998	2003	2008
Our worldly possessions:										
Cash	$ 520	$ 546	$ 601	$ 662	$ 730	$ 886	$ 1,075	$ 1,305	$ 1,665	$ 2,163
Notes and bonds	500	1,500	3,600	6,200	11,200	24,200	47,000	75,000	132,000	220,000
Stocks	–	6,740	14,490	25,795	45,400	93,000	174,000	296,000	532,000	880,000
Car	1,400	1,200	2,500	1,600	3,500	3,000	3,500	5,500	4,000	8,000
Furniture and household equipment	800	880	1,100	2,300	3,000	4,300	6,000	8,200	12,000	16,000
Clothing and jewelry	600	660	800	970	1,177	1,723	2,600	4,400	7,090	11,200
Home	–	–	–	40,000	44,100	53,500	72,000	85,500	102,000	122,000
Boat	–	–	–	–	–	4,500	5,000	5,000	5,500	3,200
Total	$3,820	$11,526	$23,091	$77,527	$109,107	$185,109	$311,175	$480,905	$796,255	$1,262,563
Our debts:										
Notes payable	$ 500	–	–	–	–	–	–	–	–	–
Car payments	–	–	–	–	–	–	–	–	–	–
Installments due on furniture	–	–	–	–	–	–	–	–	–	–
Installments due on home	–	–	–	$24,000	$22,600	$ 19,400	$ 9,600	–	–	–
Total	$ 500	–	–	$24,000	$22,600	$ 19,400	$ 9,600	–	–	–
Our true worth	$3,320	$11,526	$23,091	$53,527	$ 86,507	$165,709	$301,575	$480,905	$796,255	$1,262,563
Our estate:										
Insurance protection	$5,000	$10,000	$15,000	$15,000	$ 20,000	$ 25,000	$ 35,000	$ 50,000	$ 70,000	$ 90,000
Total estate	$8,320	$21,526	$38,091	$68,527	$106,507	$190,709	$336,575	$530,905	$866,255	$1,352,563

Table 3-12 (Continued).

	1979	1980	1982	1984	1986	1990	1994	1998	2003	2008
Our income:										
Narco's earnings	$5,700	$12,500	$15,000	$17,000	$ 19,000	$ 26,000	$ 36,000	$ 46,000	$ 59,000	$ 73,000
Natalie's earnings	2,000	5,000		9,000	9,730	11,370	13,300	15,500	18,400	
Interest	15	25	125	250	410	1,000	2,000	3,400	5,900	9,600
Dividends		20	113	200	362	800	1,550	2,650	4,750	7,980
Total	$7,715	$17,545	$15,238	$26,450	$ 29,502	$ 39,170	$ 52,850	$ 67,550	$ 88,050	$ 90,580
Our expenses:										
Home and insurance	$2,400	$ 2,000	$ 2,200	$ 8,000	$ 4,300	$ 4,700	$ 12,100	$ 4,800	$ 3,900	$ 4,400
Food	1,500	1,560	1,770	2,000	2,160	2,500	2,900	2,800	2,900	3,400
Car	800	825	2,500	1,040	3,500	2,050	2,300	4,000	2,700	3,600
Clothing	600	630	700	770	840	1,050	1,250	2,500	1,950	2,500
Vacation and recreation	600	625	675	725	825	5,425	2,580	8,000	5,000	1,600
Medical	200	500	500	400	440	520	600	1,000	850	975
Insurance premiums	60	160	200	200	250	300	400	750	750	950
School	550		200	300	1,250	1,450	1,650	4,000	4,300	
Furniture		100	500	2,400	400	800	1,000	1,300	1,550	1,800
Taxes	955	3,410	2,780	5,920	7,150	11,240	17,460	25,900	37,500	38,180
Total	$7,665	$ 9,810	$12,025	$21,755	$ 21,115	$ 30,035	$ 42,240	$ 55,050	$ 61,400	$ 57,405
Savings	$ 50	$ 7,735	$ 3,213	$ 4,695	$ 8,387	$ 9,135	$ 10,610	$ 12,500	$ 26,650	$ 33,175

48

RECORDS

The importance of keeping adequate records has been noted previously. I would suggest that you obtain a file cabinet and appropriate folders to keep your financial material available for easy reference. Your budget data may be divided into three sections: Balance Sheet, Income and Expenses, and Long-Range Financial-Health Plan. For further details on budget format, you may wish to obtain a copy of my book titled *Personal Finance Guide and Workbook: A Managerial Approach to Successful Household Recordkeeping.*[1] Your local credit union, bank, or savings and loan association can also be helpful in providing you with budget forms and other appropriate information.

PERSONAL FINANCE MANAGEMENT

The value of the budget process is that it forces you to devise a plan to meet your various objectives. It can be a valuable servant or a Frankenstein's monster. Make sure you are not caught in a morass of petty details. Furthermore, as earnings increase, you need be less exact in meeting your budgeted expenses in each category. Keep in mind that they are guidelines only.

The most important point is to deduct your savings allotment *first.* Either have an automatic deduction for investment purposes or do it yourself on receipt of each salary check. Second, be sure to make an annual review of your long-range plan and a monthly check on your yearly projection. Remember that the budget process is far more useful than for planning purposes only. As we saw in Figure 1-2, personal finance management draws on the functions of planning, organizing, and controlling. Basically, these functions may be translated into personal finance terms as follows:

1. Plan what you are going to save and spend in relation to your income.
2. Implement your plan.
3. Check to see that what you spent and saved were in accordance with your budget.

The control aspect cannot be overemphasized: It permits verify-

[1] The publisher is Pelican, 630 Burmaster Street, Gretna, Louisiana 70053.

ing your actual expenditures against your plan. Where appropriate, make the necessary modifications to face the realities of the current situation. For example, assume you have allotted $50 a month for rent in 1982 because your company plans to send you to Paris and will subsidize most of your living expenses. It is essential that you revise your budget if you quit your job in June 1982 to accept a government post in New York City.

It is also desirable to provide an adequate cash reserve in your budget for unexpected emergencies. As with death and taxes, you can be sure of their occurrence — like what happened to me recently. One Saturday afternoon, my wife and children went shopping and the house was peaceful, until the phone rang.

> *She:* I'm at the parking-lot garage — the car won't work. I left it with the attendant, and he gunned it up the ramp. When we came back, I tried to drive away but couldn't release the clutch. The gear shift is OK, but the clutch won't budge. The attendant didn't even tell me about it, and I complained to the manager that the car worked fine when we drove in. He will do nothing about it.
>
> *Me:* Let me talk to the manager.
>
> *Manager:* We are not responsible for any mechanical difficulty. You will have to get your car towed away.
>
> *Me:* It's a bit difficult to obtain service on a Saturday afternoon — particularly since it's a foreign car.
>
> *Manager:* That's your problem.
>
> *Me:* Thanks so much. [Thinking, "You dirty so-and-so!"]

After a weekend spent checking on insurance coverage, towing service, and mechanics, I finally had the car taken to a garage Monday morning. The repair bill, as usual, was higher than the estimate. My insurance did not apply in this situation, and the garage was not held responsible because there was no proof of damage on their part. I had to pay the bill, and since my budget did not allow for this expense, I had to use the funds in my cash reserve. You can understand my opinion that an adequate cash reserve is a must.

"Don't worry about it!" is the advice I often receive from my son when I express concern about having a cash reserve or a viable budget. I don't go all the way with that statement, but I do think that this budgetary process is a way to keep from *having* to worry about one's personal financial burdens.

ACTIONS YOU CAN TAKE TO COPE WITH INFLATION AND THE ENERGY SHORTAGE

1. Review objectives annually and make appropriate modifications.

2. Develop and maintain a balance sheet and income-and-expense statements. Compare estimated income and expenses, each month, with actual income and expenses.

3. Review energy expenditures for such areas as heating, cooling, electricity, gas, and car to determine where reductions can be made. Make a list of planned savings and then check monthly to see if they have been accomplished.

SUMMARY

This chapter presents a concept designed to achieve and maintain financial health. This concept I call the budget process may be divided into five phases: (1) determine where you stand today (net worth), (2) estimate income and expenses for the current year, (3) develop a long-range plan based upon your primary objective and intermediate goals, (4) maintain records indicating actual income and expenditures, and (5) compare your plan with actuality and modify your estimates where appropriate.

It is desirable to have a well-organized system of keeping financial records. Such a system can save you much time. A file cabinet and appropriate folders can assist you by making your financial material available for ready reference.

Preparation of the various budget documents are essential tools of a successful money manager. They permit you to *plan* what you are going to save and spend in relation to your income, to *implement* your plan, and they serve as a *check* to see that what you spend and save is in accordance with your budget.

He who goes a borrowing, goes a sorrowing.

—BENJAMIN FRANKLIN

IF YOU MUST BORROW MONEY

"Get out of debt and stay out of debt" was a guideline listed in Chapter 1. If followed, this advice can be an important factor in achieving financial success. The facts of life, however, indicate that nearly 50 percent of all families living in the United States are in debt. Therefore, this chapter will look at the various sources for borrowing money in order to determine how to obtain the best deals. In my view, there should be only three situations requiring you to borrow money: to obtain an education, to meet an emergency, or to buy a home.

DETERMINING BORROWING COSTS

It is important to determine the cost of renting money in order to obtain the best possible loan to suit your needs. The best deal from an interest standpoint can be computed easily. However, it is also essential to do business with a reliable company that has a good reputation. Let us see how to compare loan costs.

The Truth-in-Lending Law requires every firm to list its yearly charges on a percentage basis. In loan shopping, you may wish to make a list as follows:

Firm	Annual Finance Charge	Other Expenses	Total Cost	Name of Organization (Person to Contact, Address, Phone)
A				
B				
C				

If you desire to check on the annual percentage charged by the lending agency, you can use the following formula:

$$\frac{2AB}{C(D+1)} = E$$

where:

A = Total finance charge in dollars
B = Number of payment periods in one year (use 12 if monthly payments, or 52 if weekly, irrespective of the months or weeks specified in the loan agreement)
C = Dollar amount of the loan
D = Actual number of payments to be made
E = Annual finance charge, in percent.

Let us now apply the formula. Assume you obtain a $300 loan and agree to repay the lending agency $342 in 24 monthly payments. By utilizing the formula above, you obtain the answer of 13.44 percent as the annual finance charge:

$$\frac{2 \times 42 \times 12}{300(24+1)} = \frac{1008}{7500} = .1344, \text{ or } 13.44\%$$

Remember that when you are quoted an add-on rate of interest, it can be misleading. For example, if a loan officer states, "It's an 8 percent add-on," this does not mean that you will be paying $8 on a one-year loan of $100. The vast majority of personal loans are made on an installment basis.[1] This type of loan requires the borrower to pay back the money in equal amounts during the life of the loan; so on a one-year loan, you are in possession of only six-twelfths of the principal ($50) at the end of six months. Therefore, to determine

[1] There is such a thing as a single-payment loan, but this is normally made only by lending agencies to corporations.

what you actually have to pay in interest, let us use the formula on page 53, applying it on a $100 loan repayable monthly over a one-year period at a cost of $8.

$$\frac{2 \times 8 \times 12}{100\,(12+1)} = \frac{192}{1300} = .148, \text{ or } 14.8\%$$

Tables are available that calculate this interest. Ask your lending agency to let you see them. These tables often include interest costs for life, accident, and health insurance. Lending agencies like to sell these extras because it means added profit. The life coverage also protects the lender in the event of your death.

LOAN SOURCES

Let us now look at available sources from which to secure a loan.

Friends and Relatives

You may be able to obtain the necessary money at no interest from a relative or a friend. Perhaps that rich aunt may make the loan at a nominal rate. Personal sources can be particularly helpful if you are going to college and run into difficulty securing money elsewhere. But this type of borrowing can turn friends into enemies. It is extremely important to pay back such loans in accordance with a written agreement.

Government Agencies

Government funds are available to students who need financial assistance in order to secure an education. There are two major programs — the federal student-loan program and state aid.

Student-Loan Program
The National Direct Student Loans (NDSL) program is authorized under the National Defense Education Act (NDEA). It enables eligible persons to obtain up to $5,000 over a four-year period for the purpose of attending a college or university for an undergraduate degree. Up to $5,000 additional is authorized for graduate schooling.

Scholastic records are examined in addition to family income.[2] There must be a demonstrated need for the money. No repayment of principal is required and no interest is charged as long as the person is attending school at least half time. After leaving school, the borrower must begin repaying the loan within nine months in principal installments of not less than $30 per month. There is an interest charge of 3 percent per year on the unpaid balance. Payments may be made over a 10-year period. An extension is granted if a recipient goes on to graduate school or enters the military.[3]

State Aid
State Guaranteed Loan (SGL) programs make it possible for needy students to borrow funds from participating private loan agencies. The state will guarantee such loans and with federal assistance pay interest on the loan while the students are enrolled in school. One state, for example, has a top limit of $1,500 per year for undergraduates and $2,000 for graduate students. To be eligible these students must have a family adjusted gross income of less than $25,000 per year.

Both the federal and state programs enable eligible students to obtain a college education. Further information on these loans can be obtained at school student financial aid offices. All schools have such an office.

Life Insurance Policies

Life insurance policies with a cash surrender value provide a good source of money because the interest rate is reasonable — 5 to 6 percent. You may borrow most of the policy's cash surrender value.[4] The Veterans Administration, for example, permits you to borrow

---

[2] People with exceptional financial need may be eligible to receive money under the Basic Educational Opportunity Grant Program. This provides up to $1,600 in financial assistance for those who need it to attend post–high school educational institutions. Recipients of this grant obtain it free. Normally it is insufficient to meet all educational costs and requires other financial assistance, such as a scholarship, job, or loan. There is also a plan for those with *very exceptional financial needs*. This Supplemental Educational Opportunity Grant Program provides up to $1,500 per year but not more than $4,000 over four undergraduate years.

[3] Those who desire a career in teaching receive an added inducement from the U.S. government. After graduation they are required to pay back only the principal. However, teachers who perform their services in approved institutions may have up to 100 percent of their loan cancelled.

[4] Cash surrender value is the dollar amount a policyholder would receive from his (or her) insurance company if he cancelled his policy.

up to 94 percent on government life insurance. The loan statement in
their policy reads as follows:

> At any time after the expiration of the first policy year, and be-
> fore default in payment in any subsequent premium, and upon
> execution of the loan agreement satisfactory to the Administra-
> tor of Veterans' Affairs, the United States will lend to the In-
> sured on the sole security of this policy, any amount which
> shall not exceed ninety-four per centum of the cash value and
> any indebtedness shall be deducted from the amount advanced
> on such loan. The loan shall bear interest at the rate not to ex-
> ceed six per centum per annum, payable annually, and at any
> time before default in payment of premium the loan may be re-
> paid in full or in amounts of five dollars or any multiple thereof.
> Failure to pay either the amount of the loan or the interest
> thereon shall not void this policy unless the total indebtedness
> shall equal or exceed the cash value thereof. When the amount
> of indebtedness equals or exceeds the cash value, this policy
> shall cease and become void.

It is apparent from the statement above that you should understand the conditions outlined in the policy before making the loan.
You buy life insurance for its protection. It is essential, if you borrow money on it, that you should not then be forced into a position
of having the policy voided. You must also keep in mind that if
death should occur during the time a person has borrowed on his
policy, the money due the beneficiary will be reduced by the amount
of the indebtedness.

Some insurance companies do not specify in the policy itself
any information on loans. If this is the case, you should write the
company or contact the local agent in order to obtain details on its
loan policy. Let us look at the rules established by one company:

> After two years of membership a member may borrow up to
> 100 percent of the cash value of his insurance computed on the
> last preceding anniversary of the date he joined the Association.

> *Provisions*
>
> (a) No loan may be granted if the loan plus interest for one year will ex-
> ceed the loan value for the following year.
> (b) Only one loan may be in existence at any one time. If a loan is re-
> quested, it will be automatically combined with the old loan.
> (c) Interest will be charged at the rate of 5 percent compounded annually.

Interest is computed annually on the anniversary date of the loan unless the loan is to be paid in full or replaced by a new loan.

(d) Payments may be made at any time.

(e) Interest is due for the day a loan is granted but not for day of repayment.

(f) Notice of interest due will be mailed 30 days prior to the due date. Payments received after the close of the month in which interest is due are credited to loan principal account.

(g) Unpaid interest will automatically be carried as principal for the following year.

Although loans are permitted and the Association will make every effort to facilitate payment of loan values, we caution each member that his life insurance coverage is reduced by the amount of the loan. Keep in mind that the primary function of insurance is to provide an adequate estate for a beneficiary and that any action reducing the level of coverage may affect this estate.[5]

Now let us note how relatively simple it is to borrow on your life insurance. All that is required by one company is to sign copies of the Loan Agreement and Certificate of Assignment (Figure 4-1), indicating the exact amount you wish to borrow. This type of borrowing is much easier to accomplish than are other loans that will be discussed later in this chapter.

In my view, insurance companies should not charge interest for letting you use your own money. This same money would be paid to you, at no charge, in the event that you desired to cancel your policy. The 5 to 6 percent interest charge seems unfair and perhaps someday the rules will be changed so that all insurance companies permit a person to obtain the loan at only the cost of the paperwork involved in making the transaction.[6]

Credit Unions

Credit unions should be given careful consideration as a source of loans. You have to be a member in order to be eligible. The prime advantage of borrowing from a credit union is that the total cost of your loan is often lower than at other lending institutions. One credit union points out to members its cost advantage over a bank, dealer

[5] Army Mutual Aid Association, Fort Myer, Arlington, Va. 22211. Reprinted with the permission of the Army Mutual Aid Association.

[6] Insurance companies may argue that this is money removed from their interest-earning investments.

Army Mutual Aid Association

FORT MYER

Arlington, Virginia 22211

LOAN AGREEMENT AND CERTIFICATE ASSIGNMENT

I, the undersigned, insured by the Army Mutual Aid Association under Certificate of Membership No. __P-D-17855X20__ , hereby certify that I have this day borrowed from the Association the sum of $_____ and hereby assign to said Association the Certificate of Membership to secure the repayment of said loan and the interest thereon. It is Understood and Agreed:

First: That said Loan shall bear interest at the rate of five per cent per annum, payable at the end of each loan year, and that the interest, unless duly paid, shall be added to the above loan and bear interest at the same rate and be subject to the same conditions.

Second: That should membership be surrendered, forfeited in any manner, or allowed to lapse, the amount of the loan, including all unpaid interest, shall be deducted from any surrender value of the membership. Any indebtedness shall operate to reduce the amount of any paid-up or the terms of any extended term insurance that would otherwise be available.

Third: That if any membership certificate shall mature before the amount of any loan and interest indebtedness shall have been paid, said indebtedness shall be deducted from the amount otherwise payable by the Association.

Fourth: That if the loan plus interest shall at any time become equal to or exceed the loan value of my membership, the membership shall automatically be forfeited or void unless total indebtedness is reduced to said loan value within thirty days after notice to that effect has been mailed to the last known address of the person to whom the loan is made.

Fifth: The loan may be repaid in whole or in part at any time prior to maturity, provided the membership is not in default.

Sixth: I warrant and certify that no person, firm or corporation has any interest in or claim to my pecuniary interest in said Certificate of Membership and that I have the sole right to assign the same and am under no legal disability to assign said Certificate to the Association.

In Witness Whereof, I have hereunto set hand and seal this _____ day of _____ 19__.

APPROVED:

_____
SIGNATURE

__Richard J. Stillman__
NAME TYPED OR PRINTED

_____   _____
TREASURER   ADDRESS
ARMY MUTUAL AID ASSOCIATION
_____

Figure 4-1. Loan Agreement. (Source: Army Mutual Aid Association, Fort Myer, Arlington, Virginia 22211.) Reprinted with the permission of the Army Mutual Aid Association.

financing, finance company, small-loan company, and department store. It stresses the fact that interest is the only finance charge, with no added-on services or credit reports to raise the total cost. This credit union also pays the premium for credit life insurance and does not impose a finance charge on any amount you have already repaid. Finally, you can pay ahead of schedule without having any penalty imposed.

Credit unions may provide money to purchase a car, motorcycle, truck, truck camper, motor home, mobile home, trailer, camping trailer, boat, or airplane.

The loan application of a credit union asks for considerably more detail than you would have to supply if you borrowed on your life insurance. However, it is less detailed than the form required by other lending agencies.

Commercial Banks

Reputable commercial banks provide a good source to contact if you require a loan. Their finance charge is more reasonable than those of small-loan companies. However, they do require a stronger financial position. There are two types of loans that these banks usually offer. One is the unsecured loan, which means that you obtain the money based upon your signature alone. The unsecured loan costs more than the secured loan, which requires the borrower to put up collateral. This collateral may be in the form of bonds, stock, or savings account. If the loan is made for the purchase of a car, refrigerator, TV set, or major home improvement, that item would normally serve as the collateral. If the borrower fails to meet his or her loan obligation, the lending agency may sell the merchandise for the amount due. The remainder, if any, would be returned to the borrower.

If money is borrowed against a savings account, it can usually be obtained at 2 percent above what the bank pays its savers in interest. For example, a local bank currently pays 5 percent on its savings accounts and permits its savers to borrow up to the amount of their savings at 7 percent. In contrast, those with no such accounts are charged twice that amount.

But why keep your money in a bank at 5 percent and pay 7 percent to borrow it? Withdraw your savings for this purpose. By using your savings, you cut the costs. You will also save considerable time and effort that must be spent in filling out the loan application and personal financial statement. Awaiting approval can also be frustrating. Finally, there are the weekly or monthly repayments to be made and the worry should an emergency arise. There may, however, be a situation when you can save a good deal of money with a passbook loan rather than a withdrawal. This could be true if you need a loan for only a short time and your bank does not pay interest from date of deposit to date of withdrawal.

Banks, like other lending agencies, furnish the borrower a coupon book indicating the number of each payment, amount, and date due. A late-charge penalty is usually levied in the event that the regular monthly payment is ten or more days past due. This late fee is normally 5 percent. On an annual basis, this means a 60 percent extra expense, so it is important to make those payments on time.

Prior to signing a loan agreement with a bank, *read it with care.* Have the loan officer explain any points that may not be clearly understood. Thanks to the Truth-in-Lending Law, a complete disclosure of all costs is required of the lending agency. Be sure you find out the amount of rebate for prepayment and the specific default charge. Credit insurance is not required, *nor is it a factor in the approval of the extension of credit.* If you find that pressure is exerted on you to take out this insurance, report it promptly to the Better Business Bureau (BBB) and the appropriate consumer advisory agency in your area. You must realize that if your loan is secured by collateral, your failure to meet payments could result in the loss of *all your household goods and appliances of every kind located in or about your premises.*

Savings and Loan Associations

These institutions make collateral loans comparable to those of commercial banks in such areas as home improvements and mobile homes. They will also make signature loans against the amount of money people have saved in share accounts. A check with one association indicates that the differential amounts to 2 percent. For example, if your passbook account is paying you 5¾ percent, the association will charge you 7¾ percent. In contrast, if you have no savings account with the association, their charge on a secured loan is currently 9½ percent.

Personal-Loan Companies

Small-loan companies charge the highest rate of interest authorized within legal limits. This is an expensive way for borrowers to obtain money. In every sizable community in the United States there are small-loan companies actively seeking your business. These firms make large profits because they may charge from 24 to 42 percent interest per year, with the exact rate regulated by the individual states.

Personal loans totaled over $50 billion in 1979. Of this total, 40 percent, or $20 billion, was provided by small-loan companies. The remainder came from banks, savings and loan associations, and credit unions. The primary users of small-loan companies are individuals in the 21 to 35 age group who do not wish to defer purchases of economic goods and services.

Pawnbrokers

Pawnbrokers are available in many communities. They require a borrower to leave an item of value and will then lend an amount against this merchandise. Failure to repay the loan will permit the pawnbroker to sell the collateral to repay the loan and interest.

In order to protect themselves, pawnbrokers normally lend only a small portion of the retail value of the item pawned. A word of caution: You pay a high rate of interest (24 to 120 percent) and may lose an item of sentimental value if the loan cannot be repaid on time. One person reported the following experience.

I needed money and pawned a four-month-old automobile quad stereo tape player with an FM stereo radio. It cost me $205 and I received only $25. I was to pay it back within 90 days at $2.50 per month interest. I couldn't do it, and he sold my equipment that meant so much to me for only $38. I got back $5.50.

Loan Sharks

These are illegal lenders who charge whatever the market will bear. One of their games is to loan $10 for one week and charge $2 interest. This amounts to an annual rate of 1,040 percent. Loan sharks like to keep their clients in a position where they are just able to meet their interest payments. This is a dangerous game to play, and you should never use their services.

IMPACT OF INFLATION AND TAXES ON BORROWING

Inflation and taxes can reduce your borrowing costs and should be taken into consideration. The annual erosion in the purchasing power of the dollar can be expected to continue. There are, however, two unknowns: the annual percentage increase and the specific items that will rise. Let us assume that a dining-room set, which could be bought for $1,000 last year, rises to $1,050 twelve months later. In this case, your dollar power has been reduced by nearly 5 percent ($1,000 ÷ $1,050). If you had borrowed the $1,000 last year to buy the furniture, you could pay the money back with cheaper dollars.

Let us assume your $1,000 loan could be obtained at 12 percent, with the entire interest and principal to be paid at the end of the twelfth month. In such a case the impact of inflation would in theory result in your paying 7 percent interest [$1,120 − $1,050] ÷ 1,000).

The actual interest savings will depend on the amount of inflation that may take place with respect to your particular purchase. It could be zero for the dining-room set in question.

The second point to consider is the possible income tax advantage. Let us assume that you are in the 30 percent bracket. If you use the long form, the federal government permits you to deduct interest charges from taxable income. Using the furniture example, it would enable you to save $36 of the $120 interest charge. However, the majority of Americans take the standard deduction. If you do not have sufficient expenses to exceed the $3,400 standard deduction, this furniture loan would not benefit you from a tax standpoint.

YOUR LOAN ELIGIBILITY

If you desire to borrow money, whether you will receive it (and at what interest rate) is dependent upon your past record. What factors determine whether you pay a fair price for using a lending agency's money? A senior bank official informed me that his officers examine with care the loan application and the personal finance statement. They give special consideration to the following points:

1. *Current employment.* Particular attention is paid to the number of years on the job and present salary. Past positions are also studied. The bank wants to be sure a borrower can keep a job and is earning enough money to make payments.

2. *Indebtedness.* A hard look is taken at the list of creditors, unpaid balances, and monthly payments. The bank also looks at your response to an important question: Have you been in bankruptcy or had any judgments, garnishments, or other legal proceedings against you?

3. *Home ownership.* If a person owns his or her home and has a reasonable down payment, the fact indicates responsibility. Likewise, renters that have lived in one place for a period of time are looked on with favor.

4. *Net worth.* The financial statement is reviewed to see that assets clearly exceed liabilities. Savings accounts, stock, bonds, and other liquid assets are helpful. It is advantageous to have an account at the place you desire to borrow money.

5. *Other considerations.* The size of the family is taken into account, since a large family requires a healthy income. Prompt payment of credit card accounts, charge accounts, and other bills is a favorable factor.

6. *Credit-bureau check.* Prior to the bank's granting any loan, the bank official emphasized, the applicant must be checked out with the credit bureau. This bank is currently granting credit to only those with a high credit rating.

LOAN SHOPPING

If you must borrow, be sure to shop around for the loan. For example, a local savings and loan association charges 12 percent for a home improvement loan. In contrast, a finance company advertised real estate loans at 14.1 percent. The ad read, "Homeowners, now you can get $3,000 to $30,000 when secured by a first or second mortgage."[7] The rates were spelled out as follows:

Amount Financed	Monthly Payment	Months to Pay	Total of Payments	Annual Percentage Rate
$3,000	$ 70.00	60	$4,200.00	14.1%
$5,000	$116.66	60	$6,999.60	14.1%
$7,000	$163.33	60	$9,799.80	14.1%

If you select a finance company, your loan must normally be secured by a mortgage to obtain their lower rate. Otherwise, it could cost up to 42 percent. Length of payment is listed as five years. Note also how interest charges mount up: If you borrow $7,000 for 60 months, it costs you $2,799.80.[8]

[7] "Associates Financial Services of America, Inc." New Orleans *Times Picayune*, May 22, 1973, p. 5.

[8] You may be asked to take out a life insurance policy for $534 (if not, you would be required to assign a $7,000 portion of your present policy for the life of the loan). An accident and health policy is encouraged, amounting to $602. Thus, your cost would be increased to $3,936.

The loan habit is a series of bad trips. Once you are in its grip, it is difficult to break out. There is a real effort on the part of lenders to keep you in this cycle of debt. In my view, your objective should be to get out of debt and stay out of debt. Keep in mind that borrowing for emergencies can become a way of life. Unfortunately, if you borrow to the hilt, it may become virtually impossible to obtain money when it is of crucial importance, as the following story proves.

> I never paid any real attention to money matters. If we had any extra expenses, I easily got a loan from our bank. But this changed when I lost my 24-year job with Boeing. There was no work in Seattle, and I found meeting my bills costing me a frightful rate of interest from small-loan companies. My "good friend" at the bank cut me off when I couldn't get a job. Then one crisis happened after another. My wife became seriously ill. My son was in an auto accident, and we were hit with injuries and lawsuits. My mother had to move in with us. My need for money became a nightmare. I sold off everything, including pawning our most precious heirlooms. In desperation, I turned to loan sharks. This resulted in threats, beatings, and unbelievable mental anguish. Thank God I finally got a decent job,but it took me seven years of struggling to pay off my debts.

How to Get Out of Debt

"How do I get out of debt?" This question is frequently asked in my classes. One approach that has proved successful is to start by preparing a balance sheet, income statement, and budget as presented in Chapter 3. An examination of your balance sheet will permit you to see how deeply you are in debt. Let us assume you find it to be $5,000 that may be itemized as follows:

Amount	Finance Charge	Source	Payment Due
$1,000	36%	X Loan Co.	Monthly, for 1 year
$3,000	6%	U.S. govt. policy	Monthly, for 10 years, beginning 4 years from now
$1,000	5%	Y Insurance Co.	Entire amount 2 years from today

You then should proceed to study your income statement and find out where savings can be made. Also, consider the possibility of augmenting your salary. Your balance sheet and income statement will help you to prepare a budget for a one-year period. This document should be worked out so that your income will exceed your expenses by a reasonable amount, which should be applied to your loan. If we assume that the savings in the first year amounts to $500, this should be utilized to reduce your most expensive debt — the 36 percent finance charge.

Examination of your balance sheet might indicate $500 in a bank that earns 5 percent. Some people like the security of a savings account for emergencies. But it is poor money management to earn 5 percent and pay up to 42 percent for a loan. If you have to obtain money in a hurry, as a result of paying off a debt, your improved credit rating should enable you to obtain money promptly. Furthermore, in lieu of going to a small-loan company at 15 to 42 percent interest, you should be able to obtain funds from a bank at a lesser cost. You can also use a credit card (at no interest) to meet plane fare and other emergency expenses.

The key to getting out of debt is yourself. You have to make the decision and follow up with the necessary will power to carry it out. The hazards of borrowing are apparent from the following experiences reported by two former students:

My worst financial experience started out as a dream. My dream began when I went to ____ Loan Company and asked to borrow $2,735 to buy a car. The manager was such a nice person. He spelled out the interest on the loan and told me there would be small extra charges for other services. I signed the agreement and received my money a week later. The sad part is that I didn't check the monthly payments until my first visit to the company. The three-year loan would cost me $4,178. I lost my job six months later and the "nice" loan manager took my car and kept my payments.

Last summer, I got a decent job, but it required furnishing my own transportation. I found a car for $800 but had to borrow $500. I hurried to ____ and got ripped off in less than 20 minutes. An employee pointed out how their interest worked and handed me a pen. I signed and now own a little payment book. There are eighteen months' payments, each for $43, for a grand total of $774.

SUMMARY

There should be only three situations that require you to borrow money: (1) to obtain an education, (2) to meet an emergency, and (3) to buy a home. It is to your advantage to determine the cost of renting money in order to obtain the best possible loan to suit your needs. This can be done easily since the Truth-in-Lending Law required every firm to list its yearly charges on a percentage basis. Also, make a policy of doing business with a reliable company that has a good reputation.

There are a variety of loan sources, and it is helpful to be familiar with them. Loans may be secured from friends and relatives, state and federal agencies, life insurance companies, credit unions, commercial banks, savings and loan associations, personal-loan companies, pawnbrokers, and loan sharks.

In order to obtain money at a fair rate of interest, you need to have a healthy financial position. Lending agencies will have you fill out information forms that permit them to look at your current employment record, net worth, size of family, home ownership, and current indebtedness. They will also contact the local credit bureau, which acts as the central depository for financial information on individuals. Your record will be reflected in a credit rating that will range from 1 through 9. The lower the number, the better your credit rating.

Make every effort to "kick" the loan habit. It is a series of bad trips that is difficult to break out of. There is a real effort on the part of the lenders to keep you in this cycle of debt. In my view, your objective should be to get out of debt—and stay out of debt.

One successful approach to breaking the loan habit is to prepare a balance sheet, income statement, and budget as presented in Chapter 3. An examination of your balance sheet will permit you to see how deeply you are in debt. Then you should proceed to study your income statement and find out where savings can be made. Also consider the possibility of augmenting your salary. Your balance sheet and income statement will help you prepare a budget for a one-year period. You should work it out so that your income will exceed your expenses by a reasonable amount. Excess income should be applied to reducing your loan. If this approach is followed over the necessary period of time, it should enable you to get out of debt.

My life, my joy, my food, my all the world.

—WILLIAM SHAKESPEARE

FOOD

Allocations for food make up one quarter of the budget of the average family living in the United States. Thus, in order to make funds available for savings and other budgeted expenditures, it is essential to spend your money wisely at the grocery store.

Here again, good management is the key.

This chapter will consider the techniques of good grocery management, for shopping carefully and well plays a vital role in ensuring your family's physical and mental well-being.

PLANNING YOUR FOOD PURCHASES

Your health is your most precious asset, and nutritious meals can be an all important factor in maintaining it. It is, therefore, essential to allocate sufficient funds to guarantee you and your family a proper diet.

In order to purchase food successfully, you should apply the concepts laid down in Chapter 1, remembering to *plan* wisely, *implement* your plans and *check* to see that your plans have been accomplished. Let us first examine the planning aspect of food purchases keeping in mind three factors: facilities, budget, and preshopping hints.

Facilities

Start your planning by assessing your capacity for home storage of staples and frozen items. Do you have a freezer? How much storage space do you have in your refrigerator? How convenient are grocery stores? How often do you eat out?

Budget

Review your budget to determine the amount of money allotted for food. Table 3-3 shows that a four-person family in the urban United States spends 24 percent of its total budget for this purpose. Thus, if such a family earns $20,000, it would spend $4,800[1] for food. On a weekly basis, this amounts to $92.31.

Once the weekly expenditure ceiling has been established, you should develop nutritious menus for this time period. Itemize the food required, such as meats, poultry, fish, bakery products, beverages, fruits, vegetables, eggs, fats and oils, prepared foods, baking ingredients, and desserts. Remember to allow for parties and visits by friends — including your childrens'.

After estimating the quantity of food required for your weekly meals, you should determine its cost. Prices can be determined on the basis of prior experience. You may also call reputable supermarkets and check ads in the local newspaper. The price of snacks at ice cream and fast-food establishments and planned dining out must also be determined. If your total exceeds the budget, modify your menus and away-from-home eating.

In making a yearly food budget, remember that grocery prices can be expected to increase. I would allow a 10 percent rise annually. Food purchased for the family away from home — restaurant meals and snacks — must also be included in the budget. The sharp rise in food costs over the past several years seems to affect every type of food outlet.

Preshopping Hints

Let us assume that your current week's food cost is estimated to be $90. Your grocery list is now completed, and the money required has

---

[1] This total includes food costs at home and away from home.

been set aside from your weekly budget. However, before you go shopping, it is wise to check the following points:

1. Are you taking advantage of specials advertised on radio, on TV, and in newspapers? Find out what stores have unadvertised specials. Some post announcements in their windows; others make loudspeaker announcements. *But do not automatically buy these items if they are not within your planned budget.* At the same time be flexible. For example, if you have a freezer and an outstanding beef special is announced, you may wish to buy a sufficient quantity for the next three weeks' menus. Likewise, if you discover a vegetable selling at bargain prices when you get to the store, consider substituting it for the planned purchase.

Keep in mind that the store's objective is to sell you the maximum amount of food and that it employs techniques such as unadvertised specials to lure you into spending, much of which is unwise and unnecessary.

2. Do not spend more than you save by driving long distances for a single bargain. It does not make sense to drive an extra ten miles to save 25 or 30 cents. The cost of gas and other expenses will far exceed the food savings.

3. Try to do volume buying. Make it a point to shop weekly instead of daily. Your time is valuable and should be taken into consideration.

4. Patronize quality discount facilities. If you belong to an organization that has stores providing considerable savings, be sure to take advantage of this. The armed forces, as noted previously, have commissary privileges that enable them to save up to 30 percent, and recently, wholesalers in certain communities opened their doors on weekends to people making sizable purchases. In cases involving large grocery orders, it pays to drive a few extra miles.

5. Do not go grocery shopping when you are hungry. You are far more tempted to make extra purchases when shopping on an empty stomach. Perhaps you have noticed thirsty customers taking orange juice or other beverages from the cooler and drinking a few sips en route to the checkout counter. Others can be seen sampling cookies or tasting fruit while shopping.

6. Buy quality merchandise. It does not pay to buy food that the store wishes to dispose of because of its inferior quality. How many times have you come home and found a packaged special on fruit to be overripe or the berries under the top layer inedible?

7. Shop with a neighbor or friend. This not only cuts your transportation cost in half and saves energy but provides you with an oppor-

tunity to exchange views on good buys and stores that give you a fair deal.

8. You may find it wise in this era of energy shortage to take a team approach and shop with two or three people. One group of four wrote me:

> Our group meets weekly to plan our food shopping strategy. This involves determining the items to purchase, estimating costs, and choosing the store with the best specials. We are so well organized that our time spent in the supermarket has been cut in half from when we first started a year ago and we need to shop less often. One person has a calculator; two of us act as runners to obtain the merchandise — this includes a careful inspection of each item. The fourth member handles the money. The savings from this team approach, we found, approximates 10 percent as compared to when we shopped separately. More important, it gives us more time to do other things. It is desirable to have a compatible group to do this food shopping. We are truly a mini-food cooperative without the headaches of such a formal organization.

9. Buy unbranded or house-brand products whenever quality is comparable. In almost every instance it is more reasonable. Major grocery chains obtain price savings because of quantity buying and no advertising costs. Some of these savings are passed on to you.

10. Buy meat, fish, and poultry when prices are low. Freeze them. It may pay to store other bargain specials as well if you have adequate space. You might also can or freeze fresh fruits and vegetables in season.

11. Health is a paramount factor when buying food. Keep nutrition in mind at all times. Fresh vegetables and fruits in season are cheaper and may be more healthful than canned items.

12. Shop around and compare stores in your general area in terms of quality, service, location, cleanliness, and price. Other things being equal, it pays to shop where you obtain the best financial deal. In this respect, remember that the saving stamps offered by some grocery stores cost the owners money. They must pass this extra cost on to their customers. So do not let yourself be enticed by the stamps unless the food items you desire to buy are equal to, or less than, the price elsewhere.

There are important price differences among stores in every locality. A survey of 198 stores in the Greater New Orleans area emphasized this point. The Louisiana Consumers' League checked items considered to be a well-rounded grocery list. More than 100 volunteers inspected groceries of similar size, weight, and brand in every store. The result of this survey pointed out that prices ranged from $20.00 to $33.65, a difference of more than 68 percent. A family that spends $4,000 a year on food could save as much as $2,720 a year by buying at a local chain store instead of the convenience shops.

13. Familiarize yourself with unit pricing. It enables you to pick out which of a number of comparable items is the least expensive by providing a common unit of measurement.

You may, for example, believe you have found the lowest price on an 18-ounce can of Del Monte peaches, as a result of checking newspaper ads from three stores. However, when you arrive at the store with the best deal, you find they have five different brands of peaches, in various-sized containers. A look at your shopping list will indicate the price for the Del Monte brand advertised in the paper. But in order to compare this brand with the four others, you must have a common denominator — in this case, it is the *price per pound.* This unit price should appear on the shelf under each brand and permits you to make a valid comparison (see Table 5-1). In this case you can quickly determine that Brand E sells for the least cost — 17½ cents per pound.

It does not necessarily follow however, that you should buy the cheapest brand. The can may be too large to store satisfactorily (Brand E is a 12-pound item); the contents may not taste as good to you or your family as those of another brand; there may be fewer peaches than in a competitor's brand. (The total weight is utilized in unit pricing and includes the liquid contents.) Still, in spite of its limitations, unit pricing can be a helpful device that should be considered in arriving at your buying decision.

14. Stay alert for unusual bargains. For example, the water used in

Table 5-1. Comparative Unit Prices.

Brand	Total Price	Total Weight	Unit Price per Pound
A	$ .72	4 lbs.	18¢
B	.18	1 lb.	18¢
C	1.20	6 lbs.	20¢
D	.57	3 lbs.	19¢
E	2.10	12 lbs.	17½¢

some communities has been suspected of being a health hazard. Bottled water from deep artesian wells has been suggested as an alternative. Some enterprising people in New Orleans (where water is suspect) buy their milk in one-gallon plastic containers. (The cost for the nonreturnable carton is 5 cents). When they have saved up a goodly number, three or four friends get together and drive one car 35 miles to obtain bottled water free at a public artesian well. The savings is sizable because a gallon of this water costs from 29 cents to 49 cents in the supermarket.

15. Save your coupons. They provide anywhere from 5 cents to 75 cents off on the purchase of food items resulting in savings of 5 to 25 percent. These coupons appear in newspapers and magazines, are placed on or in boxed foods, and are sent through the mail. When you have collected a good supply, take your coupons to the stores where you normally shop and receive the best prices. But do not fall into the same trap as one shopper: "I use all my coupons, but unfortunately I don't use many of the items. But they seem like such bargains, I can't refuse." Two final thoughts: Check the expiration dates of the coupons, if any, and consider swapping coupons with friends.

IMPLEMENTING YOUR PLAN
AT THE GROCERY STORE

Once the planning aspect is complete, you are ready to tackle the stores with confidence. So let us turn to points you should consider in implementing your grocery shopping plan.

1. Follow your marketing list. It is one thing to itemize your grocery needs, but *the real challenge is to abide by the list once you are in the store.* Why is this so difficult? Supermarkets are set up to encourage you to maximize your purchases. For example, the narrow checkout counters at which you may be forced to linger are loaded with all sorts of goodies that encourage you to do impulse buying. The longer the line, the greater the opportunity for the store to make such sales. Once forewarned, however, you can foil this game plan.

Abiding by your shopping list is also in the best interest of your health. The majority of Americans overeat and are overweight. Dr. Nathan Shock of the National Institute of Child Health and Human Development has stated, "If you could . . . eliminate all the obesity in the population, you'd be more likely to increase life span than by almost any other means."

And besides, what is the point of making a budget if you do not stick to it when you get to the store?

2. Look at each packaged item to be sure it is undamaged and what you are looking for, both in brand and quantity. It is disappointing to arrive home and find you have an 11-ounce package when you wanted 15 ounces of a particular item. Also see if the box contains a usage date, such as, "Better if used before Jan 05, 1981" Be sure to select the freshest item, with the longest life. And keep an eye out for merchandise for which you have a coupon, estimating the percentage savings if you buy it.

3. Examine fruits and vegetables carefully for possible damage. It is better to do this at the store than to come home and find that your produce is spoiled. At the same time, consider your grocer, respecting his or her attractive display and perishable merchandise.

4. Be systematic. Proceed in an orderly fashion from the time you enter the supermarket until your departure, noting the overhead signs that label the aisles. Your time is valuable — use it wisely.

5. Watch carefully while your purchases are being tallied. Be sure the cashier takes adequate time, and be alert as the prices are being rung up. Major mistakes can be made; after all, supermarket cashiers are neither certified public accounts nor mathematics majors. In addition, they are human.

During the pricing of your groceries at the checkout counter you should be watching the register rather than talking with a neighbor or friend. Prior to leaving the counter, make a point of examining your total bill, including tax. It should approximate the sum you had estimated. If there is a sizable difference, recheck every item. Also, keep an eye on how your groceries are packed. Do not hesitate to speak out if the bagger attempts to put fragile items on the bottom.

CHECKING YOUR PURCHASES

The final function in good grocery management is to *check* what you have bought. This should be done as follows:

1. Return home promptly after shopping and unpack your groceries. Examine each item for possible damage. Any defect should be noted, and the merchandise should be returned on the next visit, if not perishable. This inspection might include checking eggs and other perishables by opening a carton as well as inspecting packaged meats, poultry, fruits, etc. Food is expensive and you have paid good money

for it. You are entitled to good groceries! Do not be timid about returning unsatisfactory items. Perishable items should be returned as soon as possible.

2. Post the amount of money spent on food. Check it against what you had planned in your budget. If you have overspent, you will have to make up for it the following week. This can be painful, but it is essential in order to achieve your financial objectives.

FOOD AND HEALTH

It cannot be overemphasized that your health is your most precious asset and that proper diet is essential to its maintenance.

The U.S. Department of Agriculture (USDA) has prepared an excellent daily food guide geared to ensure your family an adequate diet (see Table 5-2). USDA categorizes food into four major groups — meat, milk, vegetable-fruit, and bread-cereal, giving daily requirements for each. As a further aid, USDA has prepared a complementary chart (Table 5-3) that presents ways to use the food groups. Once you have studied the charts you should proceed as follows, in accordance with management technique established earlier in the chapter:

1. Plan meals for a one-week period that will give you a healthy diet. (Use Tables 5-2 and 5-3 as guides.)

2. Determine the cost of this menu. Check the cost with the money available in your food budget. Make appropriate modifications to stay within the budget. *In no case should you sacrifice a healthy menu for your family.* If necessary, make a savings elsewhere in your budget.

3. Utilize the list you prepared in 2 above in doing your weekly shopping. Most families use similar foods each week. You may wish to use the format shown in Table 5-4 to help you itemize your needs as to quantity and cost.

4. Check your purchases against the list when you arrive home.

If you have special health problems, your doctor is the best person to advise you on a diet tailored to meet your needs. You, however, are the only person capable of implementing the recommendations. Doing so takes will power but pays off in a trimmer figure and greater zest for living. It should also reduce your grocery and medical bills.

Table 5-2. A Daily Food Guide.

Servings Recommended	What Counts As a Serving[a]
Meat Group 2 or more	*2 to 3 ounces of lean cooked meat, poultry, or fish.* As alternates: 1 egg, ½ cup cooked dry beans or peas, or 2 tablespoons of peanut butter may replace ½ serving of meat.
Milk Group Child, under 9 . . . . . . 2 to 3 Child, 9 to 12 . . . . 3 or more Teenager . . . . . . 4 or more Adult . . . . 2 or more Pregnant woman . . 3 or more Nursing woman . . . 4 or more	*One 8-ounce cup of fluid milk* — whole, skim, buttermilk — or evaporated or dry milk, reconstituted. As alternates: 1-inch cube cheddar-type cheese, or ¾ cup cottage cheese, ice milk, or ice cream may replace ½ cup of fluid milk.
Vegetable-Fruit Group 4 or more, including: 1 good or 2 fair sources of vitamin C 1 good source of vitamin A — at least every other day	*½ cup of vegetable or fruit; or a portion,* for example, 1 medium apple, banana, or potato, half a medium grapefruit or cantaloupe. *Good sources:* Grapefruit or grapefruit juice, orange or orange juice, cantaloupe, guava, mango, papaya, raw strawberries, broccoli, brussel sprouts, green pepper, sweet red pepper. *Fair sources:* Honeydew melon, lemon, tangerine or tangerine juice, watermelon, asparagus, cabbage, cauliflower, collards, garden cress, kale, kohlrabi, mustard greens, potatoes and sweet potatoes cooked in the jacket, rutabagas, spinach, tomatoes or tomato juice, turnip greens. *Good sources:* Dark-green and deep-yellow vegetables and a few fruits, namely; Apricots, broccoli, cantaloupe, carrots, chard, collards, cress, kale, mango, persimmon, pumpkin, spinach, sweet potatoes, turnip greens and other dark-green leaves, winter squash.
Bread-Cereal Group 4 or more	*Count only if whole-grain or enriched:* 1 slice of bread or similar serving of baked goods made with wholegrain or enriched flour, 1 ounce ready-to-eat cereal, ½ to ¾ cup cooked cereal, corn meal, grits, spaghetti, macaroni, noodles, or rice.
Other Foods as Needed *to round out meals and* *meet energy requirements*	Refined unenriched cereals and flours and products made from them; sugars; butter, margine, other fats. Try to include some vegetable oil among the fats used.

[a] Amounts actually served may differ — small for young children, extra large (or seconds) for very active adults or teenagers.

Source: U.S. Department of Agriculture, *Daily Food Guide*, Washington, D.C., 1978.

Table 5-3. Use of Food Groups: Some Ways to Use in Family Meals.

Meat Group

Foods from meat group usually appear as the main dish, the "meat," at a meal; or as an ingredient in a main dish — a soup, stew, salad, casserole, or sandwich. Small amounts of two or more foods from the group used during the day can add up to a serving. Egg used in custards and baked goods counts too.

Milk Group

Milk may be served as a beverage at meals or snacks. Some may be included on cereals and in preparation of other foods — soups, main dishes, custards, puddings, baked goods. Cubed or sliced cheese (plain, on crackers, or in sandwiches) and ice cream or ice milk (at meals or in between) may replace part of the milk.

Vegetable–Fruit Group

Vegetables or fruit are part of most meals. Serve some raw and some cooked, some with crisp textures and some with soft; and contrast strong flavor with mild, and sweet with sour for variety in meals. Brighten meals with color — a slice of red tomato, a sprig of dark greens, or other colorful vegetable or fruit. Both vegetables and fruit are used in salads and as side dishes; some vegetables in casseroles, stews, and soups; and some fruits raw, as juices, and in desserts, such as cobblers, pies, or shortcakes. Many families include their vitamin-C food as a citrus fruit or juice, as melon or strawberries (when in season) at breakfast.

Bread–Cereal Group

Foods from this group are served at breakfast as toast, muffins, pancakes, or grits; cereals, cooked or ready to eat; at lunch and dinner as macaroni, spaghetti, noodles, or rice in a casserole or a side dish; as any kind of bread and as a baked dessert, such as cake, pastry, and cookies. Because breads and cereals are well liked, usually inexpensive, and can be served a number of ways, they are used more than four times a day in most households.

Other Foods as Needed

Some of these items, such as flour, sugar, and fats, are ingredients in recipes. Some may be added to other foods at the table — sugar on cereals, dressing on salads, and spread on bread.

Source: U.S. Department of Agriculture, *Food Groups*, Washington, D.C. 1977.

Table 5-4. Food-Shopping List.

Food	Brand	Price per lb/oz	Quantity	Est. Cost	Actual Cost
MEAT GROUP					
Beef					
Calf liver					
Corned beef					
Beef roast					
Beef ribs					
Beef steaks					
Soup meat					
Stew meat					
Ground beef					
Ground chuck					
Ground round					
Pork					

Food	Brand	Price per lb/oz	Quantity	Est. Cost	Actual Cost
MILK GROUP					
Butter					
Margarine					
Cheese					
Cottage					
Cream					
Swiss					
American					
Other					
Milk					
Ice Cream					
Eggs					

Other

Bacon

Chops

Ham

Pork loin

Sausage

Lamb

Chops

Roast

Chicken

Cornish hens

Turkey

Fish & shellfish

Trout

Catfish

Shrimp

Oysters

Table 5-4. Continued.

Food	Brand	Price per lb/oz	Quantity	Est. Cost	Actual Cost
Lobster					
Sandwich meat					
Bologna					
Frankfurters					
Other					
Subtotal					
VEGETABLE-FRUIT GROUP					
Peas					
Green pepper					
Potatoes					
Spinach					
Squash					

Food	Brand	Price per lb/oz	Quantity	Est. Cost	Actual Cost
Subtotal					
BREAD & CEREAL GROUP					
Biscuits					
Flour					
Muffin Mix					
Cake Mix					
French Bread					

80

Sweet potatoes	White Bread
Tomatoes	Rye
Turnips	Rolls
Apples	Wholewheat
Applesauce	Dry Cereal
Bananas	Grits
Berries	Oatmeal
Cantaloupe	Pancake Mix
Cherries	Spaghetti
Dried Fruits	Macaroni
Grapefruit	Noodles
Grapes	Rice
Oranges	Other
Peaches	
Pears	
Pineapples	

81

Table 5-4. Continued.

Food	Brand	Price per lb/oz	Quantity	Est. Cost	Actual Cost	Food	Brand	Price per lb/oz	Quantity	Est. Cost	Actual Cost
Plums											
Tangerines											
Watermelon											
Fruit juices											
Jellies											
Other											
Subtotal						Subtotal					
OTHER FOODS						NONFOOD					
Cola						Cleanser					
Cocoa						Detergent					

Coffee	Paper															
Cooking oil	Toilet															
Frozen dinners	Towels															
Olives	Soap															
Peanut butter	Other															
Pepper																
Pickles																
Pies																
Pizzas																
Popcorn																
Nuts																
Salt																
Soups																
Spices																

83

Table 5-4 (Continued).

Food	Brand	Price per lb/oz	Quantity	Est. Cost	Actual Cost	Food	Brand	Price per lb/oz	Quantity	Est. Cost	Actual Cost
Sugar											
Tea											
Other											
Subtotal						Subtotal					
						TOTAL					

Note: This sample format was based upon the weekly food and non-food items purchased by a four-family unit. It will help you to design a form that will be suitable for your family. Please note that a column is available to indicate the brand. Some shoppers find this helpful because when they make a list of specials from the newspapers they find that only certain brands of an item are on sale. Often these sale items are not clearly marked; thus having brand designations on a shopping list can be a time saver.

FOOD CO-OPS

One good way to save money in your food budget is to be a member of a consumer-owned and operated food co-op. (If there is not one in your community, it is relatively easy to organize one among your friends and neighbors.) A food co-op is a group of people who buy groceries collectively, and in bulk quantities, at wholesale for their own use, doing all the work necessary to purchase and distribute the food. By this means the "middle" function in the food distribution chain (the grocery store) is eliminated. In order to secure money to buy items, each member of the co-op contributes a small amount, the amount being determined by the co-op members.

The typical consumer co-op provides a limited number of items. It is neither a supermarket for one-stop shopping nor the corner grocery store. Often it starts out selling only produce. As the membership increases, dairy products, eggs, and some grains might be added. There are large well-organized co-ops that do offer canned goods, spices, fish, meat, and other products.

Co-Ops in Action

Co-op members may be organized into five working groups: buyers, weighers, storekeepers, transporters, and cleaners. Sharing duties ensures that no single member ends up with too much to do. Willingness to work and cooperate are essential if the co-op is to work.

In a food co-op there are specific jobs that must be done each time food is bought and distributed:

1. Collect the orders of members.
2. Buy the food from wholesalers and bring it to a convenient distribution point.
3. Separate the purchases into categories: potatoes, rice, beans, tomatoes, etc.
4. Weigh and price items sold by weight. Price items sold by the piece.
5. Open the doors for business only after the above tasks are completed. At that time members can pick up their orders for the week. (Open promptly at the time that had been specified.)
6. Assure that the "storekeeper" is available to accept payment for goods and record sales and that he or she has the financial records available for members to review.
7. See that the members turn in their order for the next week when making their pickups.
8. After all orders have been picked up, clean up the distribution area and store the co-op equipment until the following week.

Importance of Good Management

Like any other successful business venture, a food co-op must be well managed. It should be operated in accordance with the three principles emphasized throughout this book. Members must (1) *plan what they are going to do*, (2) *carry out that plan*, and then (3) *check to see that it has been done properly*. In regard to a food co-op, *planning* involves establishing money needs, arranging for the necessary personnel to perform the various duties, acquiring space for the needed storage and operation of the co-op, establishing contacts and contracts with wholesalers, maintaining (and perhaps broadening) membership, deciding what items to purchase, and determining what written instructions are required. The *implementation* of the plan calls for a good plan of organization that spells out who does what. And *checking* includes keeping a close watch on the money, equipment, and membership.

Advantages of Co-Ops

What benefits are there to members of a successful food co-op? A co-op can obtain food at a lower price because purchases are made in bulk at wholesale prices and then sold to the members at that price plus a markup covering operating costs. Since members share the work, the primary costs are transportation, rent (if any) of a distribution site, paper to keep records, and an adding machine (or perhaps an inexpensive pocket or desk computer). There are no expenses for salaries or allowances for profits. The more conscientious the group members, the more money can be saved. However, it must be noted that even though the co-op may buy in bulk and at a wholesale price, it may not always be able to sell every item at a lower price than a chain store.

A HOME GARDEN

With the high cost of food these days, growing your own fruit and vegetables would appear to be a great way to save money. Home-grown produce also has an appeal to the health-minded and the environmentalists. Attractive as it sounds in theory, however, home gardening in reality can be demanding, discouraging, and expensive. One family planted a small vegetable garden, specializing in tomatoes, anticipating not only saving money but also savoring the taste of tomatoes straight from the garden. But insects ate the green fruit before they could apply protective measures. Things then went from bad to worse, and after six months they gave up the project.

In contrast, another family has maintained a successful vegetable garden for years and much of their spare time is spent with this hobby. Anyone interested in starting a vegetable garden should contact the local county agent. He or she can give good advice on preparing and maintaining the soil, advise what crops do well in the area, and provide many other helpful suggestions.

HOME CANNING

Home canning can be a money saver, but requires extreme care. This fact is highlighted from time to time when people die from botulism (a type of food poisoning) as a result of improper canning. If you decide to do home canning, be sure to select appropriate foods and sterilize and seal your foods meticulously.

COOKBOOKS AND OTHER GUIDES

In order to plan menus wisely, you should own a good cookbook. Today bookstores and libraries are well stocked with general basic books to the exotic and special-purpose volumes dealing with such topics as low-calorie, meatless, sugar-free, poultry, hamburger, Chinese, leftover, salad, or French meals to name only a few. In spite of the recent flood of cookbooks, I still recommend that old favorite, *Joy of Cooking*.[2] Well written and easy to follow, it features a myriad of splendid recipes as well as separate chapters on "The Foods We Eat," "Entertaining," "Menus," "Canning," "Salting and Smoking," and "Freezing." Another good seller is *Weight Watchers Cookbook*, with daily menus that enable you to reduce.[3] People who like to count their calories should also enjoy *The Low-Calorie Diet*.[4]

How Sex Can Keep You Slim[5] received much publicity when it appeared in 1972. The author, Dr. Abraham Friedman, has treated metabolic diseases and obesity for over 25 years. His recommenda-

---

[2] Irma S. Rombauer and Marion Rombauer Becker (Indianapolis: Bobbs Merrill Co., Inc., latest edition).

[3] Jean Nidetch (Great Neck, N.Y.: Hearthside Press, lastest edition).

[4] Marvin Small (New York: Pocket Books, latest edition).

[5] Abraham Friedman (Englewood Cliffs, N.J.: Prentice-Hall, Inc., 1972).

tions include "reaching for your mate instead of your plate." He also prescribes essential foods that he calls R.S.V.P.:

Raw fruits — three servings per day. (Be sure to include at least one citrus fruit or juice daily.)
Salads — all you want. Use vegetable oil (1 tablespoon) and vinegar dressing.
Vegetables — three servings per day, especially the green or leafy vegetables.
Proteins — three servings per day.

Dr. Friedman states that "proper nutrition plays an important role in our general health and well-being. It is essential for proper performance of all our body functions and activities, including sexual activity. A proper diet will help keep you fit and slim, and even enhance your sexual potency."[6]

There is an abundance of current literature on cooking that can be obtained free. For example, most public utilities furnish their customers with pamphlets that contain menus, recipes, and suggestions helpful to the homemaker. These are frequently available at public libraries as well as directly from the utilities.

Another potential source of information on diet and nutrition is the dietitian at your local hospital who can offer good advice on menus and may have literature available. Public Health officials and librarians can also provide helpful material on cooking. Be on the alert for new recipes appearing in newspapers and magazines. TV also offers several good programs on food preparation.

ACTIONS YOU CAN TAKE TO COPE WITH INFLATION
AND THE ENERGY SHORTAGE

1. Check the percent of your budget spent annually for food. If your expenses exceed the norm (about 25 percent), consider such methods as: a garden of your own; substituting less-expensive but equally nutritious items; shopping less frequently; car pooling; taking advantage of specials; buying unbranded or house-brand products; cooking outdoors whenever possible, using charcoal in lieu of the electricity or gas needed for indoor cooking; eliminating junk foods; and avoiding high-priced specialty stores.

2. If you have a freezer, are you actually using it or could the appliance be sold and the store act as your storage place? And speaking of storage space, can you cut down on the number of items stored at home in order to avoid spoilage?

---

[6] Ibid., p. 104.

SUMMARY

Food makes up about one quarter of the budget of the average family living in the United States. It is essential to spend your money wisely at the grocery store so that adequate funds are available for savings and other budgeted expenditures.

Your health is your most precious asset and appropriate food can be an important factor in maintaining it. Having nutritious menus within your available budget requires good management. This involves performing three functions: *planning* your food purchases wisely, *implementing* what you plan, and *checking* to see that what you planned has been accomplished. Initially, you should review your budget to determine the amount of money allowed for food. Once the weekly expenditure has been established, the required menus should be developed for this period. By itemizing the food needed for each of the weekly meals, you can arrive at your grocery requirements.

Points to consider prior to shopping for food include: taking advantage of specials; not spending more than you save by driving long distances; shopping when you are not hungry or thirsty; buying quality merchandise; becoming familiar with unit pricing; shopping with a neighbor or friend; buying house brands; buying items like meat when prices are low and freezing them; buying nutritious foods; and shopping where you obtain the best financial deal — other things being equal.

While doing your shopping you should: follow your grocery list; examine your purchases carefully; be systematic in moving through a store; watch the cashier's adding machine as your purchases are being totaled.

The final function in good grocery management is to check on what you have purchased. Return home promptly after shopping and examine each item for damage or spoilage. Do not be timid about returning unsatisfactory items. And be sure to check the money spent on food against what you planned in your budget.

When I feel a desire to exercise, I lie down until it goes away.

—ROBERT HUTCHINS

CLOTHING AND PERSONAL HEALTH

Clothing and personal care make up about 9 percent of the budget of the average family living in the United States. As in the case of food, it is essential to spend your money wisely in these areas so that adequate funds are available for savings and other expenditures.

Here again, good management is crucial. Performing the management functions of wise *planning,* *implementing* these plans, and *checking* to see that what you have planned has been carried through will help you meet your clothing and personal health needs within the allotted budget. This chapter will investigate techniques for maximizing your clothes-buying power and keeping you as fit as possible. A word of caution: *do not* skimp on health care — it is far less expensive to take preventive health measures than to pay for operations.

CLOTHING

Planning Your Clothing Purchases

Before considering specific purchases, sit down and reexamine your budget in terms of the *total sum* you have allotted to clothing and personal needs. The majority of such expenditures will not be made in equal amounts throughout the year. Therefore, you must itemize your specific requirements on a weekly basis. Certain personal-care expenses such as visits to the barber shops, beauty parlor, and drugstore for sundries may occur regularly, each week or month. Such expenses should be easy to estimate accurately. In contrast, your expensive outer clothing may be bought on a seasonal basis. These expenditures will be rather difficult to determine, but do your best. It is helpful to develop a checklist itemizing the entire family's clothing needs from the skin out (see Table 6-1). Your estimated cost should allow for a 10 percent increase during the year.

Once you have decided upon the amount of money needed for clothing, you may wish to consider the following guidelines, which can help you stay within your budget.

1. *Shop around.* Before you buy, compare stores in your community as to quality, service, location, cleanliness, and price. Other things being equal, it pays to shop where you can obtain the best price — but, again, I stress, "other things being equal."

2. *Consider reputation!* Choose a store that is known for its quality merchandise and willingness to accept returns (within a reasonable period of time) graciously. It is surprising how pleasant some stores can be at the moment of purchase but how disagreeable at the time of return. A number of stores, however, have fair return policies and place competent people in their adjustment departments.

Since many items of clothing are expensive, the possibility of returning unsatisfactory merchandise is important. A dollar saved on a costly item is meaningless if upon examination once back home the garment turns out to be shoddy and unfit to wear. Return privileges should include receiving your money back, obtaining full credit, or exchanging the article in question. The choice should be yours.

3. *Take advantage of legitimate specials* as advertised on radio, on TV, and in the newspapers. Stores will often reduce prices on clothing before or after each season. But be sure that these specials will not soon be going out of style and are not faulty. Sales are not announced for your benefit; they permit merchants to bring in business at slow times or unload merchandise that it is not to their advantage to retain.

4. *Beware of buying from stores going out of business.* There is no opportunity to return merchandise after the owners have liquidated their stock. Such "bargains" also permit some unscrupulous merchants to restock their shelves with inferior merchandise.

5. *Patronize quality discount facilities.* Many communities have quality discount stores which offer sizable savings. Again let me

Table 6-1. Clothing Shopping List of _____ as of _____
_____, 19 _____.

	Estimate	Actual	Store (name, address, phone)
Outer Garments			
Undergarments			

Table 6-1 (Continued).

	Estimate	Actual	Store (name, address, phone)
Personal Care			
Total			

stress the importance of checking the return policies of any firm you deal with.

6. *Do not buy garments that are too highly styled.* Manufacturers and retailers realize that by changing styles frequently, they will increase sales. The higher styled the item, the quicker it will be outdated. Try to purchase a dress or suit that can last for a reasonable period of time, so that it will wear out and not "style out."

7. *Consider usefulness.* Before buying a piece of expensive clothing, question its versatility. For example, the color of a jacket should permit it to be worn with more than one pair of slacks. And do not forget that basic black dress which can be used for morning, afternoon, or formal wear with an appropriate choice of accessories.

8. *Plan to make some of your clothes.* It is surprising how much you can save by buying material and making your own garments. The earlier in life you learn to sew, the greater the savings. You should, therefore, allow for a sewing machine in your budget. This investment can pay for itself many times over, not only in terms of sewing new garments but by permitting you to do your own repairs and alterations as well.

There is considerable satisfaction in creating your own models. Furthermore, the workmanship in most clothing today is not comparable to what you can do at home. Patterns are readily available in stores and by mail order. Sewing lessons can be obtained in most communities.

Over the years, my wife has made dresses for herself and our daughter at considerable savings. She has also designed drapes, curtains, and bedspreads. Recently she saw a dress that was selling for $44 in a prominent department store. Here is what it cost her to duplicate it:

Material (polyester knit), 3 yards @ $3.95 per yard	$11.85
Buttons	2.50
Zipper	1.00
Pattern	3.00
Thread	.50
Trim and interfacing	2.10
Total	$20.95[1]

[1] In arriving at your total, you may wish to pay yourself a fair return and include this figure in your overall price. My wife enjoys sewing as a hobby and is a homemaker. However, other individuals who could obtain a paying job in lieu of the time spent sewing must add this hourly return to arrive at the total cost. There may also be gas or other transportation expenses involved. Time is money and in such cases it might be more cost efficient to do other work. Good money management includes managing time and determining the cutoff point below which it doesn't pay to make your own clothes.

This well-confected dress required ten hours to complete. Simpler patterns, such as sports clothes, take her three to four hours. It is apparent that adequate time is needed to do a good job, but my wife says, "I love to sew. It's fun to design my drapes or improve on a dress I've seen in a store. The extra loving care of quality workmanship pays off in ample seams, regular topstitching, wide hems, quality materials, and good fit. It's fun to wear my creations to parties and have friends guess where I bought them."

9. *Know your fabrics.* Whether you make your own clothes or buy them ready-made, beware of materials that are not washable, durable, or easy to work with. Watch for fabric sales — particularly for good remnants, material that is flawless but has only a few yards remaining in the bolt. It is often available at half price because of its limited quantity.

10. *Buy practical clothing.* Garments should be wrinkle resistant and ready to wear after coming out of the washer and dryer. There is no need to spend time ironing today. How delightful to pack all your clothing in one small bag that can be slipped under the seat of the airplane!

Implementing Your Plan at the Shops

What are the points you should keep in mind while shopping?

1. Abide by your list of planned clothing purchases. Bring along a list of the items you plan to buy and stick to it. When you walk into the store, go directly to the department where you intend to make your purchases. Stores will make every effort to induce you to buy additional goods. Their displays will be attractive, and their salespeople are trained to push their wares. When you buy shoes, for instance, you may be encouraged to select a matching bag or other coordinated accessories including scarves and hats. Don't waver from your planned list.

Salespeople in some stores receive bonuses (often a 5 to 10 percent commission) for selling old merchandise — items that may have been in the store for several years. Therefore, be suspicious of items that are not in style. Several of my students also work for department stores where they receive a splendid on-the-job education on how to encourage sales. One young woman who sells ladies' apparel told the class, "I have been taught to play to a person's vanity. This approach is highly successful. Sometimes it requires my calling the store manager to assist in closing a flattery sale. He's good-looking, and the customers love his approval."

2. Shop with someone whose judgment you respect in order to find

out what really looks best on you. The salesperson's advice may prove costly, as he or she may automatically favor the most expensive item.

3. Shop during a quiet time of day whenever possible. This permits you to examine the merchandise more carefully. Salespeople are also more helpful when they are not being harassed.

4. Check carefully on the alteration policy of the firm prior to making a purchase. Are alterations made free of charge? Do the tailors do first-class work? Faulty workmanship can ruin an expensive suit. If you have to return to the store several times for a proper fit, you may decide it is not worth the effort. The garment then remains in your closet until given away or thrown out.

Checking On Your Purchases

1. As soon as you get home, reexamine your merchandise for defects. If the color or style has lost its appeal in the light of day, you may decide to return your purchase. If so, do it promptly. Keep all your receipts and leave the tags on the garments so that there is no question as to when and where you bought them.

2. Maintain your clothes by keeping them neat and clean and making minor repairs. But once they go out of style or look worn, eliminate them from your wardrobe! It may not pay, for example, to have shabby shoes half-soled. The repair cost is too high compared to the price of buying a new pair. You may be able to sell your old clothes to a thrift shop or include them in a garage sale. The Salvation Army or other charitable organizations will be happy to pick them up. Remember, if you give them away, there may be a tax benefit based on their fair value at the time.

3. Keep your clothing needs to a minimum, reviewing your wardrobe frequently. If you have a limited amount of storage space, it is foolish to fill it with dust collectors. Do not overbuy and make yourself a storage center. Styles change too quickly, and more practical garments are being created each year. You do not need the stockpile your parents required because it is so easy with wash-and-wear clothing today.

4. If you have received a "bum deal," keep after the store until it makes a fair settlement. This may require going to the Better Business Bureau, local consumer agency, or small-claims court. And tell your friends about your experience. Here is how one person won out:

Last year, I bought a pair of tennis shoes. They had been used only eight times in three weeks, but both shoes wore out in the inside heel.

I took the shoes back to the store in hopes of exchanging them for another pair. The manager of the shoe department kept me waiting for 45 minutes. He then told me the shoes would have to be returned to the manufacturer, who had to OK the exchange. A reply was promised within six weeks. The manager told me that I would be called when he received the word.

After waiting eight weeks, I finally called the store and was informed that no answer had been received. I called several times in the next two months and was given the same story, "No word yet."

Two more weeks passed, and I decided to visit the store with my roommate, who is an attorney. When I introduced my friend, the manager informed me of receiving authorization for me to select another pair of shoes. It took perseverance, but sometimes this seems to be the only way to get results.

PERSONAL CARE

Major personal-care items should include a yearly medical examination, dental checkups, health club membership and physical-fitness programs, beauty and barber shop visits, and sundries for good grooming. *Do not skimp* on these expenditures. Periodic visits to your physician and dentist, as well as keeping you fit, can help you avoid expensive medical bills (see Chapter 10 in regard to health insurance). Furthermore, by keeping physically fit you can be more productive and this increases your earning potential.

Annual Physical Examination

An annual physical examination[2] and other visits to your doctor as required can be your best single investment. It is surprising how many people will spend more on car checkups than on assuring their own health. If you do not have a family doctor, contact the local

---

[2] The yearly physical for healthy individuals has been questioned by some writers. They claim that few diseases can be detected by the usual annual examination, and others develop so quickly (e.g., certain breast cancers) that one would have to be checked every six to eight weeks to assure that one did not have them. Thus, a "good" physical could give a false sense of assurance. There are some exams that *are* desirable (e.g., pap smears for women, blood pressure), but these can often be reasonably had at screening clinics.

hospital director for the name of a physician. Everyone should have a doctor who considers him (or her) a regular patient. A first-class medical examination can be obtained at reputable hospitals in your area. There are a number of hospitals in the United States that have obtained national recognition for the thoroughness of their physical examinations. Among them are the Mayo Clinic in Rochester, Minnesota; Ochsner Clinic, New Orleans; the Lahey Clinic in Boston; the Scripps Clinic and Research Foundation in La Jolla, California; and Duke University Hospital, Durham, North Carolina. You normally spend one or two days in the hospital, with the cost ranging from $195 to $450 plus travel and accommodations. The advantage of going to a quality hospital is that it has specialists in many areas. Thus, a problem that might go undetected elsewhere could be diagnosed properly and corrective measures taken promptly.

The best time to have a physical examination is when you are well. A detailed health check can permit the physician to advise you of possible danger signals. He or she can then prescribe courses of action to improve your health, thus preventing costly and debilitating illness.

Dental Checkups

Periodic dental checkups are also important. They permit problems to be detected before they become serious. At the same time, have your teeth cleaned. This enhances your personal appearance as well as preventing serious trouble. Checkups and cleanings should be done every six months. Most tooth loss is due to periodontal disease, caused by tartar buildup. Even the best "flossers" need to have this removed. Dental checkups are needed maintenance, not purely preventive checks.

Health Club Membership and Physical-Fitness Plans

The importance of physical fitness was emphasized in a *Newsweek* article entitled "Tips on How to Stay Younger"[3] It pointed out the advantages of keeping your weight down, avoiding alcohol and tobacco, and having a sound exercise program, regular physical examinations, and a healthy mental outlook that permits useful and satisfying activities. An enjoyable way to fulfill the exercise part of the bill is to join a health club.

[3] April 16, 1973, p. 63.

Health Clubs

Health-club memberships at the YMCAs throughout the country vary in price from $200 to $400. The facilities available for this fee normally include steam room, sunlamp, sauna, exercise room, indoor track, weight equipment, swimming pool, gymnastics, basketball, volleyball, handball, squash, fitness testing, and counseling. Massages; yoga, dance, and exercise classes; and special fitness classes such as "The Y's Way to a Healthy Back" or the Fitness Finders Program (see below) are usually offered to members for a nominal extra fee. There are many private health clubs, as well, that have ample exercise facilities; however, some have proved to be promotional come-ons, so be careful to read and understand any contract before signing it.

Fitness Finders Program

Today, the importance is recognized of having an exercise program that strengthens the heart and improves the cardiovascular system. An outstanding fitness program, currently being sponsored by the YMCA, is based on the Fitness Finders system of conditioning exercises. The pilot study was headed by Glen Suelymes, Director of Program Development for the President's Council on Physical Fitness and Sports. The significant results of the 12-week program were lower pulse rates, decreased body weight and increased muscular strength and endurance. The program also proved to be fun.[4]

If you devise a fitness program of your own or enroll in one of the many programs being offered, be sure to check with your doctor first to be sure that your physical condition is up to such a regimen.

Personal Exercise Program

Last year I did a TV commercial for the YMCA, describing the series of exercises that keeps me in shape. My three times-a-week workout includes the following routine: (1) head stand, 1 minute; (2) skip rope, 200 times; (3) sit-ups, 50; (4) pull-ups, 6; (5) jog, 2 to 5 miles.

A history of nutritious meals and appropriate exercise permitted me to establish a physical-fitness record in the military and made it easy to complete the paratrooper course as a senior officer.

Today, exercise and proper diet help me to meet my commitments as a teacher and author. At times, I may be tempted to skip my exercise routine. But my friend and jogging companion, Martin Klein, M.D., will encourage me, saying "Come on and run — you'll

---

[4] Over the years, a fitness-and-diet regimen pays off financially as well as in terms of good health. A reformed two-pack-a-day smoker can save more than $300 a year. Savings on liquor and drugs are likely to be even greater.

feel a helluva lot better afterwards!" Marty's medical advice always proves to be right.

Track Clubs
In recent years there has been increased interest in competitive track events for people in their middle and senior years. Mr. Ted Haydon is presently coach at the University of Chicago Track Club. It has about 200 members ranging from Olympic-level competitors to "ordinary" individuals in their sixties. Haydon was an assistant track coach of the U.S. Olympic track teams in 1968 and 1972. His specialty is developing long-distance runners.

A *Wall Street Journal* article featured Coach Haydon and quoted the views of a 58-year-old Chicago lawyer who began running at the club for exercise in the early 1960s.

> "Ted let me go on my own for a while, but pretty soon he started asking me to get into one of his meets. He said I'd get more out of it if I had a competitive goal," says Mr. McLendon. "I told him that nobody wanted to see some old guy stagger in after everybody else had gone home. He said that no matter how slow I was, there'd be somebody out there slower. He was right."
>
> Mr. McLendon now enters about a dozen meets a year, competing in everything from the 220-yard dash to the marathon. "Every once in a while I catch some kid by surprise," he says with a laugh. "It does him a lot of good, you know? He figures that if a man my age can beat him, he'd better start working harder."
>
> Mr. Haydon, too, still competes in track despite his 62 years; he runs fairly regularly and holds several age-group records in his speciality, the hammer throw. For the ordinary middle-ager, however, he prescribes moderation in exercise. "It's better to do too little than too much, especially at first," he says.[5]

Please note Coach Haydon's advice: "Better to do too little than too much."[6] The cost of membership in Haydon's club is un-

[5] Fredrick C. Klein, "To Be on This Team You Needn't Be Great To Enjoy Yourself," *Wall Street Journal*, February 25, 1975, p. 1.
[6] I learned the hard way. I joined the New Orleans Track Club last year and participated in a meet on a June morning. My events and times: 100 yards—13.2 seconds; 440 yards—1.23; ½ mile—3.15; 1 mile—6.49; 2 miles—15.43. Won three firsts and two seconds in my age group. And my Achilles tendons were sore for a month. Now it's back to jogging in moderation.

believably low. There are no dues. Entry fee for each meet is $1 no medals are awarded. If medals are presented, the fee is $1 for each event entered.

Most sizable communities have track or running clubs. New Orleans, for example, has the New Orleans Track Club, Inc., and its membership, too, costs very little. Last year it held 22 meets. Investigate the track clubs in your area if such sports appeal to you. Joining will benefit you not only physically, but also socially and mentally (somehow, when you are fit you seem to think more clearly). If running is not your "cup of tea," there are other sports that have clubs for the amateur hobby athlete in such fields as tennis, bicycling, and walking.

Proper Diet

In addition to new developments in exercise the diet prescribed by experts has been modified. The cardiovascular system, in particular, has received much attention recently, in view of the fact that heart attacks are a major killer. There have been studies with respect to the limits of saturated fats in the diet. Now doctors are talking about unsaturated and polyunsaturated fats.

Saturated fat has been cited as a possible cause of coronary heart disease. Foods rich in such fat include eggs, cheese, whole milk, butter, coconut and palm oils, pork, chocolate, and avocado. *Reduce and Stay Reduced on the Prudent Diet*[7] is a book written by Dr. Norman Jolliffe, head of New York City's Bureau of Nutrition, to help combat heart attacks. His diet reduces the consumption of saturated fats and increases the intake of unsaturated fats. He suggests limiting the number of eggs eaten to four per week and including fish frequently as part of the menu.

For a more complete discussion on diet, refer to Chapter 5. In particular, study Table 5-2 (A Daily Food Guide) and Table 5-3, which presents ways to use the food groups.

Barber and Beauty Shops

What about beauty or barber shop visits and sundries for good grooming? They can be good for your morale (mental health) and good for those who look at you if you are well groomed.

It is important to select a hair stylist with a good reputation. Your friends and relatives can give you sound advice. Prices vary con-

[7] S & S Enterprises, Los Angeles, California, 1964.

siderably so obtain charges *prior* to a visit. And do not forget to add the cost of a tip. Salons may offer such varied services as cutting, washing, blow drying, coloring, setting, conditioning, permanent waves (straight, body, curl), shampoo and sets, facial, manicure, pedicure, hair pieces (to include cleaning and styling), straightening, hair analysis, and hair-care products.

In view of the many services available at hair salons for both men and women, it is easy to exceed your budget allotted for personal care. After a recent visit to a beauty shop my daughter Ellen remarked: "I intended to spend $20, but my hair stylist was cute and said I needed a conditioner plus a number of hair-care products. His friendly persuasion resulted in my spending $39."

If you are handy you may decide on the do-it-yourself approach for much of your personal grooming. And many parents have become proficient at hair cutting and styling for members of their family. It is important to shop wisely for hair-care products and other sundries in a manner suggested earlier in the chapter for clothing.

ACTIONS YOU CAN TAKE TO COPE WITH INFLATION AND THE ENERGY SHORTAGE

1. Have a health checkup when required and take other preventive measures to avoid illness wherever possible. Begin a physical-fitness program, using a facility like the YMCA.

2. Clothing-conservation measures might include: wearing a sweater and/or thermal clothing to cut heating costs; drying clothes on the line whenever possible, instead of using the clothes dryer; eliminating fad clothing; and sewing clothes yourself.

SUMMARY

Clothing and personal care comprise about 9 percent of the budget of the average family living in the United States. It is essential to spend your money wisely for clothes and personal items so that adequate funds are available for savings and other expenditures.

Buying clothing, like purchasing food, calls for good management in order to meet your clothing needs within the allotted budget. This can be accomplished by performing the management functions of *planning* wisely, *implementing* what you plan, and *checking* to see what you planned has been completed.

Your appearance is important in both social and business contacts. In view of the high cost of many clothing items, it is essential to make good use of money available for this purpose. A major factor in keeping your costs down is to make your own clothes. It is also economical to minimize the size of your wardrobe.

The most essential personal-care item can be an annual physical examination and other visits to your doctor as required. It is far less expensive to take preventive health measures than to pay for operations. Appropriate expenditures on physical fitness also can be helpful in maintaining your health — your most precious asset.

TRANSPORTATION: CARS HIGHLIGHTED

A car is a major investment. It is also a recurring purchase, made at frequent intervals.

If you buy 20 cars in your lifetime, you could easily spend $100,000 for this purpose. In addition, another $30,000 could be spent on finance charges. The primary purpose of this chapter is to present facts that could enable a car buyer to save up to $50,000 of a potential $130,000 outlay. We shall also discuss how to maintain and sell a car most advantageously. Alternate forms of transportation, such as motorcycles, bicycles, public transportation, and our own two feet, are covered as well.

One car buyer once told me, "I have owned 16 cars, including Fords, Cadillacs, and Mercedes, keeping them from one to six years. Most were good buys, but one was a disaster. My first purchase was an emotional thing; I had to have that car, and it cost me a bundle. I gradually learned, however, that in order to obtain a good deal, I needed to take my time and examine all aspects of the transaction."

A careful reading of this chapter should provide you with the information needed to follow his example.

CAR BUYING
AND THE MANAGEMENT APPROACH

The Planning Phase:
Determining Your Objective

Successful car purchasing not only requires time and study but profits from a management approach. As explained in Chapter 1, and emphasized since, to arrive at a sound decision, you should first *determine your objective*, answering the questions what, when, where, how, and why.

First, *what* type of car is best for you? Factors to consider include size of family, purpose for which the car is to be used, and availability of funds for both the initial purchase and the upkeep. It can be helpful to prepare a checklist of points that you wish to consider in making your purchase. Table 7-1 presents a format that can be modified to meet your requirements.

If your checklist indicates that economy and ease of parking are of prime importance, a subcompact may be the answer. Contrariwise, if money is not a main concern and luxury is paramount, you may select one of the expensive models. A Cadillac, Continental, or other large car will give you a comfortable ride. You will pay for this privilege, however, in such areas as greater initial cost, limited gas mileage, considerable annual depreciation, sizable maintenance charges, and increased parking problems. Likewise, the number of service agencies available may be fewer than for the popular low-priced automobiles.

Given the current concern about energy shortages and pollution, manufacturers of luxury automobiles may be subjected to greater pressure in the future to reduce the size of their products. In Europe the most expensive cars are considerably smaller than comparably priced vehicles built in the United States. The trend to small cars may influence your decision because of the reduced resale value of large luxury cars in the event that they are no longer manufactured.

The question of size recalls a conversation between my wife and the president of a major automobile company. We had recently returned from living in Europe for three years. She inquired why his company did not manufacture a small car like the European models, which we found to be so practical and economical. He replied, "Well, you see, we make our largest profit per car on our biggest and most

Table 7-1. Format to Help Determine Which Car Is Appropriate For You.

	1	2	3	4	5	6	
Size of family	___		___	___	___	___	___ over 6
Purpose	___ business		___ pleasure		___ business and pleasure		
Yearly mileage	___ less than 5,000		___ 5,000–15,000		___ over 15,000		
Funds available:							
Initial purchase	___ less than $1,000		___ $1,000–2,999		___ $3,000–4,999		___ over $4,999
Annual upkeep	___ less than $1,200		___ $1,200–2,599		___ $2,600–3,799		___ over $3,799
Reputation of dealer	___ outstanding		___ good		___ fair		___ poor
Availability of service	___ outstanding		___ good		___ fair		___ poor
Resale potential	___ outstanding		___ good		___ fair		___ poor
Features desired	___ ego satisfier		___ comfortable ride				
	___ ease in parking		___ fast acceleration				
	___ good mileage		___ immediate delivery				

Accessories

1.
2.
3.
4.
5.
6.
7.
8.

expensive vehicles. From an economic standpoint, it would be foolish to make a small car."

This large differential in profit between larger and smaller cars was pointed out in a comment in *Consumer Reports:*

> The production cost difference between a Chevrolet Caprice and a Cadillac de Ville with comparable equipment is $275 to $300. But the selling price differs by $2,700, giving GM a $2,400 extra gross profit on the Cadillac.[1]

Let us examine the next aspect of the objective. *When* is it desirable to buy your car? Do you want one of the first new models off the line? It may be fun to show off the latest thing, but new models can present real problems due to their very newness. This is particularly true if the model has been radically altered. Regardless of tests, there are frequently bugs uncovered in the early production that are corrected later in the model year.

Suppose you buy a car at the end of the year, when the manufacturer is converting to its new model. Your initial cost should be less, but you will have a car that—even though "new"—is in fact one year old. Thus, the depreciation factor will be greater than if you waited a short time and bought a current model. If you trade in such a buy within a couple of years, you may lose more than if you had bought the model shortly after it was introduced.

Where do you want to purchase your car? If you can obtain a fair price in your neighborhood, there is considerable advantage from a service standpoint in buying close to home. If you have traveled long distances to get the best financial deal, you will not normally go back to your place of purchase for service but will patronize a local agency for minor repairs and upkeep. Should major problems arise, it is aggravating and expensive to be forced to take a long trip. Therefore, it is wise to deal with a local agency from the start. Neighborhood dealers are likely to make a special effort to keep your business.

In deciding where to buy, you should also consider the reputation of the dealer. Has he or she been in business a long time? A respectable neighborhood dealer may charge you a few dollars more than another source, but it may be worth it.

How do you plan to purchase your car? With cash or on credit? By making a minimum down payment and borrowing the remainder? If you borrow, how long should it be for? Will you trade in your old car or try to sell it yourself? These and other questions will be dis-

---

[1] "Quote Without Comment," as quoted in *Consumer Reports.* February 1975, p. 82, from *Business Week.*

Table 7-2. Application of the Management Objective to Automobile Buying.

Component	Car Case
What?	Buy a subcompact
When?	Upon graduation
Where?	Neighborhood dealer
How?	Cash
Why?	Essential for job

cussed later in this chapter, under the subheading "That Car Loan."

Why do you need to buy a car? Is it really the most economical means of going to and from work? Perhaps it is a second car you are considering. Whatever your requirements, before purchasing, weigh such alternatives as public transportation, taxi, bicycle, motorcycle, or boat. There is also the possibility of leasing a car in lieu of buying it.

You should not purchase an automobile until you have clarified your objective by answering the questions what, when, where, how, and why. Let us assume that you determine your objective as follows: I will buy a *subcompact*, upon *graduation*, for *cash*, from a *neighborhood dealer*, because it will be *essential for my job*. Table 7-2 documents this application of the management objective to car buying.

Implementing Your Plan: Buying a New Car

Negotiating for a New Car
Once you have determined your objective, you are in a position to be a tough negotiator. Some people pay the sticker price without questioning it. This delights the salesperson and the dealer because the latter buys the vehicle for about 75 to 85 percent of the manufacturer's suggested list price. Furthermore, the profit differential on accessories may run up to 40 or 50 percent. To obtain a good deal, you may have to do some homework and resort to tough bargaining.

1. Obtain the facts about costs on a used car[2] from a current manual (*Used Car Guide*) published monthly by the National Automobile Dealers Association (NADA) of Washington, D.C. Look at both wholesale and retail prices on cars that you would like to purchase. If you want to make a trade-in, be sure to have your car appraised. Facts about new-car dealer costs and retail prices can be obtained

[2] For further information on costs of used cars, see page 114.

from current issues of two books, *Edmund's New Car Prices*[3] and *Car/Puter's Auto Facts.*[4] Armed with this information and a knowledge of the markup, you are prepared to discuss a deal.

2. Visit several dealers to secure their prices. At times it may help to talk directly to the owner of a small firm. Keep in mind that when you come to the closing, the boss has the final word.

3. Buy at the time when dealers are "hurting." In a period of economic recession and high inventories, you can get a much better bargain. And, take your time closing the deal. The dealer will be anxious to complete the sale, so set your price and stick with it. Dealers have been schooled in sales techniques and have all the answers. They are not above playing on your sympathies. If you cave in, it is just that much more money in their pockets. One successful dealer told me, "I size up every customer. Over the years, I have found what gets to them. Selling is a game, and I love to win."

The dealer's need to win was pointed out by the following experience of a student in my recent class:

I went to a Dodge dealer to purchase a new Charger after determining the car that best met my objective. The salesman was ready for me.

Salesman: Good evening, may I help you?
      Me: I'm looking for a good deal on a Charger.
Salesman: We have just the thing!

He showed me a pretty black-on-red model which he said was sold quickly for $5,543. I then informed him the daily paper advertised it for $5,185. He told me the price had been changed and then went into his act about what a great car I was buying which aroused my suspicions. He concluded, "I need this sale. My wife is in the hospital." I then decided to do my own act, remarking, "I can get a much better deal from your competitor. My cousin lives in Detroit and I may visit her and buy it through Nationwide."

After two weeks of negotiation with the salesman and the owner, I ended up buying the car for $4,753. Instead of being outsmarted, I came out with a fair deal. A check of the dealer's

[3] Prepared by Edmund Publications Corporation, West Hempstead, New York, and distributed by Dell Publishing Company, New York City.
[4] Published by Davis Publications, New York City.

cost for the car and equipment indicated he made $205 on the sale. However, he does a high volume and may have received an additional discount.

How sad the salesman looked as I walked out the door with the keys to my new car! He proved to be an actor to the end.

4. Use friendships to help you get that special discount from a reliable dealer or to save on such accessories as air conditioners.

5. Recheck all figures *prior* to closing. The importance of such a review cannot be emphasized too strongly. And be sure you receive the estimate *in writing*. A former student of mine related the following story about his high school graduation present.

My Dad was friendly with the fleet manager at the Ford dealership in town. We made a visit to his office and were informed that the cost for my new Pinto would be $100 above wholesale. The car of my choice was quoted at $2,750.26. Without checking other agencies, or asking to look at the figures, my father accepted the deal and gave his friend a check for $100 deposit. Two days later I picked up my Pinto Three-Door Runabout after paying the remaining $2,650.26. The following week, Dad saw an ad in the paper announcing a new Runabout for $2,610 (plus tax and license). We decided to check it out and found precisely the same car (including an AM radio). Dad then proceeded to find out how his friend arrived at his price and compared our price with the manufacturer's suggested retail price (Table 7-3).

After reviewing the figures it was apparent we hadn't received the $100 above wholesale. We did slightly better than the ad although this might have been subject to negotiation. And we saved $226 over retail. But Dad's friend had added on a $50 service charge. Likewise, the tags and title cost $9.50 but friend charged $15.00. Dad was also informed the agency received a 5 percent rebate for this end-of-month sale.

Next time, I'll check all figures prior to purchase because recently my cousin went to our dealer friend, armed with my facts, and saved the $50 service as well as $5.50 by buying his own tag and title.

Buying A New Car at $125
Over Dealer's Cost
After talking with dealers in your area you should be able to determine how much you will have to pay over cost for a new car. You

Table 7-3. Comparative Prices for Ford Pinto.

Our Price	Retail (Sticker) Price	Ad Price
$2,226.21 Dealer cost[a]	$2,568.00 Base price	$2,610.00 (Included
20.00 Preparation and	61.00 AM radio	freight, service,
conditioning	2,629.00	& AM radio)
25.00 Ford dealers	105.00 Freight	157.80 Sales tax
advertising fund	2,734.00	9.50 Actual cost of
2.40 Gas (there was	50.00 Service and	tag and title
so little gas in	handling	$2,777.30
the tank the car	$2,784.00	
barely reached	177.04 Sales tax	
the station)	15.00 Tag and title	
51.82 AM radio	$2,976.04	
2,325.43		
105.00 Freight		
2,430.43		
100.00 Markup		
50.00 Service and		
handling		
2,580.43		
154.83 Sales tax		
15.00 Tag and title		
$2,750.26		

[a]Because the car was sold near the end of the month and the manufacturer was anxious to move cars in a slow month, he provided the dealer another 5% below this normal cost of $2,226.21.

may wish to utilize a checklist to post your facts (see Table 7-4). As mentioned previously, the dealer cost and manufacturer's suggested retail price can be obtained from *Car/Puter's Auto Facts* or *Edmund's New Car Prices*.

If the price you receive from a dealer exceeds his or her cost by $125 or more, you may wish to consider an alternative.

Buy through an organization that will "deliver the car you want for $125 over dealer cost." Car/Puter, the company that prepares *Auto Facts*, located in Brooklyn, New York, does just that. For $10 it will provide a printout of the retail prices and dealer costs for the car you are considering as well as its various options. If you are unable to obtain a satisfactory price from your local dealer, "Car/Puter will arrange the purchase (and delivery to your city) [of the car of your choice] through our participating national network of authorized new-car dealers. You pay only $125 over dealer cost, even on cars retailing for $6,000 or more. The only exceptions are foreign makes and a few limited-production, luxury and specialty models like

111

Table 7-4. Price Comparison Chart.

	I Manufacturer's Suggested List	II Dealer's Cost	III Dealer's Best Price A	B	C	IV Nationwide Purchasing, Inc.	V Car/Puter
Initial cost:							
Car X (base price)							
Accessories:							
Air conditioning							
Power-disc brakes							
Power steering							
Radio, AM							
Destination charge							
Dealer preparation							
Gas and oil							
Dealer advertising							
Tax							
Total initial cost							
Annual cost:							
License							
Oil and gas							
Insurance							
Maintenance and repairs							
Depreciation							
Finance charges							
Total annual cost							

Cadillac, Corvette and Mark IV. Some of [these models, however] are available at a substantial discount through Car/Puter."[5]

Informing your dealer that you are aware of the conditions offered by Car/Puter should help you obtain the best possible price. If you post all initial costs on a price comparison chart (Table 7-4), it becomes apparent where you can obtain the lowest price.

Once the dealer has established a selling price for the new car, you can discuss a trade of your present car — but *not* before. To check on your car's present retail value, you can consult a current NADA manual. If you do not obtain a fair offer for your used car, you may prefer to sell it yourself using Car/Puter. However, for simplicity's sake, you may choose to sell to your local dealer.

Selling Your Car

Let us assume you decide to sell your car in the retail market. How do you go about it? The following points should be considered by prospective sellers:

1. *Appearance.* See that your car is clean and neat. Take time to wash and wax it. Vacuum the interior. Clean under the hood.

2. *Condition.* Be sure that the car is in satisfactorily working condition. Check the paint, battery, brakes, tires, etc. Make minor repairs yourself when possible. Replace deteriorating items such as a failing battery or a smooth tire.

3. *Pricing.* Set a fair dollar value on your car based upon the current market price of a comparable model. Check several dealers to see what they are asking as well as consulting the NADA manual.

4. *Advertising.* Utilize free facilities, such as school and business bulletin boards. Talk to friends. Place a sign on your car. If this free advertising does not bring you a buyer, consider using the newspaper. Place your ad when it will be read by the largest audience — perhaps in the weekend editions of your local paper. Ask the paper to help devise an effective ad.

5. *Timing.* Try not to sell when the used-car market is depressed.

6. *Selling techniques.* Be on time for appointments. Be honest about the good and bad features of your car. Make certain you have all of the necessary papers, including title and bill of sale. If the bill of sale must be notarized, know where this service can be done. Accept only cash, a money order, or a certified check.

---

[5] Car/Puter Auto Facts Department, 1603 Bushwick Ave., Brooklyn, New York 11207. Extract of advertisement appearing in *Car/Puter's Auto Facts* (New York: Davis Publications, Inc., 1978), p. 41.

Implementing Your Plan:
Buying A Used Car

Buying a used car successfully requires the same management approach that has been presented for purchasing a new car. In addition, however, the car's condition must be carefully assessed. When you buy a new car from a reputable dealer, you can be sure that no one has used or abused it. But in purchasing a secondhand vehicle, you run the risk of choosing a "lemon." I regret to report that normally, the less you pay, the greater the risk.

The major advantage in buying a quality used car is the considerable savings in price. Once you have driven a new car around the block, it becomes used and depreciates as much as 30 to 35 percent off the list price. If you can find a used vehicle in first-rate condition, it can be a good investment. People who cannot afford a new car because of the initial down payment and monthly finance charges may find the used auto a feasible alternative. There are two major sources for buying used cars — dealers and owners.

Dealer Buying
If you purchase a car through a dealer, be sure to check out his (or her) reputation! How long has he been in business? Verify his record with your Better Business Bureau and local bank. Is he a member of the National Automobile Dealers Association? And remember, there is no substitute for satisfied customers. Contact people who have bought his cars and ask for their views. This information can be very helpful. The advantage of buying through a reputable dealer is that he may provide some type of warranty. In contrast, if you make the purchase through a private individual, you cannot take the car back for free service, once the factory-established warranty period has expired.

Private Sales
An established dealer normally makes some repairs on a vehicle that he or she takes in on a trade. In purchasing from an individual, however, you take the car as is. There are two advantages in buying from a private party: (1) You may well obtain a lower price because the middleman has been eliminated; (2) since you know the owner, you can probably ascertain whether he or she has given the car tender loving care. Such knowledge is extremely helpful.

In order to obtain a fair deal, you should check the current NADA *Official Used Car Guide*[6] to price the used car of interest to

[6] Published by the National Automobile Dealers Used Car Association, 2000 K Street, N.W., Washington, D.C. 20061.

you. Your local bank loan officer should have a copy of this monthly publication. Three prices are shown for each domestic and imported car: average retail, average loan, and average trade-in. The *Guide* also lists the additional charges for certain equipment, such as air conditioning, power steering, AM/FM stereo, and automatic transmission. Read this NADA pamphlet carefully. It includes tables on the effect of different mileages on the value of various cars. There is also information on the insurance designation for each vehicle: high performance, intermediate performance, sport, rear engine.

Negotiating For A Used Car

When used-car shopping, you should utilize the same bargaining procedures suggested for buying a new car. A Better Business Bureau pamphlet "offers several tips that will increase the odds that purchasing a used car can be as satisfying as buying a new one." This BBB publication includes the following six suggestions on which used car to buy:

1. The make of used car is not as important as its condition.
2. Forget the mileage shown on the odometer. It could have been altered or disconnected by the former owners.
3. Ask to see the car's service record. Be sure the car has received service as recommended by the manufacturer.
4. Try to talk with the former owner. Ask him [or her] about the mileage reading. Why did he trade the car? What problems did he have with the car?
5. Do not overlook the manufacturer's warranty. How much of the warranty is still in effect? Has it been kept up to date?
6. If you know little about automobiles, have a good mechanic check the car. It is well worth the investment.[7]

A final cautionary note on used-car buying is provided by a colleague and friend:

Some used-car dealers have cars that may look OK on the outside, but that are certain to break down quickly and need expensive repairs. They are sold on credit with a very small down payment. These cars are called Lassies because they always come home. The victim quickly finds out that the car is no good and stops making payments. The dealer repossesses the car. He then sells it at auction to satisfy the debt of the victim. The auction is poorly publicized, and the dealer or a friend of his

[7] "How to Buy a Used Car," Better Business Bureau of Greater New Orleans Area, Inc., New Orleans, Louisiana 70130.

buys the car for a scrap value price or even less. No one who knows what he is buying would pay more. The victim learns that he still owes his debt on the car less what the dealer got for it minus his selling costs. Often the debt has already been sold to a finance company or other holder in due course which claims no responsibility for the quality of the car. The courts will force the debtor to pay. Meanwhile the dealer sells his Lassie to his next victim, and the process repeats itself. I am told that it is not uncommon to have eight or ten people paying off debts on the same Lassie at one time.[8]

ANNUAL COST OF A CAR

Prior to buying a car you should give serious thought to its upkeep. What facilities do you have for storage, both at home and at work? If, for example, you will be keeping your car outdoors in extremes of weather, you do not want a model with a reputation as a temperamental starter.

Take the case of a friend of ours who bought a luxury foreign car to be used in North Dakota. At home he keeps it in a heated garage. When he is at work, however, it stays in the outdoor parking lot. In cold weather the only way he can be sure it will bring him home at night is to leave the motor running all day. More than once, he has received a call over the loud-speaker system: "Will the owner of a car with license number 99999P report to the information desk immediately." Needless to say, our friend's extra fuel consumption adds up to a sizable bill on an annual basis and the waste of precious fuel is really unpardonable, but despite the added cost and inconvenience, he refuses to sell the car because it fulfills a lifelong desire. What are the annual costs that you should compute before purchasing an automobile? The lower segment of Table 7-4 can be helpful in estimating the various yearly expense car owners face. Let us examine them in detail.

License Fees

You might begin by checking on the cost of the license and any additional state or city tax on the car. In some states such taxes vary considerably based on the price of the vehicle.

---

[8] Joseph Horton, Chairman, Department of Economics and Finance, Slippery Rock State College, Slippery Rock, Pennsylvania.

Fuel

Gasoline has become a costly item, and the amount you spend on it each year will depend greatly upon the car you select. Mileage per gallon on various makes of cars range from 12 to 34 miles per gallon for city driving. Carefully check the mileage differential in cars that interest you. The most helpful guide I have found is a report by the U.S. Environmental and Protection Agency (EPA).

A recent EPA report pointed out the following factors that influence gasoline consumption:

Vehicle weight and engine size are the most important items affecting overall fuel consumption. Generally speaking, in city driving, a 5,000 pound car will require twice as much gasoline to run as a 2,500 pound car. Optional equipment not only adds weight to the car but also requires power from the engine and thus requires fuel to operate. For example, using an air conditioner can reduce gas mileage by more than 10 percent in city driving.

An automatic transmission usually reduces gas mileage as compared with a manual transmission.

Rapid acceleration can reduce fuel economy by 15 percent over moderate acceleration.

The best fuel economy occurs at speeds between 30 and 40 miles per hour with no stops and no rapid speed changes.

Using radial tires, instead of conventional or bias-ply tires, can result in a 3 percent improvement in gas mileage. Improper front-end alignment and tires inflated below the recommended pressure will reduce gas mileage.

An idling engine burns about a half-pint of gas every six minutes, so don't idle your engine needlessly.

A tuned car will average 6 percent better mileage than an untuned one. And a properly maintained car also helps reduce air pollution.

Unnecessary braking, excessive driving in low gears, dragging brakes and short trips all reduce fuel economy.[9]

A copy of the EPA *Gas Mileage Guide for New-Car Buyers* may be obtained by writing to Fuel Economy, Pueblo, Colorado 81009.

[9] *EPA Gas Mileage Guide for New-Car Buyers*, Pueblo, Colorado 81009.

Insurance

Be sure to determine what the insurance will be on the car of your choice. Shop around for the best deal. Car insurance will be discussed in detail in Chapter 10.

Maintenance and Repairs

Today maintenance and repairs are expensive items and can be expected to rise in cost. If you plan on buying a high-priced car available through only a handful of authorized dealers, you can expect to have costly charges for maintenance and repairs. Be sure to budget an adequate amount for this purpose. We shall examine automobile maintenance more closely later in this chapter.

Annual Depreciation

The expense of annual depreciation can be easily determined by finding out what your car is currently selling for in the marketplace. Then consult the NADA manual for the price of a car one year older. The difference between the prices for the current and the older model should provide a fair depreciation figure. Another approach is to use one of the depreciation methods suggested by the Internal Revenue Service in their current Federal Income Tax Forms package. Normally, the higher the price, the greater the dollar depreciation.

Yearly Finance Charges

Cost of finance charges should be checked with care. Be sure you obtain the necessary information from the various lending agencies in your area.

It is important to estimate accurately your total annual cost (Table 7-4). Time and again, I have been told, "My car is being repossessed — I couldn't make my monthly payments." In each instance the car owner had failed to consider what it would cost annually to maintain the car.

THAT CAR LOAN

If you must borrow money to buy a car, make the maximum down payment and pay off the loan in the shortest time. A typical credit unit posted the following rate for a car loan in this era of high interest:

Annual Percentage Rate is 10.8%; the Periodic Rate is 9/10 of 1% per month on the unpaid balance: and the Finance Charge is $5.84 per $100 per year, provided equal monthly payments are received every 30 days from the date the loan is disbursed.

Advantages of borrowing from a credit union were listed by one as follows:

1. Loan-protection insurance.
2. Financing of up to 90 percent of the actual purchase price (after discount) of a new car.
3. The right to select your automobile insurance carrier in order to secure the best rates on collision and comprehensive insurance.
4. Acceleration of your loan payments in any amount at any time in order to reduce the cost of financing.
5. The privilege of moving your car to a new assignment anywhere in the world.
6. No extra charges or fees of any kind.

Before accepting a credit-union loan, you should check with other sources, including your car dealer, local bank, insurance company, and a loan company.

It is important to determine exactly what any extra charges and fees include. Recently Mr. A. obtained the following information from a bank loan officer:

> *Mr. A:* What is your current new car-loan rate?
>
> *Loan Officer:* It's 7½ percent, plus 1 percent for credit life coverage and another 1 percent for accident and health.
>
> *Mr. A:* Is this the annual rate?
>
> *Loan Officer:* No, this amounts to 13.69 percent on a three-year loan.
>
> *Mr. A:* What is the maximum length of time I can borrow this money, and what is the cost per $1,000?
>
> *Loan Officer:* We are presently making 42-month loans. The total payment on $1,000 for 42 months is only $287.80; life, $48.47 and accident and health $48.47. The total note, all costs, will be $1,384.74.
>
> *Mr. A:* Are there any other facts I should know?
>
> *Loan Officer:* Yes, you must have an active account with us, and in view

of the tight money market, we like you to carry a compensating balance of 20 percent. This means that for every $1,000 we lend you, you should have $200 in some type of account with us.[10]

Let us assume that you have decided on car type and place of purchase, and have completed the loan arrangements. Once you have taken possession of the vehicle, it is essential to have necessary insurance protection. Do not wait until the last minute to buy car insurance. Its purchase requires the same careful study as any other sizable investment. Again, for details on car insurance, see Chapter 10.

AUTOMOBILE MAINTENANCE

It is important to keep your car in good condition from the moment you purchase it. Good maintenance will cut your costs, reduce your need for repairs, and help your car run smoothly. If you have done a good job in choosing a car, maintaining it should not present an undue problem. If you have purchased a "lemon," however, your repair costs can be unreasonable. So buy carefully.

How do you go about taking care of your car? The following pointers and suggestions may help.

1. Read the warranty booklet provided by the manufacturer. Follow recommendations for service checks, tire pressure, etc. Be sure you understand all important facts presented. If you have any questions, contact the dealer or the dealer's service manager.

2. Take your car to a respected authorized dealer for the recommended inspections within the mileage and times specified. His or her mechanics work exclusively on your make of car and should be factory-trained.

3. Use the proper gas and oil. Be sure to change your oil when it is dirty and make sure it comes up to the required level. Engines can be — and have been — ruined by inadequate oil. Economize on your gasoline consumption; you will save money, reduce pollution, and conserve our natural resources.

4. Make *periodic* preventive *maintenance checks* yourself. Your personal inspection is the best way to prevent costly repairs. You may

---

[10] This compensating balance requirement, in fact, increases the interest rate by reducing the value of the loan in this case from $1000 to $800.

wish to make up a reminder list of items to look at weekly. This might include the following points:

a. *Battery.* Does it have sufficient water? If not, add distilled water to the desired level, and do not spill it elsewhere. You should also see that the terminals are clean.

b. *Tires.* Buy a good gauge. Check the pressure on all tires, including the spare. Examine each tire for wear; if it is uneven, take the car to a service station and find out if the wheels need to be aligned and/or balanced. Also, look at your tires carefully to determine if any are worn enough to be replaced. It is false economy to drive with unsafe tires. Learn how to change a tire.

c. *Oil.* Keep an extra quart on hand, so that you can add oil if necessary.

d. *Water.* Check the water in the radiator. In cold climates, make certain you have adequate antifreeze for the lowest readings.

e. *Appearance.* Wash and wax the car yourself whenever possible. It is a good form of exercise and saves money. More important doing it yourself gives you an opportunity to examine your car and find problems before they can become serious. It is much easier and cheaper to tighten a loose screw than to replace a piece of equipment that has fallen off.

5. When repairs become necessary, take the car to that respected authorized dealer. Do it promptly, before the car can no longer be used. Obtain an estimate in writing before any work is done, and require the service manager to notify you if any increase is necessary after work begins. Finally, check out the repair work carefully with the service manager prior to payment. This may require a test drive. Owners become very unhappy when their cars break down shortly after being repaired. An on-the-spot inspection immediately after the work has been done can alleviate the problem.

6. What should you do if you encounter serious trouble with a dealer in regard to repairs? First, bring it to the attention of the service manager. If this fails, put it in writing to the owner. Next, write the car manufacturer and send copies to the local Better Business Bureau and appropriate consumer affairs office. Finally, you may wish to take the matter to a small-claims court yourself. If it is important enough, hire a lawyer. Stay with it until you get a fair deal.

FUTURE OF THE AUTOMOBILE

There are currently more than 130 million cars in use in the United States. Automobiles caused over 50,000 deaths in 1978 and more than 3 million injuries. By the year 2000 our population will increase by 50 percent to 300 million. At that time we can expect 210 million cars on our highways and in our cities.

The car problem is all too obvious today, what with pollution, auto accidents, gas shortages, acres of unsightly car cemeteries, and cities glutted with vehicles. What will the situation be a quarter of a century from now? Much worse — unless we use smaller and more efficient cars and develop other forms of first-class transportation. Perhaps electrical vehicles will replace some of our gas-driven engines.

It behooves all of us to think in terms of what we can do to improve the situation in the years to come. If more forceful action is not taken, vehicular deaths will increase, the energy crisis will worsen, pollution will become unbearable, and driving will become a nightmare. Surely American ingenuity can devise cars that are virtually pollution free, safer, longer lasting, and more economical. The annual model changeover is ridiculous. It results in failure to eliminate deficiencies that could be worked out if cars remained virtually unchanged for several years. The recall of large numbers of vehicles today is due in considerable measure to the manufacturers' modification policy.

The time has come to focus on improving alternate means of transportation, thus lessening the need for automobiles. We must also demand more positive action by our political leaders.

READ BEFORE YOU BUY

Buying a car is an expensive investment. An astute person can save hundreds of dollars by having the facts prior to making a purchase. In order to obtain the facts, it is essential to read the latest editions of certain publications. I particularly recommend that you read the following literature:

1. *Edmund's New Car Prices.* This book, mentioned earlier in the chapter, is distributed by Dell and is available for $1.95. It lists new-car prices (foreign and domestic), showing the base cost to the dealer and the manufacturer's suggested list price. It also gives good advice on "choosing the right car for you." Other topics presented include questions and answers on importing a car, discount buying, and vehicle registration statistics.

2. *Car/Puter's Auto Facts* is published three times a year and provides information somewhat similar to Edmund's. It is a Davis publication and sells for $1.95. As noted earlier, it gives you dealer cost and manufacturer's suggested price. Car/Puter also includes informa-

tion on insurance needs, discount buying, a coded freight chart, and how to get the best financing deal.

3. Consumers Union frequently publishes valuable material on cars in their monthly *Consumer Reports*. These findings are based on their own tests of various vehicles. Current articles should be read with care before making a purchase.

4. The Ford Motor Company has prepared a helpful booklet entitled *Car Buying Made Easier*. The first section gives you general information about cars; the second concentrates on vehicles produced by Ford. It can be obtained free of charge by writing to Ford's Customer Service Division, 19855 West Outer Drive, Dearborn, Michigan 48124.

ALTERNATE FORMS OF TRANSPORTATION AND THE MANAGEMENT APPROACH

Henry Ford, II, chairman of Ford Motor Company, pointed out in an interview the need for conservation, saying:

We're still living in a fool's paradise in this country. We have always thought that we could have an endless supply of cheap energy and we can't. We've got a major energy problem, but the American people don't believe it. We waste so much. We waste everything in this country. . . . I wonder, theoretically, if it's right that the auto industry should chew up as much raw materials as it chews up.[11]

A good way to consume fewer raw materials is to turn to other means of transportation. Some alternate approaches that could benefit our pocketbooks, society, and health are motorcycles, bicycles, mass transit, and person power (jogging and walking).

Once again, I suggest you use a management approach to help you obtain the type of transportation best suited to your needs at the most reasonable price.

In order to reach a decision about the appropriate form of alternate transportation for you, you must first determine your objective. What will best suit your needs? This requires providing answers to the questions what, when, where, how, and why. First, what type of

[11] *Time*, February 10, 1975, p. 71.

Table 7-5. Format to Help Determine Which Alternate Mode of Transportation is Best For You (*Assumption: A serviceable car is presently owned*).

	Motorcycle	Bicycle	Mass Transit	Walk/Jog
What is the initial cost?	$	$	$	$
	4_3_2_1_	4_3_2_1_	4_3_2_1_	4_3_2_1_
What is the annual upkeep (including insurance)?	$	$	$	$
	4_3_2_1_	4_3_2_1_	4_3_2_1_	4_3_2_1_
What are clothing costs?	$	$	$	$
	4_3_2_1_	4_3_2_1_	4_3_2_1_	4_3_2_1_
How well does it meet my objective?	4_3_2_1_	4_3_2_1_	4_3_2_1_	4_3_2_1_
Will it be available in all weather?	4_3_2_1_	4_3_2_1_	4_3_2_1_	4_3_2_1_
How safe is it?	4_3_2_1_	4_3_2_1_	4_3_2_1_	4_3_2_1_
Are outlets available nearby to provide parts and service?	4_3_2_1_	4_3_2_1_	4_3_2_1_	4_3_2_1_
Is it a convenient and comfortable service?	4_3_2_1_	4_3_2_1_	4_3_2_1_	4_3_2_1_
What are the risks of theft or mugging?	4_3_2_1_	4_3_2_1_	4_3_2_1_	4_3_2_1_
What does it do for my morale upon arriving at at my destination?	4_3_2_1_	4_3_2_1_	4_3_2_1_	4_3_2_1_
Total				

Scoring: 4 Best rating
         3 Second best
         2 Third best
         1 Fourth best

transportation should you utilize? Let us assume you have already decided that a subcompact is required for your wife for her work. Factors to consider in determining what further form of transportation you need include purpose for which it is to be used and availability of funds for the initial purchase as well as for upkeep. In determining your objective it can be helpful to use an approach similar to that presented for car buying (Table 7-2). Likewise, preparing a format similar to Table 7-5 can assist you in deciding what mode of transportation is best suited for you.

ACTIONS YOU CAN TAKE TO COPE WITH INFLATION AND THE ENERGY SHORTAGE

1. Buy subcompact and stripped-down-model cars whenever appropriate.

2. Minimize your current car investments in view of breakthroughs that could render present models obsolete and greatly reduce their resale value.

3. Carefully schedule your daily activities to save on mileage and gas costs. Students should arrange class schedules for three days instead of five days if possible. If you can see the doctor as well as shop for food and clothing in one trip, do so.

4. Consider alternate forms of transportation: motorcycling, bicycling, walking, jogging, and using public transportation. Likewise, consider car pooling, pumping your own gas, reducing your speed, and budgeting your gas consumption.

SUMMARY

A car is normally the second largest investment that a person makes in a lifetime. It is a repetitive purchase that may involve a lifetime expenditure of $100,000 plus another $30,000 in finance charges. Therefore, considerable time and study should be given to selecting the appropriate car.

A management approach can be utilized to obtain a fair deal. This necessitates adequate planning prior to purchase. First, determine your objective. The type of car to best meet your needs can be arrived at by your answers to five components of the objective — what, when, where, how, and why.

After you have determined your objective and done your planning with care, you are in a position to be a tough negotiator. Keep in mind that a dealer buys cars at 75 to 85 percent of the manufacturer's suggested list price. Furthermore, on accessories the profit differential may run up to 40 to 50 percent.

In lieu of buying a car through your local dealer, you may consider two alternatives: First, buy it from an organization in Detroit at a sizeable discount. Second, purchase the car through a company that will deliver it to you at $125 over dealer cost.

The management approach used in buying a car should also be used in purchasing other means of transportation, such as a motorcycle or bicycle. In view of the energy situation, considerable thought should be given to selecting alternative forms of transportation in the years ahead — including greater use of person power, which is economical and healthful.

His name was George F. Babbitt and he was nimble in the calling of selling houses for more than people could afford to pay.

—SINCLAIR LEWIS

HOME: RENT OR PURCHASE

"We want a place of our own." This seems to be the consensus of most people — be it young or old. The type of dwelling desired, however, varies from living on a rented boat to buying a camper and moving to Canada. In this chapter, we shall look at the two major approaches to housing — rental or purchase — and the choices available in these two categories.

RENT OR BUY?

The most basic question to decide is whether you intend to sink your roots deep into a particular community or to travel extensively and take on a job that requires frequent changes. Some young people will sacrifice higher pay and job promotions in order to remain at home. The family ties, familiar climate, pace of life, pleasant living, and local sports opportunities may be factors that influence this decision to stay put. In such a situation it would appear that the purchase of housing is the wise decision. In contrast, it is normally better to keep mobile by renting if you plan to enter the Foreign Service, work for the Peace Corps, join the military, or accept a position with an international corporation.

127

It is important to spend an appropriate amount of time selecting the right housing to suit your needs. The risk factor is much greater when you purchase a home or apartment than when you rent. But even in a rental situation, certain precautions are necessary. Try not to become involved in a long-term lease. There should also be an escape clause in any lease because of the chance of transfer, military service, or other possibilities. The greater your ability to move quickly, the greater your opportunity for accepting new and exciting challenges.

SINGLE OR MARRIED?

A significant factor in the selection of living accommodations is marital status. If you plan on marrying shortly after graduation, you will need more spacious accommodations than if you stay single.

What type of accommodations do you desire? The range of standards varies from one room on Skid Row to luxurious condominiums. In a recent class of mine, one member who was going into social work said he had already selected a room in the ghetto in order to relate better to the people he would be associated with. Then I spoke to the class about luxury apartments in Miami, with gold-plated plumbing fixtures, swimming pools, tennis courts, gymnasiums, and cabanas. This, I presumed, would be a long-range goal. However, one young lady spoke up: "My husband-to-be is taking over as manager of a condominium in Fort Lauderdale this summer. We plan to enjoy all the benefits you mentioned because his remuneration as the resident manager includes a one-bedroom apartment." Not surprisingly, 76 percent of the females in my class desired to own a home of their own once they were married. In contrast, only 41 percent of the males wanted to be saddled with a house after taking on a bride.

ADVANTAGES: RENTALS VS. PURCHASES

It is easy to list the advantages of both rentals and purchases, but often the area you live in has much to do with the decision. You may have little choice because of a housing shortage, or you may find low rentals and homes at bargain prices in locations such as Cape Canaveral (formerly Cape Kennedy) was shortly after the NASA cutback.

However, the housing boom that began in California in 1976 spread eastward and resulted in waiting lists for homes under construction in a number of communities. This scarcity, coupled with inflation, caused new home prices to rise over 10 percent in one year. (New homes doubled in price between 1970 and 1977.)

The selection of a dwelling is such a personal matter that a husband and wife must arrive at a decision based upon their own personalities, irrespective of advantages and disadvantages. Whatever you prefer, within your means, should be the deciding factor.

Rent

First let us look at the six advantages that may accrue to the renter:

1. *Mobility.* The key advantage to rental on a monthly basis is the mobility it provides. You can leave at any time, with no financial worries about selling the property. But don't get tied up in a long-term lease with no escape clause unless you plan to stay put. If you have found a fine apartment or house and are reasonably sure to remain for, say, three years, then it may be to your advantage to have a lease for that period. It prevents the landlord from either raising the rent or kicking you out before your lease is up.

2. *Community living.* If you enjoy friends close at hand, apartment living offers a delightful opportunity for sharing experiences.

3. *Funds for other investments.* The home down payment and closing costs, as well as major maintenance expenses, can be used for business, real estate, hobbies, the stock market, or other purposes.

4. *Less work.* There is much less work in apartment living, and even in house rentals, than for the homeowner who is responsible for all house and yard maintenance activities.

5. *Security.* Because of the increase in all types of criminal activity, a number of apartments now provide first-class security. Although homeowners can make their residences more secure through burglar alarm systems, special locks, dogs, or other security methods, they do not normally have the funds to afford the overall protection available to some apartments.

6. *Timesaver.* It usually takes a lot more work to buy than to rent. The problems of securing the land, going through the closing, and worrying about the soundness of the investment all take time from other activities. And I am sure you know people who become virtual slaves to their homes and devote all their time to maintenance of them.

Purchase

From a buyer's viewpoint, the advantages of home ownership may be itemized as follows:

1. *Freedom.* You can be "king of the castle" and do as you please. My neighbor, who moved recently from an apartment, put it bluntly: "How sweet it is to have no landlord giving me a list of rules and regulations!"

2. *More living space.* Most homes provide more indoor space than most apartments and have a yard as well. This permits greater privacy for the family and more outdoor space for the children to play in.

3. *Pride of ownership.* This intangible value can mean much to the peace of mind of families.

4. *Good Investment.* Houses are now increasing in value faster than the cost of living. You are building an increasing equity with each monthly payment.

5. *Community roots.* Owning your own home gives you a greater opportunity to sink your *roots* deep into the community. Neighbors who buy with the same intentions tend to have common interests.

COST COMPARISONS

Cost comparisons may be made utilizing the format in Table 8-1. This hypothetical case assumes a family of three and is based upon comparable living areas in a local community.

This cost comparison indicates greater overall dollar expenditure

Table 8-1. Rental–Purchase Cost Comparison.

	Rental (3-Bedroom Apartment)	Purchase ($52,000 3-Bedroom House)
Monthly payment	$450	$336[a]
Taxes (property)		55
Insurance (house)		50
Upkeep		60
Utilities (gas, electricity, water)	135	135
Phone	20	20
	$605	$656

[a]Includes principal and interest, but little goes to principal in early years.

for the homeowner. Keep in mind, however, that property taxes and much of the monthly payment (interest) are tax deductible for home-owners. Over a year's time, this makes buying little more expensive than renting. In some areas, even without the tax advantages, it is cheaper to buy than to rent.

These figures will vary from locality to locality. Furthermore, they are not completely valid, because of differences in types of dwellings, locations within the community, floor plans, age of build-ings, and other factors. Therefore, such a comparison should be used primarily as a guide to indicate amounts required for this purpose.

TYPES OF HOUSING AVAILABLE FOR PURCHASE

In the event a decision is made to buy, several kinds of accommoda-tions are available. Let us look at the most common ones.

Conventional Home

The conventional home continues to be the most popular form of accommodation. In 1978, 1.81 million such homes were built, a number that was less than had been anticipated, owing to the high cost of mortgage money, land, and materials. The future demand for conventional homes will be tremendous. The nation's goal for hous-ing was stated in the Housing and Urban Development Act of 1968: "A decent house and a suitable environment for every American family." The Ninetieth Congress felt that this objective could be reached in 1978, with the construction or rehabilitation of nearly 28 million housing units. The plan called for construction of 20 million private houses, rehabilitation of 1.7 million, and government-assisted construction of 6 million new dwellings. There was a considerable shortfall of the congressional goal, because of the rising home prices, energy shortage, and high interest rates that first became apparent in 1973.

A conventional home is the goal of the majority of families in this country. The choices available are dependent on financial re-sources. Many lending agencies say you should spend no more for a house than 2½ times your yearly salary before taxes. Thus, if you make $20,000, you can afford a $50,000 home. The U.S. Department of Housing and Urban Development states that "a homeowner should not pay more than 25 percent of income for monthly housing expense (payment on the mortgage loan plus average cost of heat, utilities, repair and maintenance)."[1]

Virtually all homes are purchased with the assistance of some loan arrangement. Let us look at the principal sources available.

G.I. Loans

Since the end of World War II in 1945, more than 10 million people have purchased homes with the assistance of G.I. loans[2] under the guaranteed home-loan program of the Veterans Administration (VA). For those of you in school who are veterans, or who may be eligible for a G.I. loan, this topic is worthy of your study.

The present rate of interest on a G.I. loan is 11½ percent. The VA will guarantee no more than 60 percent of a loan, the top portion of the loan, in an amount not to exceed $25,000. Eligible persons first apply to a lending agency. The major firms doing this type of business are mortgage bankers. If the lender agrees to the loan, the VA orders an appraisal, normally by an independent appraiser who sets a value on the property. Although a G.I. loan can be for more than the appraised value, any differential must be paid for by the purchaser.

In determining how much you should pay for a house, it is essential that you make a thorough inspection of it. It is a good idea to utilize a checklist such as the one in Figure 8-1. And it is helpful to estimate your financial payments by itemizing the costs listed in Figure 8-2.

Let us assume that your inspection indicates the house is a good buy, your financial estimate convinces you that there should be no trouble meeting payments, and you qualify as a veteran. It would then be advisable to utilize the G.I. loan, which provides the following advantages:

1. The interest rate is normally lower than the going rate at the time. For example, the VA charges 11½ percent, whereas in most areas, conventional loans are running between 12 and 14 percent.
2. With a VA guaranteed loan, you have the right to repay your loan at any time without penalty.
3. An independent appraisal is made by the VA for $60. This appraisal is made known to you.
4. No down payment is required.

---

[1] U.S. Department of Housing and Urban Development, *Wise Home Buying* (Washington, D.C.: U.S. Government Printing Office, current edition).

[2] The phrase "G.I. loan" means "a loan made by a private lending institution to a veteran for any eligible purpose, pursuant to Title 38, United States Code" (from "Loans for Veterans," VA Pamphlet 26-4, current edition).

CHARACTERISTICS OF PROPERTY (Proposed or existing construction)

Neighborhood

Consider each of the following to determine whether the location of the property will satisfy your personal needs and preferences:

Remarks

Convenience of public transportation	☐
Stores conveniently located	☐
Elementary school conveniently located	☐
Absence of excessive traffic noise	☐
Absence of smoke and unpleasant odors	☐
Play area available for children	☐
Fire and police protection provided	☐
Residential usage safeguarded by adequate zoning	☐

Lot

Consider each of the following to determine whether the lot is sufficiently large and properly improved:

Size of front yard satisfactory	☐
Size of rear and side yards satisfactory	☐
Walks provide access to front and service entrances	☐
Drive provides easy access to garage	☐
Lot appears to drain satisfactorily	☐
Lawn and planting satisfactory	☐
Septic tank (if any) in good operating condition	☐
Well (if any) affording an adequate supply of safe and palatable water	☐

Exterior Detail

Observe the exterior detail of neighboring houses and determine whether the house being considered is as good or better in respect to each of the following features:

Porches	☐
Terraces	☐
Garage	☐
Gutters	☐
Storm sash	☐
Weather stripping	☐
Screens	☐

Interior Detail

Consider each of the following to determine whether the house will afford living accommodations which are sufficient to the needs and comfort of your family:

Remarks

Rooms will accommodate desired furniture	☐
Dining space sufficiently large	☐
At least one closet in each bedroom	☐
At least one coat closet and one linen closet	☐

Interior Detail —Continued

Convenient access to bathroom	☐
Sufficient and convenient storage space (screens, trunks, boxes, off-season clothes, luggage, baby carriage, bicycle, wheel toys, etc.)	☐
Kitchen well arranged and equipped	☐
Laundry space ample and well located	☐
Windows provide sufficient light and air	☐
Sufficient number of electrical outlets	☐

CONDITION OF EXISTING CONSTRUCTION

Exterior Construction

The following appear to be in acceptable condition:

Wood porch floors and steps	☐
Windows, doors, and screens	☐
Gutters and wood cornice	☐
Wood siding	☐
Mortar joints	☐
Roofing	☐
Chimneys	☐
Paint on exterior woodwork	☐

CAUTION: Cracking, peeling, scaling and loose paint on stairs, decks, porches, railings, windows and doors may contain amounts of lead which are harmful if eaten by children under seven years of age. Examine these areas carefully.

Interior Construction

Plaster is free of excessive cracks	☐
Plaster is free of stains caused by leaking roof or sidewalls	☐
Door locks in operating condition	☐
Windows move freely	☐
Fireplace works properly	☐
Basement is dry and will resist moisture penetration	☐
Mechanical equipment and electrical wiring and switches adequate and in operating condition	☐
Type of heating equipment suitable	☐
Adequate insulation in walls, floor, ceiling or roof	☐

The following appear to be in acceptable condition:

Remarks

Wood floor finish	☐
Linoleum floors	☐
Tile floors—vinyl asbestos, asphalt	☐
Sink top	☐
Kitchen range	☐
Bathroom fixtures	☐
Painting and papering	☐
Exposed joists and beams	☐

Figure 8-1. Checklist for Buying or Building a Home. (Source: *To the Home-Buying Veteran*, VA Pamphlet 26-6, rev. ed. [Washington, D.C.: Veterans Administration, 1977], pp. 17–19.)

5. The loan may be made for up to 30 years.

6. The veteran has the right to sell his (or her) home to whomever he pleases and whenever he desires.

The disadvantages you may encounter are these:

1. There will undoubtedly be red tape involved in dealing with the government.

2. Add-on points[3] are often charged that may absorb much of the savings

[3] A one-time charge, based upon the amount of the mortgage, that may be made by lending agencies. One point is equal to a 1 percent additional cost for one year.

133

Relate these figures to your assets now and what you estimate you can pay for housing in the years to come.

Downpayment	_____	Add these
Closing charges:		to get your
Title search and clearance	_____	TOTAL
Various legal fees	_____	INITIAL
Other charges	_____	CASH
TOTAL INITIAL COST	_____	OUTLAY
Size of monthly payment on mortgage	_____	
Monthly payments on taxes and assessments	_____	
Monthly payments on insurance	_____	
TOTAL MONTHLY PAYMENT	_____	Add these
Probable fuel cost (average per month)	_____	to get your
Probable monthly utility cost (lights, water, gas, etc.) . .	_____	TOTAL
Estimated monthly maintenance and repair expenses . .	_____	MONTHLY
TOTAL MONTHLY COST	_____	COST

Figure 8-2. Format for Estimate of Costs of Purchasing a Home. (Source: To the Home-Buying Veteran, VA Pamphlet 26-6, rev. ed. [Washington, D.C.: Veterans Administration, 1977] p. 23.)

gained from the lower interest rate. The VA will not permit point payments legally by the veteran except in refinancing and a few other situations. However, there are ways to do this "under the table." For example, if a home builder charges $60,000, he or she may hold this price for the G.I. purchaser but lower it to $57,600 for a conventional 13 percent loan. This means the builder has cranked in a four-point charge, or $2,400, to compensate for the lower rate of interest.

FHA

The Federal Housing Administration (FHA) also provides an opportunity to obtain a loan at less than the going rate. The FHA, like the VA, guarantees a loan for the lending agency. The procedure is similar, in that you go to a lending agency first to get its approval for a loan. The next step is for the FHA to make the appraisal. Anyone who has good credit, steady work, and the necessary cash down payment is eligible for an FHA loan. At the present time, the maximum mortgage that the FHA will guarantee for a single-family dwelling is $60,000.

The FHA calculates the maximum insurable loan by taking

97% of the first $25,000 (the appraisal value)
95% of the excess.

The advantages of the FHA loan are as follows:

1. There is a smaller down payment than with the regular loan. As is apparent from the figures above, if a person purchases a $60,000 home, his or her down payment is only $2,500. But the buyer may have to pay closing costs similar to those in a conventional loan. However, no down payment is required if the home buyer is a veteran.
2. The interest rate is normally more reasonable. It is currently 11½ percent plus ½ percent FHA mortgage insurance.
3. The period of payment may be longer, with a 30-year maximum.

The prime disadvantage that I found, from talking with people who have gone the FHA route, is the amount of time consumed in the bureaucratic delay that can be so exasperating.

On the other hand, the established standards can be helpful in preventing you from buying a "lemon" or suffering a heavy loss on resale owing to such factors as poor structure and inferior equipment.

Conventional Loans
The key advantage to the conventional loan is that it eliminates the governmental red tape. However, it is often more costly; and also, in periods of high interest rates, the lending agencies are more selective and these loans may be difficult to get.

In the 1979 capital market, it was generally not possible to secure the best deal on a conventional loan. Two examples illustrate the picture in one area: First, the branch manager of a large savings and loan firm told me he was making no G.I. or FHA loans — money was too scarce and there were better opportunities in the regular home loan. He was making conventional loans up to 80 percent of appraised value. On a $60,000 home, this means a $48,000 maximum loan, with an interest charge of 12 percent and monthly payments to be completed in 20 years. So a buyer had to have $12,000 of his or her own money available or secure a second mortgage from some other source — at a higher rate of interest.

In the second case, a prominent lending institution on the West Coast was requiring a 25 percent down payment on a new $80,000 house. Although the bank would loan $60,000 at a 12 percent rate, they stipulated that if the prime interest rate was raised before the contract was closed, the borrower had to pay the higher price. In addition, they would not grant the loan for a period in excess of 20 years. Consequently, monthly payments, including interest, taxes, insurance, and so on approximated $950. Other costs of closing the deal amounted to an added $3,000 (tax reserve, title company fee, recording fee, etc.). In this situation the buyer had to muster at least $23,000 to obtain the $80,000 house, aside from the cash he or she may have needed for furniture, drapes, and other necessities.

Real Estate Settlement
Procedures Act
In regard to closing or settlement charges, a recent law requires complete disclosure of all these costs.

The Real Estate Settlement Procedures Act of 1974 (Public Law 93-533), as amended in 1975, requires use of a standard form for advance disclosure of settlement costs and as a record for actual charges incurred at settlement in all mortgage transactions involving federally related loans. This law, which became effective in June 1975, is, in my view, very helpful to the home buyer because it enables the buyer to know exactly what costs must be paid prior to the actual closing time. The HUD (Department of Housing and Urban Development) form dated June 10, 1976 (QMR-No. 63-R-VHO), requires that all disclosure settlement costs must be itemized for both the borrower and seller.

HUD's first printing of their *Settlement Costs* booklet contained a statement that made realtors very unhappy. The comment appeared in the section titled: "Understand the Role of the Real Estate Broker" and reads: "The broker's principle interest at settlement is to get the transaction closed and his fee or commission disbursed."[4]

The action taken by the realtors was reported in our local newspaper under the caption "Book Offensive, HUD Changes It." The article stated that

National Association of Realtors president Art Leitch huddled with HUD general counsel Robert Elliot, NAR's publication reports, and so now future copies of the little book will read:

"It is up to you to review the documents carefully. Although the broker may offer helpful advice, keep in mind that you are the one who is spending the money to buy a home and are entitled to a full understanding of the costs. The broker has a substantial interest at settlement to complete the transaction. Also bear in mind that the obligation of the seller's broker is to represent the seller and in this connection, the seller may be interested primarily in closing the transaction as soon as possible."[5]

The power of NAR is apparent from the prompt action taken by HUD to modify its booklet. This points up the importance of consumers having a strong national organization to look after their interests.

[4] U.S. Department of Housing and Urban Development, *Settlement Costs* (Washington, D.C.: U.S. Government Printing Office, 1975), p. 19.
[5] The New Orleans *Times Picayune*, November 19, 1975, p. 15.

Energy Conservation

Every potential home buyer or home builder should give serious consideration to the future energy situation in the United States. It is apparent that this problem will increase in the years ahead. President Carter said that the energy shortage "is the greatest challenge that our country will face during our lifetime." How does this affect the potential homeowner of tomorrow? He or she should check with care the size and energy efficiency of a home prior to purchase. Does it have adequate insulation? (Approximately eight inches of fiberglass in the ceilings and six inches in the exterior walls are the minimum requirements.) Are the windows and other glass areas insulated or double glazed? Are the exterior doors adequately insulated? Are heating and cooling units the most efficient and economical? What about location in relation to work? Do you need all this floor space? What are current and projected utility rates? Questions on energy conservation should be answered to your satisfaction prior to purchase.

Present homeowners should study with care the possibility of providing better insulation and making over energy-saving improvements. You are entitled to a credit of 15% of the first $2,000 you spend on components to conserve energy in your home. You are eligible for the credit when the original installation of the components is completed. The full $2,000 of energy-saving items need not be installed in a single tax year. However, if the qualifying items are installed over a period of more than one tax year, the 15% credit must be claimed for the tax years in which the items are installed. For example, from April 20, 1977, through the end of 1978 must be combined in computing the 1978 credit. A new $2,000 limit applies to each subsequent principal residence in which you live.

Cooperative Apartments

A cooperative apartment, as the name implies, is one whose purchase involves the sharing of ownership of a building and land. The building is constructed for a group of people who incorporate for this purpose. Their ownership is reflected in their shareholdings, which enable them to reside in their apartments. Each owner also has the privilege of using the land and sharing the common building facilities. The responsibility for maintenance of the building, including payment of taxes, rests with the corporation. It obtains funds for upkeep from the apartment dwellers. Each apartment owner has a single vote in management affairs. An individual owner in a cooperative cannot sell his or her apartment to another person without the consent of the other members of the cooperative, a restriction that sometimes presents harsh problems with respect to contemplated sales. The method of financing a cooperative is similar to that previously discussed with respect to a conventional housing loan.

Condominiums

Condominiums are apartment buildings, often of the luxury type, in which title to each apartment rests with the purchaser. Ownership also includes a pro rata share of all land and improvements. Often the builder can borrow virtually all the money required and sell each of the apartments before the construction is completed.

During a recent visit to Miami, Florida, I looked at a number of condominiums. Although some of the cheapest units could be purchased for as little as $20,000, the majority ranged far in excess of this figure — not surprisingly, in view of the location. One luxury unit published a proposed price schedule for its apartments that ranged from $90,500 to $142,500, and this did not include the annual maintenance cost, which ran upward of $210 per month.

Although a condominium, in contrast to a cooperative, does permit you to sell to whomever you please, there is always the problem of finding a buyer. In the meantime, you have made a heavy fixed investment with money that could be earning interest, and in periods of high yields the interest can be a considerable sum. Your monthly assessment may approximate the cost of apartment rent, and as the building ages, these maintenance expenses increase.

Financial Arrangements
Financing arrangements on condominiums vary. I found that some of the luxury units were asking 50 percent of the total selling price as a down payment, with the remainder to be paid within 20 years. In contrast, others were advertising small down payments with long-term settlement dates. One such ad read, "Purchase price of $25,990; with 10% down payment of $2,600 and monthly payments at $213 per month for the first 7 years and then $160 per month for the next 23 years. Each payment includes principal and interest — annual percentage rate of 8½% per annum."

Mobile Homes

There has been a healthy rise in the use of mobile homes beginning in the 1960s. Mobile units accounted for only 8 percent of all new single-family dwellings in 1960, but sixteen years later, they had increased to over 36 percent. Over 900,000 mobile homes were sold in

1978; families living in this type of unit numbered 10 million. The majority of purchasers, accounting for over 50 percent, were young married couples.

Costs

A primary advantage of mobile-home living, in contrast to conventional residences, is the lower initial cost. The average two-bedroom unit can be purchased for $10,000 to $12,000, although prices range from $8,000 to $50,000, and even higher for custom jobs. A problem in purchasing a mobile home is choosing from among the myriad of manufacturers in the business — more than 200 of them. It is important not only to obtain a good-quality home, but also to make the purchase from a reputable dealer who will stand by his or her product. If you buy a used mobile home, check the going rates as published in the *Official Mobile Home Market Report.*

As you know, the mobile home is not mobile at all. You cannot move the average one with your car; a sizable truck is required for that purpose. Before you buy, be sure that you have found a suitable park or lot to move your home to and that the dealer will pay for all setup costs. If you are in a hurricane area, make certain that the mobile home is properly grounded so that high winds do not turn it over. And be sure the dealer is reliable; it is one thing to have a 90-day factory warranty, but another to get the dealer to provide the services within that period.

Recreational Homes

Outdoor living beckons to an increasing number of Americans each year. The facilities they occupy are usually used only for recreational purposes, although some people make this kind of dwelling a year-round home. I know a young college instructor who has a small houseboat as a permanent abode. These recreational homes range from tent campers costing $400 to elegant motor dwellings with price tags that exceed $100,000.

Motor Homes

A relatively recent innovation is the motor home, which is truly mobile and is used primarily during vacations. This is normally an expensive investment. The cost may range from $15,000 to $100,000, or more.

A motor home permits the owner to stop in any locality without needing to use the motor-park facilities. It is a completely self-contained unit. The method of financing is similar to that for a mobile home. The only different aspect is that insurance rates are higher for this vehicle on wheels. This is not normally an item purchased by the recent college graduate, because of its high cost and limited use.

The energy crisis also has had an adverse impact on motor homes. A full-sized motor home averages approximately 7 miles per gallon.

Other Choices
There is a wide variety of other types of recreational "homes." One student enjoys living in a tent and, in the balmy southern clime, he makes it his year-round home. A young teacher spends each summer vacationing in her camper. Other potential home choices include standard trailers, houseboats, truck campers, van conversions, and tent campers.

RENTALS

If you decide to go the rental route, there are much the same options available in the way of housing — apartments, houses, duplexes, boats, motor homes, and mobile homes. As in a purchase, you must decide from among alternatives what is available that best meets your needs.

In the current housing market there are opportunities to rent with the option to buy. That is, if you like a home or condominium that you are renting, you can buy it later; freedom of choice rests with you. This situation permits a thorough check of the house while renting it, an opportunity to raise down-payment money, and time to decide if you really like the community.

"Singles" Apartments

For the socially minded single person just graduated from college, there is a fairly recent development that has been well received in a number of localities — apartment rentals for single people. They provide a social atmosphere with swimming pool, clubhouse, bar, and entertainment. A visit to one building supported the fact that it provides an active and enjoyable social atmosphere. A local apartment advertises, "For Young Singles. Where the Action Is."

Motor Homes

If you are interested in a motor-home vacation, you may wish to rent a vehicle. Our neighbor has a family of eight and finds it a delightful way to vacation each year. In 1978 his rental cost (not including a refundable deposit of $400) for a four-week trip from New Orleans to California was as follows:

$300 per week × 4	=	$1,200
12 cents per mile × 4,000	=	480
		$1,680

ACTIONS YOU CAN TAKE TO COPE WITH INFLATION AND THE ENERGY SHORTAGE

1. The smaller home may be the better buy with appropriate energy-saving devices, such as: an automatic-timer thermostat (it regulates home temperatures automatically), inside window insulation or storm windows, weather stripping for doors and windows, doorstops and thresholds, a timer for the electric water heater, an attic ventilator, and wallboards and insulation.
2. Keep furnishings simple and buy only items that are needed and practical. Conserve whenever possible. For example, buy stainless-steel utensils instead of sterling silverware.

SUMMARY

The purchase-or-rent decision is never a completely black-and-white situation. If you are considering a career that requires frequent moves, you may find renting is the better approach — particularly in the first few years. This will give you a better feel of whether such a career is to your liking, and it will also provide an opportunity to build a money base for a healthy down payment. Nevertheless, there are situations in a career requiring frequent change where buying is the better deal. For example, some companies pick up the tab for all moving expenses and will permit you to buy a home on a no-loss basis. Upon your transfer, the corporation will reimburse you for your original purchase price, although you have the option of trying to sell the house yourself at a profit.

In careers such as the foreign service and multinational corporations, the personnel accept the fact that frequent moves are inevitable. These transfers are a financial hardship for most people, but a few have made their moves a source of profit.

Both in the United States and overseas there are communities where housing is critical. Frequently there is a considerable waiting period for appropriate rentals, and this involves an additional move, with its attendant expenses and other tribulations. Although recent apartment building has alleviated the shortage in some measure, the rentals may be inadequate in size and overpriced in relation to value received.

In certain areas rents are high when compared to the cost of owning a home. In others it may be more advantageous to rent. Before making a decision, consider the following points: (1) adequate shopping for rentals and homes available for sale, (2) estimated duration of current assignment, (3) available funds, (4) the money market — that is, the current interest rates, and (5) the personal desires of the family.

It is generally better for young people to rent initially instead of buying a residence. However, in some situations it is not feasible to rent. To maintain a desired standard of living, purchasing may be more practical. Also, for those who are in the area where they plan to spend their lives, buying may be the best solution.

What about the desirability of buying with the idea of renting out the property upon being transferred? This approach can be costly. It is advisable to be close to the property you own. Absentee ownership is difficult. Maintenance problems, sudden transfer of tenants, and delinquent accounts are difficult problems to solve from a distance of hundreds or thousands of miles.

If purchase is decided upon, the buyer should make the lowest down payment possible as a general rule, except for the home he or she plans to occupy for a minimum of three years, because when a new position is accepted, it is far easier to sell the property. It is hard to find someone who has the large lump sum to buy you out if you have made a considerable investment. Furthermore, your monthly payments should be spread over a long period of time, so that they are lower and more potential purchasers will be able to meet them. Take advantage of GI and FHA loans where appropriate. In contrast, if you have found your ideal locality, make the maximum down payment on a home and pay the balance off as rapidly as possible.

Experience indicates that when you are subject to transfer, it is invariably the wrong time to sell. It is important to remember that property will bring a seller whatever price a buyer is willing to pay. Usually, it does take a fair amount of time and effort to obtain a good deal in either buying or selling. For those subject to frequent transfer, this "shopping opportunity" is not always feasible, and it may result in their being forced to "dump" their homes on the market at a considerable loss in order to get back a part of their equity that is needed for other things.

A prominent bank and lending real estate firm in your community are good places to secure appropriate home-buying and -selling information. However, you may wish to avoid using real estate brokers initially. This could save you a 6 percent commission on each end of the transaction. For example, a used home listing at $50,000 may cost an extra $3,000 if bought or sold through a realty firm. If you cannot make a direct sale or purchase, you can always turn to the real estate agent.

Houses, like securities, should be purchased only after adequate background and understanding of the problems confronting the buyer. It pays to investigate well before purchase.

In addition to conventional homes, there are alternative dwellings, such as condominiums, cooperative apartments, mobile homes, recreational homes, motor homes, and apartments. You should review your budget and goals in life in order to arrive at a sound decision as to what type of dwelling is appropriate for your lifestyle.

The essence of social insurance is bringing the magic of averages to the rescue of the millions.

—WINSTON CHURCHILL

LIFE INSURANCE AND SOCIAL SECURITY

HOW MUCH INSURANCE?

A key concern for each draft-eligible man during the Vietnam conflict was "What insurance provisions should I make, in view of possible combat duty?" At one university certain unscrupulous people were selling insurance to service-bound men. Some agents were wounded veterans and others born hucksters. They would invite students to a free dinner at the local hotel and perhaps give them a ballpoint pen. The young people would end up buying endowment-type commercial insurance policies. These high-premium policies earned splendid commissions for the salesmen concerned but did not give the purchasers what they needed most — adequate insurance protection at reasonable cost.

The college graduate who will be required to travel frequently by car and plane, or who expects to take a high-risk job, or who is an ROTC product, should give careful consideration to his or her insurance needs. Most other people, too, should carry some insurance. It is a reasonable way of providing money for others in the event of your death. Furthermore, there are many fine agents and able insurance companies that can be of assistance to you. However, it is important to have an understanding of various aspects of insurance before you purchase a policy.

144

I believe that insurance should be purchased solely as protection in the event that you should die before you have accumulated a nest egg to meet the needs of your heirs or provide a legacy for whatever other purposes you desire. If you accept this approach, you should buy the cheapest form — term or group. By following my investment policy, you can accumulate your own insurance in the form of cash reserves, bonds, stocks, real estate, and other assets. A check of insurance company holdings proves that these companies place their funds in such investments. For their services, the insurance firms ask a high fee. Why pay this middleman cost, other than for necessary protection?

Also keep in mind that the organization you work for may have splendid group policies at nominal rates.

A managerial approach can be helpful in the development of a sound insurance program (Chapters 9 and 10). This requires determining your insurance objectives and planning a total program to meet your needs. Once you have decided on your *plan, implement* it and then *check* to see that your plan is kept up to date.

INSURANCE PLANS

Insurance is big business in America today — *very* big. There was $2,583 *billion* worth of life insurance in force at the end of 1977.

There were 1,762 life insurance companies in the United States in mid-1977, of which 1,607 were stock companies owned by shareholders and usually not paying dividends on their policies. Mutual life insurance companies numbered 141 but accounted for slightly over half the life insurance in force. Mutuals do not have stockholders and normally issue policies that pay dividends. This fact does not lower the net cost of mutual insurance because the premiums charged reflect this dividend differential.[1]

The four major categories of life insurance are ordinary, group, credit, and industrial. The average size life insurance policy in force, in 1977, for each of these categories was as follows:

Category	Average Policy Size
Ordinary	$ 9,240
Group	$10,550
Credit	$ 1,760
Industrial	$ 590

[1] American Council of Life Insurance, *Life Insurance Fact Book*, 1978.

This chapter will deal primarily with two of the categories — ordinary and group. In the case of ordinary life insurance, each individual must decide which type of policy is best suited to his or her needs. It is far more complicated than group insurance, which is usually provided by the employer and gives the employee no choice but to accept it or not to participate.

You will encounter credit life insurance if you borrow money. Its purpose is to protect the lender in case you should die prior to repayment of the entire debt. It is utilized by such lending agencies as furniture stores, banks, and small-loan companies. From the borrower's standpoint, it is just another expense in the high cost of using someone else's money. The lender normally makes a profit on credit insurance. At the end of 1977, there was $139.4 billion worth of credit life insurance in force in the United States, an increase of $15.8 billion over the previous year.[2]

Industrial insurance policies should not be confused with the excellent group insurance available to workers in many industrial organizations. The title "industrial" is misleading. Industrial policies are in fact ordinary life insurance but they are categorized separately because they are written in small amounts and collected weekly or monthly by agents going from house to house. This is the most expensive type of life insurance — and the most profitable for the insurance salespeople and their companies.

An insurance policy is only as good as the company behind it. Therefore, it pays to take a hard look at available facts prior to signing a contract. It is wise to select a company that has been in business a long time and has a fine reputation, a healthy growth rate, and competitive prices. There is much good material on insurance companies to be found in *Life Financial* and *Life Rates and Data Reports*, published by The National Underwriter Co., 420 East 4th Street, Cincinnati, Ohio 45202. In addition to this information on specific companies, you may wish more general background on insurance. If so, I recommend your reading the *Life Insurance Fact Book*, current edition. It is published by the American Council of Life Insurance, 1850 K Street NW, Washington, D.C., 20006. Both books should be available in your library.

ORDINARY INSURANCE

Let us now examine the ordinary insurance category. It has the largest amount of insurance in force ($1,289 billion) and the greatest

[2] Ibid., p. 31.

number of policyholders (139 million). Ordinary offers a variety of policies to meet any individual need. We will discuss the four principal types and several special types.

Ordinary Life

The ordinary life (or straight life) policy provides insurance protection by the payment of a fixed premium throughout the lifetime of the insured. Ordinary life calls for the lowest premium payment of any of the permanent plans, thus affording the largest amount of permanent protection per dollar of premium paid. After the first policy year the accumulated cash value may be utilized for one of several purposes: paid-up insurance, extended term insurance, cash loans, or cash surrender. This is the most common type of insurance held by American families. Premiums continue for life, and the face value of the policy is payable at death.

The advantages of this type of policy are the relatively low cost and the accumulation of cash values. The latter permits cashing in the policy and receiving a limited amount of money in relation to the amount paid, or borrowing against it, for which insurance companies charge you 5 to 6 percent. A disadvantage of the ordinary life is that the insured may not always be able to meet the premiums. It is important to remember that these are lifetime payments. The possibility of failure to meet future payments is increased when a large proportion of earnings is placed in such insurance. There is also the inherent weakness of life insurance itself — the lack of protection against inflation.

Ordinary life may be purchased on a guaranteed-cost or a participation basis. A participation policy, while higher in initial cost, pays the insured, after the second year, dividends that may then be applied toward the premium payments. Detailed computations may be necessary to determine whether the dividend-paying or non-dividend policy is the better deal.

The disadvantage of life payments is not as much a handicap as would appear at first glance. If at some future date the insured is no longer able to maintain payments, he or she has the privilege of converting to a paid-up policy of lower value and making no further payments. The option is often taken by retirees whose insurance needs decline along with their income.

Fixed-Payment Life

The fixed-payment (or limited-payment) life policy provides insurance protection throughout the lifetime of the insured by the payment of a fixed premium for a period of 20 (20-payment life) or 30 (30-payment life) years. At the end of this period, payments cease, but the insurance continues in force, and guaranteed values continue to accumulate. Also, such dividends as may be declared on a participating policy will be payable throughout the lifetime of the insured. Premiums for the 20-payment life policy are, of course, higher than those for ordinary life, or 30-payment life, because the policy becomes fully paid up in 20 years.

The limited-payment life policy is a variation of straight life. The period of premium payments is tailored to the individual's requirement. Fixed-payment policies are of two varieties, designed to mature either at a specific time in the future or at an explicit age. These policies have the advantages of being paid up at a definite time and of building cash values more rapidly than does a similar amount of straight life. The major disadvantage is cost. Most life insurance is bought by the young family man of modest income. The amount of protection that can be bought per dollar of premium is lower than with group, term, or straight life.

There are variations of the standard policy. For example, at least one insurance company has what they call a Modified Life 5–10 Policy. After purchasing, say, a $10,000 policy, for the first 5 years the insured pays 50 percent of the annual premium, and the full premium thereafter. At the end of 27 years, the policy is fully paid up. However, if the insured continues premium payments for the next 8 years, the policy becomes an endowment that would pay, at age 65, $14,265. The total cash outlay for such a policy is $8,100. This modified policy overcomes one of the major objections about fixed-payment life: It provides good protection to the insured at a time when his or her income is low and the need for insurance may be high. A major drawback to this type of policy is the fact that 5 years after purchase the premiums will double, and it may be at a time when the policyholder can least afford it.

Endowment

A majority of endowment policies are of the 20-year variety. They provide that a fixed premium shall be paid for 20 years. At the end of this period, unless the policy matures sooner by death, the full amount is payable to the insured, either in one sum or in monthly installments normally ranging in number from 36 to 240, as he or she may elect. The premium for this type of contract is higher than the premium for ordinary 20-payment life or 30-payment life plans because the contract not only provides for full payment to the insured if he or she is alive at the end of the endowment period, but also guarantees full payment to his or her beneficiary if the policy-holder should die at any time during the 20-year period.

Another variety of this policy is the endowment at age 60. This policy, otherwise identical with the 20-year endowment, provides for fixed premium payments only until the insured is 60 years old. There are other varieties of endowment policies that can be tailored to fit your needs.

Endowment insurance is designed as a life benefit policy. In 1976, for example, life insurance companies paid out $976 million in matured endowments, as compared to $9.6 billion in death benefits. A person buying an endowment is paying for both protection and a savings account. Therefore, his or her premiums are higher than for other types for the same amount of protection. Insurance companies take both the savings and the protection portions of your endowment premiums (less a big chunk for expenses) and invest them.

How well have the insurance companies done with their investments? The rate of interest they paid in the past ten years ranged from 2½ to 4 percent for some of the mutual companies. Check your local bank and you can beat that return. Endowment policies are also prime targets for loss due to inflation. As they are long-term contracts, maturing endowments may only partially fulfill the need for which they were obtained in the first place. Like long-term bonds (see Chapter 12), they often fail to keep up with loss in the purchasing power of the dollar.

An endowment policy can be a means to encourage saving. Insurance companies do insist upon payment of your premiums on penalty of cancellation. The company has no compunction about voiding the policy.

In a Roper survey, it was found that a large percentage of the public thinks of life insurance premiums as debt similar to mortgage payments. Even during the depression, most policyholders paid their insurance premiums. However, for those who do default, the primary purpose of insurance — protection — is defeated. Default often occurs when protection is most needed.

Retirement-income insurance is like endowment insurance. It has similar strengths — such as forced savings and death benefits — and comparable weaknesses. It is expensive, there is no inflation protection, and the interest paid on the money is low in comparison to what can be obtained elsewhere.

Term

Term insurance provides for a level premium rate for a set period, often 60 months (five years), after which the policy ceases and becomes void, except when renewed or changed to some other form of policy. Payment of the premium for the sixtieth month automatically renews the term insurance for an additional five-year period, at a correspondingly higher premium rate.

Term insurance has been classified as "pure protection" insurance. What you pay for a term policy is a sunk cost; that is, there is no cash value being accrued. If you live to the end of the insurance period, you have only a pile of receipts to show for your premiums. Dollar for dollar, it's the best deal — it is similar to car or fire insurance, in that you pay for insurance protection only.

The simplest and oldest form is declining term insurance. This is very reasonable. A few years ago, there was an insurance company in the Midwest that would sell a $10,000 policy for $44 a year if the insured was under 35 years of age, and no medical examination was required. The fly in the ointment was that each year the value of the policy declined sharply.

A second type of term insurance provides for payment of the face value of the policy in case of death during the term for which the policy is issued. This type is popular with young families because of low cost, renewability, and the conversion privilege. A term policy is renewable, usually for the face value of the original, without the need of a physical up to age 65. The major mutual or stock companies normally do not offer term insurance to people over 65, and never to those aged 70 or more.

A term policy may be convertible into an ordinary life, a fixed-payment, or an endowment policy. The type of conversion varies with insurance companies. The major attraction of term insurance is low cost. A $10,000 renewable term policy can be purchased for approximately $55 at age 25. This includes not only accidental death benefits equal to the face value of the policy, but a waiver of premium due to disability as well. However, at each renewal the cost of the insurance goes up without a corresponding increase in protection. At age 30, premiums approximate $59; at 45, $116; and by age 60, a total of $350. The waiver of disability is no longer available at age 60.

The key to successful use of term insurance is to employ it early and then build your own insurance nest egg through other investments. If you go the long route in either term or convertible term, it can be costly. Let us consider the following example. At age 25 Mr. X purchases a $10,000 ten-year convertible term policy and converts at the end of the period. He would pay $58 a year for the first ten years and $245 thereafter. Mr. Y, at age 25, purchases a participating ordinary life policy for $10,000 at a premium of $183. At age 40 Mr. X has had a total insurance cost (premiums minus cash value) of approximately $1,200, while Mr. Y's cost was $885. The cost gap widens over the years.

Special Policies

In addition to the four major types of ordinary policies (term, ordinary life, fixed-payment, and endowment), there is a group that combines the features of ordinary life, term, and endowment policies. Such a combination is expensive but in theory gives greater protection and savings.

One company sells what it calls a Family Security Policy, which provides monthly income protection for 20 years, along with permanent insurance payable at death. It carries a level life premium; therefore, the cost is considerably lower in the early years than that of a straight life policy with a family-protector rider of comparable coverage. Of course, cash values accrue very slowly under such a plan. Each unit consists of $1,000 of face amount.

Another combination of ordinary life and term insurance is one that one company calls a Family Policy, under which all family members are covered. It provides for $5,000 in straight life on the head of the household, a $1,500 term policy on the wife that is in force until the insured's sixty-fifth birthday, and a $1,000 term policy on each child up to age 25. Both the term contracts are convertible into other types of policies, with restrictions, and the cost of the accidental-death benefit and disability waiver are included in the premium. The advantage of this type of policy is that each new member of the family is automatically insured at the age of 15 days, thus saving this additional expense.

There is also a "jumping-junior" policy that has a face value of $1,000 until age 21, when the face value jumps to $5,000. Premiums are payable to age 65. In addition, another $5,000 worth of permanent insurance can be purchased at age 21 without medical examination or proof of insurability. There are a multitude of other policies, and an insurance company will tailor a program to meet your desires.

Adjustable Life

An adjustable life policy is a recent innovation in life insurance that permits one to decide the amount of coverage one needs and, within limits, the amounts to be paid at various periods in the life of the policy. This concept is based on the idea that as insurance needs and income vary, there should be flexibility to increase or decrease the amount and type of coverage. Here is an example of how it works:

Steve Swift required $20,000 insurance his first two years after graduation. His income permitted only term-type protection, but he wanted the option to make changes later so bought an adjustable life policy. Two years later he married Stephanie, a teacher in special education. They decided it would be desirable to have $40,000 straight life and after reviewing their budget that they could afford the higher premiums. A year after their marriage twins arrived, and Stephanie became a homemaker. The drop in income made them decide to reduce their policy to $30,000. Steve said, "The beauty of adjustable life is that it permits us, at any time in the future, to vary the amount of insurance."

The shortest period that an adjustable life policy may be purchased for is ten years. It is called term insurance because of its duration. However, this is a technicality. An adjustable policy acquires a cash value over the years. It offers more than pure protection, but it also costs more than term insurance. An adjustable policyholder may increase coverage up to 20 percent, each three-year period, without a physical examination. However, if amounts greater than 20 percent are desired, a physical is normally required.

That Best Ordinary Policy

Which of the four principal ordinary policies is best for you — endowment, fixed-payment, term, or straight life? Obviously, each person must decide what his or her own needs are in relation to a total investment program. Factors to consider in arriving at your decision should include: your age, funds available, net worth, and family responsibilities. Likewise, whether you are married, single, divorced, or widowed normally makes a difference in your insurance needs.

I favor term (and/or group) insurance for most young people. It provides maximum dollar protections for minimum cost. The savings from lower premiums, however, should be invested as discussed in Chapters 11–14. If my total financial program is followed, a person would be reducing insurance payments over the years (other than group) and buying growth investments.

GROUP LIFE INSURANCE

Group insurance, as the name implies, is issued to a group of people under one master policy. A number of organizations, both private and public, have such policies for their employees. These group policies normally do not require medical examinations.

The major advantages of group insurance are the low premium and the splendid protection. It gives you the protection when you need it the most — during the early years of employment. I strongly urge that if you have the opportunity to participate in such a program, you take full advantage of it. By paying minimum rates for insurance with maximum protection, you can put your other savings in investment areas with a greater dollar return. With each dollar saved in bonds, banks, or other investments, you are in fact providing both savings and insurance. Let us assume that at the end of five years you have a group policy for $15,000 and another $10,000 in the bank and U.S. Savings bonds. In such a situation, you have, in fact, $25,000 in insurance. In all investments maximize the dollar to your advantage. Group insurance is one way to do this.

A number of organizations pay part of the insurance premium and some may pick up the entire tab. It pays to check insurance benefits before the time of your whom-to-work-for decision.

In one university policy, if you make $20,000 a year, your premiums are only $11.00 a month (under age 65). This is a sweet deal for $20,000 protection. At age 65 and over, the premium is only $0.51 per $1,000 protection per month.

VARIABLE INSURANCE

An interesting development in life insurance is the variable policy. It is available in limited-payment form only. People who buy such policies will find their premiums and benefits to their heirs varying over the years. The objective of a variable policy is to keep up with inflation.

Insurance companies offering such policies plan to invest the premiums in quality common stock in order to keep abreast of rising consumer costs.[3] This concept sounds great in theory, but many common stocks over the past several years have failed to show any growth, and a number have declined during this era of rapid inflation.

The variable policyholder will have protection in the event his or her company's portfolio of stocks declines below the estimated amount of the policy. The insurance firm is required to pay the beneficiary an amount at least equal to the face value. Contrariwise, if the stock investments should enhance in value, payment to the heirs

---

[3] Some mutual funds are now also selling variable life policies.

would exceed the face amount. For example, if you buy a $5,000 variable life policy, you can be assured that, as a minimum, your heirs will receive $5,000 upon your death. However, if the common-stock investments of your particular company are successful, your beneficiaries could receive $6,000, $7,000, or more. For this privilege, of course, you can expect to pay higher premiums. The higher the common stock in the company portfolio rises, the greater your premiums. It has been estimated that premiums will be about 10 percent higher than for the regular fixed-payment policy.

In addition to the higher cost, another problem with the variable policy is the inability to determine precisely its loan or cash surrender value. The possibility that one day you will want to borrow money on your life insurance policy should be taken into consideration. The stocks may go down at the time you need the loan from your insurance company. Of course, the possibility exists that the stocks will be much higher, but there is this uncertainty in a variable policy. In contrast, you always know the exact amount available in a regular policy in each of the years ahead.

From a buyer's viewpoint, it is good to know that all variable insurance comes under the jurisdiction of the Securities and Exchange Commission (SEC). This regulatory federal agency requires companies issuing such policies to be registered with the SEC and to establish prudent controls. For example, prior to buying a variable policy, a potential purchaser must receive a prospectus. In addition, an annual report must be issued to each policyholder. If you are interested in a variable policy, be sure to first read with care such literature as the prospectus and current annual report.

In planning your total personal financial program, you may consider the variable policy. It could provide your beneficiary with more money than a fixed life policy. However, in return for the possibility of a larger final payment, you would pay greater yearly premiums. In my view, it would be wiser to buy a fixed amount of insurance for a set price. The difference could then be placed directly in common stock. Otherwise, you are paying a middleman cost by having the insurance company invest in growth securities.

In addition to the sizable administrative cost charged by insurance companies, their investment program might not coincide with your specific stockmarket objective. Furthermore, the common-stock gain in your insurance policy may be subject to estate taxes. This point should be checked carefully in doing your estate planning.

Keep in mind that variable policies will show remarkable differences in growth. Their success or failure will depend largely on the managerial skill and objectives of each company. Look, for example, at the wide differences in the growth rates of mutual funds — even those with comparable objectives.

ANNUITIES AND PENSION
PLANS

In addition to the topics already described, there are two other major programs that are available from life insurance companies — annuities and private pension plans.[4]

Annuities

An annuity may be defined as "a sum of money received at specified times over a period of years." The amount of the payments are arrived at based on a written agreement (contract) between the insurance company and the annuitant (beneficiary of the annuity).

The number of individual annuities in force with United States life insurance companies approximated 4.3 million in 1977. The increase of 398,000 from 1976 was due largely to continued purchases of annuities for individual pension plans made possible by the 1974 federal pension legislation, the Employee Retirement Income Security Act.

Annuities provide protection against the possibility of outliving one's financial resources. They can be set up to pay income currently or in the future at regular intervals, usually monthly. Most annuities are intended to provide guaranteed retirement income of a predetermined amount, most often for life.

There are several sources of annuity plans. They are available on a group basis, most often as pension plans set up by employers with life insurance companies, or they can be purchased individually through a life insurance agent. The cash surrender values, the matured endowment value, or the death benefit of individual life insurance policies may also be used to set up an annuity.

In arriving at your income requirements in later years you may wish to consider an annuity. For example, if you are self-employed this may be a desirable way to supplement income from other sources such as stocks, bonds, and real estate. Or for the poor money manager it may be the appropriate investment as pointed up in the following story.

---

[4] Source for a portion of the information in this section was the *Life Insurance Fact Book '78* (Washington, D.C.: American Council of Life Insurance, 1978).

During a recent visit to southern California, I spoke with a spry nonagenarian who related this story of praise for annuities.

> I retired at age 51 and left my home in Bay City, Michigan for a warmer climate. Fishing was what I enjoyed most. My wants were limited — a modest cottage near the ocean, nutritious food, girl friend, the opportunity to fish and commune with nature daily. My life as a bachelor in Bay City had been carefree. My only problem — I was a terrible money manager barely making it from one month to the next. However, the sale of my small store in the Depression enabled me to buy three annuities. My decision to buy annuities was due to my poor record of money management. I was unable to maintain a savings account and knew nothing about stocks or real estate. With annuities I would have a fixed income for life. I was careful to select good insurance companies that had been around a long time. Each contract agreed to pay me on a weekly basis for as long as I lived. It was somewhat of a gamble. But I had no family or other expenses if I died. Most important, my mother had lived to 98 and father to 91. Although inflation was no problem in the early years, it's been tough lately. But the older I get, the more meager my wants. Some of my friends, in their declining years, became so concerned about their savings running out that they actually starved themselves. Thanks to my annuities I never had this problem.

> My goal — to set a new family longevity record. I have a year and twelve days to go. But regardless, I have been an expensive annuitant.

Variable Annuities

Annuities may be fixed or variable. A fixed annuity, as the name implies, provides the same amount of money to the recipient over a set period of time. The variable annuity, all or part of which may be based on common-stock investments or on a cost-of-living index, was first developed in the 1950s.[5] Part or all of the funds normally placed in common stocks or other investments are maintained in a separate investment account. Considerably more investment latitude is permitted with funds in separate accounts than with life insurance investments generally. One type of variable annuity has income payments

[5] A variable life insurance policy, discussed earlier in this chapter, utilizes some of the concepts applicable to a variable annuity.

that are fixed and guaranteed once they begin, although the initial size depends upon the value of the fund. Another type has income payments that vary with the current value of the investments on which the annuity is based. Many plans provide for a combination of fixed and variable incomes under one contract.

Private Pension Plans

The number of Americans covered by pension plans with life insurance companies totaled 19.2 million at year-end 1977, an increase of 2.3 million over 1976. This figure includes retired people receiving pension benefits, those who have left employment with vested pension credits, and those still actively at work. There is some duplication due to persons being covered under more than one plan.

Group annuities cover the largest number of people under pension plans with life insurance companies. The traditional type is the deferred group annuity, under which a paid-up annuity is purchased each year for each employee, with the sum of these benefits paid as monthly income upon retirement. Deposit-administration–type plans set up a single fund for all employees in the pension group; money is withdrawn to buy an annuity for an employee when he or she retires. Immediate participation guarantee plans are a variation of this type, with participation in gains or losses from mortality and investment as they occur, rather than these being spread over the life of the contract.

Under terminal funded plans, reserves are usually not set up with the insurance company until the employee is about to retire. Funding for the prospective pension prior to retirement may be handled in a variety of ways.

Individual policy pension trusts, group permanent plans, and profit-sharing plans are often used by smaller firms. Individual policy pension trusts usually involve the purchase of a whole life or endowment policy for each person to provide retirement benefits. Group permanent plans use whole life or endowment policies on a group basis keyed to retirement. Profit-sharing plans included here generally provide for an individual fund for each participant annually.

In September 1974 comprehensive federal pension legislation, the Employee Retirement Income Security Act (ERISA), was signed into law. This law relates primarily to private pension and welfare plans, and various sections of the law become effective at different times. One important section, which became effective in 1975, allowed individuals employed where there was no private pension plan under which they could be covered to set up their own Individual Retirement Accounts (IRAs). Contributions and accruals are tax free until retirement, with limits set on the amount of contributions which could be contributed and penalties for early withdrawals. Funding of these individual plans could be handled in a variety of ways, one being through contracts with life insurance companies, generally annuities or endowment contracts. The maximum annual contribution allowed is 15 percent of salary or wages or $1,500, whichever is less. Beginning in 1977, a nonemployed spouse could be covered, and the maximum IRA contribution rose to $1,750.

Another provision of ERISA increased the maximum amount that self-employed persons could set aside for themselves and their employees — from $2,500 to $7,500 — but continued the limitation of 15 percent of salary, if less. This provision applied to the Keogh plans (HR10), which had been in effect for some years. Tax-sheltered annuities, permitted for use primarily in the academic community and nonprofit organizations, have also shown substantial increases.

Public Pension and Retirement Programs

In addition to the private pension plans with insurance companies, there are major public pension and retirement programs. The largest, of course, is Social Security, which will be discussed in the next section of this chapter. It is estimated that over 50 million workers in the United States are participants in major private and public pension and retirement programs, other than Social Security. About 38 million persons were members of private nongovernment plans. This figure represents the number of persons in private plans, both active workers and those presently retired, including survivors and beneficiaries.

The Railroad Retirement System is unique in being a private system covering a single industry, but administered by the federal government. The system is now fully integrated into the Social Security program and is actually a part of that system. It covers some 1.6 million persons. Figures for the railroad employees and the beneficiaries are separately maintained and generally continue to be included as a separate item under government-administered plans.

Most people are quite concerned about having money available when they retire. Unfortunately, not enough concern is given at an early age. Recent visits by the author to retirement centers in Florida and California highlight the tragic financial plight of the elderly. One lady commented: "I should have started saving for my old age when I first went to work. But I wasn't ever going to be old so why bother. My advice to young people: Select a job with a good retirement program to include Social Security and set aside money each month to build up a nest egg of stocks and real estate. Of course, like Jacqueline Kennedy, I should have married someone rich and famous."

ACTIONS YOU CAN TAKE TO COPE WITH INFLATION AND THE ENERGY SHORTAGE—LIFE INSURANCE

1. Determine if the dollars in your current life insurance policies will provide your beneficiaries with sufficient funds to keep pace with inflation.

2. Review your policies annually to determine if you need to modify them because of a change in your family situation or a desire to substitute other forms of protection. Will any new concepts in life insurance better fit your needs in view of the inflationary situation?

SUMMARY: LIFE INSURANCE

Sufficient life insurance protection should be an essential element in the financial portfolio of young people with responsibilities. You may have this protection in the form of investments, a commercial policy, or a group policy where you work. For those going into military service after college, the government provides military personnel with excellent family benefits at little cost. This financial protection should be given due consideration in a determination of your overall life insurance requirements.

As a basic premise, I believe life insurance should be bought for the primary purpose of giving the family dollar protection in the event of the wage earner's death. The amount of dollars needed must be determined by each family, based upon individual requirements. The odds are very much against your dying as a healthy young person, but your chances of hitting the insurance jackpot increase with age. Death gets you in the end, but by that time you should have a tidy sum of savings and other investments. How much insurance you want to leave is your decision. But it is helpful to keep in mind the other assets that you will leave to your heirs. If you have no family, no obligations, and no wish to leave anything to charity, you may say, "To hell with insurance; I want to enjoy it all myself!" At the other end of the spectrum, you can skimp to maximize savings for insurance purposes, betting on dying young and leaving a sizable fortune for someone else to enjoy.

Who is Covered?

Social Security, like life insurance, is a form of protection. It protects you and your family against the risks of being without any income because of death, prolonged disability, or retirement. In addition, just about everybody aged 65 or over can count on help in paying their doctor and hospital bills. The Social Security Act was passed by Congress in 1935 in the midst of the Great Depression. Its primary purpose was to provide a retirement income to people who had money deducted from their paychecks for this purpose during their working years. This act has had many amendments over the years, and now the Social Security insurance system provides protection for millions — about nine out of ten of all working Americans. Although retirees receive the largest share of Social Security payments (over 50 percent), there are substantial amounts paid for survivor benefits, disability, and hospital benefits under Medicare.

The following examples indicate the broad coverage today:

Mrs. ____ was left with five small children when her husband, a milkman, died of a heart attack at 29. She'll get monthly checks for herself and her children until they're 18, plus checks for each child from 18 to 22 who stays in school. And when Mrs. ____ is 60, she'll be eligible for widow's checks for herself. Altogether the family may collect well over $100,000.

Or take Mrs. ____ , whose husband, a garage mechanic, died at 27 in an automobile accident. They had three small children and were expecting a fourth. Mrs. ____ and her children may eventually get more than $115,000.

Each month a check goes to Mr. ____ of Hattiesburg, Mississippi who was born on July 4, 102 years ago. Another goes to a baby girl, born 7 months after her 21-year-old father was killed in an automobile accident. A third goes to a young widow, whose husband was killed in Vietnam, leaving her with a 2-year-old boy. A fourth goes to Mr. and Mrs. ____ and eight of their children because Mr. ____ has been in a hospital bed ever since he was hit by a stray bullet during a fishing trip. A fifth goes to 19-year-old triplets, whose father retired in 1958 and who are now enrolled in college. A sixth goes to a retired lawyer. A seventh goes to a 97-year-old gentleman, and it has been his sole source of income for the past 30 years.[6]

Recent Legislation

Major amendments in the Social Security law brought greater protection and higher payments to millions of Americans beginning in 1973. This 1972 legislation provided for a 20 percent increase in Social Security payments and automatic increases in cash benefits in future years, to keep pace with increases in the cost of living. Legislation enacted in late 1977 made an important change in the way benefits are calculated, improved the financial soundness of the Social Security program, and made other changes. Following are other specific areas where the recent amendments have been beneficial.

Disability
Beginning January 1973, a person who became disabled before age 22 can receive childhood disability benefits if one parent is entitled to retirement or disability benefits or dies after working long enough under Social Security. The new law also provides that monthly benefits can be started again if a person who once got checks as an adult (disabled in childhood), and later recovered, becomes disabled again within seven years after his or her previous disability ended.

Although the new disability provision is an improvement, there is considerable criticism about the current coverage because a person must be younger than 22 in order to be eligible. Since tragic automobile accidents, for instance, occur daily on our highways and people become totally or partially disabled, many believe that all those eligible, regardless of age, who become disabled should be protected by Social Security.

Student Benefits
Starting in 1973, a full-time student's checks no longer stop when he (or she) reaches 22, but continue through the end of the quarter or semester in which he reaches 22 if he has not completed undergraduate requirements. If he attends a school that is not run on a semester or quarter basis, checks continue until he completes the course or for two months after the month he reaches 22, whichever comes first.

[6] U.S. Department of Health, Education and Welfare, *Social Security: What It Means to You* (Washington, D.C.: U.S. Government Printing Office, 1972), p. 2.

Benefits for Grandchildren
Children may now be eligible for Social Security benefits based on a grandparent's earnings if the natural parents are disabled or dead, and if the grandchildren are living with and/or supported by their grandparents.

Duration of Marriage in Accident Cases
A widow (or dependent widower) and stepchildren of a worker who died accidentally or in the line of duty while on active duty in the Armed Forces can now get survivor benefits regardless of the length of time the marriage lasted. Previously, the marriage must have lasted at least three months for any survivors to get benefits.

Benefit Increases for Widows
The benefit for a widow (or dependent widower) who starts getting benefits at age 62 or later can now range from 82½ percent to 100 percent of her husband's full benefit, instead of being limited to 82½ percent as in the past. Her benefit rate depends on her own age when she first starts getting benefits, as well as the benefits her husband would be getting if he were still alive.

Special Minimum Benefit
A special minimum benefit at retirement for people who worked under Social Security for more than 20 years. This change helps people who had low income in their working years. The amount of the special minimum depends on the number of years of coverage.

Figuring Men's Benefits
Benefits for men who reach 62 in 1975 or later are now figured the same way as they are for women. Under the old law, if a man and woman of the same age had the same earnings over the years, the woman would generally have a higher benefit rate. Under the new law, a man and woman who are the same age have equal benefits if they had equal earnings. The work credits required to qualify for benefits are now also the same for both men and women.

Delayed-Retirement Credit
A worker who does not get benefits before 65 and who delays his or her retirement past 65 will get a special credit that can mean a larger benefit. The credit adds to a worker's benefit 1 percent for each year (1/12 of 1 percent for each month) from age 65 to age 72 for which he or she did not get benefits. The credit applies only when a worker

has earnings after December 1970. The increases became effective January 1973. Benefits of dependents or survivors are not increased.

If you are 65 or over and work while getting Social Security, you can earn more without losing any benefits under the 1977 law. You can earn $4,000 in 1978 and get all benefits for the year. If your earnings exceed $4,000, $1 in benefits will be withheld for each $2 you earn above that amount. The annual exemption amount will increase to $4,500 in 1979, $5,000 in 1980, $5,500 in 1981, and $6,000 in 1982. The exempt amount after 1982 will increase automatically as wages go up.

Starting in 1982, there will be no limit on the earnings for people 70 or older. Until then, there is a limit on earnings for people under 72.

Another 1977 change restricts the use of the monthly earnings test. Before 1978, full benefits could be paid for any month that a beneficiary had earnings below the monthly exempt amount (one-twelfth of the annual amount) and did not perform substantial services in self-employment. Now, the monthly test is eliminated except for the first year in which a person's earnings both exceeds the annual limit, and there is a month in which the person neither earns more than the monthly limit nor performs substantial services in self-employment. The monthly exempt amount of earnings for people 65 and over in 1978 was $334.

If you reach 65 after 1981 and decide to delay retirement, your benefit later on will be increased 3 percent for each year from age 65 to 72 that you were eligible to receive benefits but did not take them. If you reach 65 in 1981 or earlier and delay getting benefits, the present retirement credit of 1 percent a year will continue to apply. The credit will also apply to people who received reduced benefits if they have a deduction month after 65. Also beginning June 1978, any delayed-retirement credits you earn as a worker can be payable to your surviving spouse.

The delayed-retirement benefit beyond 65 has been criticized as not going far enough. At present, a person can work after 65 up to a certain dollar amount, and receive Social Security cash benefits. Beginning in 1982, at 70, she (or he) can receive all her dollar benefits regardless of her income from work. It has been argued that every person who continues to work beyond 65 should be entitled to receive *all* her cash retirement benefits at 65 if she so desires, regardless of her income from work. After all, it was her money that was put aside, by the Social Security Administration, for this purpose (insurance protection). Why shouldn't payments be made to her at the time she desires to receive them? She may decide to accept the bonus of the delayed retirement credit and wait until age 70. But it should be her choice.

Other Improvements
The 1972 legislation also took constructive measures in regard to the disability waiting period; disability claims after death; workmen's compensation offset; new benefit for people disabled by blindness; benefits for divorced women; adoption by retired or disabled workers; and wage credits for Japanese-Americans.

If you have any questions in any of these areas, it is important to call your nearest Social Security office. Look in your phone book under "Social Security Administration." If you are in an area where there is no such office, you should write to Social Security Administration, U.S. Department of Health, Education and Welfare, Baltimore, Maryland 21201.

Cash Benefits

The higher your earnings (up to the current ceiling of $22,900), the higher your monthly Social Security benefits will be. A person who was disabled in June 1977, for instance, might have received $236.40 per month if his (or her) average yearly earnings after 1950 amounted to $3,000. In contrast, if he had averaged $6,000, his payments would have been $364.50. A retired worker (65 or older) would also be paid the $236.40 based upon $3,000 earnings, or $364.50 based upon $6,000.

Rising Costs

The additional benefits made available to Social Security recipients over the years have taken their toll in increased expenses. To cover these costs, workers' payments have been increased. This has been accomplished by increasing both the tax rate and the tax base.

In December 1977, Congress passed a Social Security funding bill that will more than triple payroll taxes for many workers by 1987. Tables 9-1 and 9-2 provide a comparison between the old and current law.

In addition to the dollar increase, there has also been a percentage increase. A projection of what this will be in the future is apparent from the contribution rate schedule under the current law (see Table 9-1).

Note that in the year 1977, the employee contributed 5.85 per-

Table 9-1. Social Security Contribution Rate.

| Calendar Year | Tax Rate | |
	Current Law	Old Law
1977	5.85%	5.85%
1978	6.05	6.05
1979	6.13	6.05
1980	6.13	6.05
1981	6.65	6.30
1982	6.70	6.30
1983	6.70	6.30
1984	6.70	6.30
1985	7.05	6.30
1986	7.15	6.45
1987	7.15	6.45

Note: Employer and employee *each* pay at this rate.

cent under the recent law. By 1987, this percentage increases from 5.85 to 7.15 percent. Let us assume that in 1977, a person earned $16,500. His or her Social Security payment for that year would have been $965.25. By 1987, a person who earns $42,600 would pay $3,045.90 (see Table 9-2). The employer must also pay into the Social Security system, in the same amount as that deducted from each employee.

Table 9-2. Social Security Payroll Taxes for Workers.

| Calendar Year | Current Law | |
	Wage Base	Tax
1977	$16,500	$ 965.25
1978	17,700	1,070.85
1979	22,900	1,403.77
1980	25,900	1,587.67
1981	29,700	1,975.05
1982	31,800	2,130.60
1983	33,900	2,271.30
1984	36,000	2,412.00
1985	38,100	2,686.05
1986	40,200	2,874.30
1987	42,600	3,045.90

165

SOCIAL SECURITY'S FUTURE

The fact that more people are living longer, with greater numbers receiving Social Security benefits, has resulted in the failure of the system to be self-supporting. When Social Security was first established, there were about 12 workers supporting one retiree. Today that base has been reduced over 60 percent. To partially compensate for this loss both the wage base ($22,900 in 1979, and the contribution rate (6.13 percent in 1979) have been increased markedly since 1935. The recent law will provide additional funds for Social Security needs, but may not be sufficient in the long run. Unless additional funds are obtained through such measures as imposing Social Security taxes on all earnings, and increasing the contribution rate, the system could be in financial trouble. And if Congress should reduce the tax rate and tax base, as a result of political pressure, the system could go broke. I feel sure, however, that the U.S. government would divert other revenue to assure that certain payments are made to all recipients who earned them. In my view, we can expect Social Security pensions to continue, to include cost-of-living increases, financed in part by higher payments from the working-age group. The federal government will make up any deficit by dipping into other funds.

ACTIONS YOU CAN TAKE TO COPE WITH INFLATION AND THE ENERGY SHORTAGE—SOCIAL SECURITY

1. Review annually the estimated money you expect to receive from Social Security. Decide if you should modify your other investments (including insurance policies) to meet your projected retirement needs. Keep in mind that Social Security is exempt from income taxes and that it increases annually in accordance with inflation.

2. Examine the possibility of working longer in order to collect higher Social Security benefits.

SUMMARY: SOCIAL SECURITY

Social Security benefits in the future can be expected to increase. Better insurance protection will be provided in the way of retirement payments, disability, health, and hospitalization. Therefore, in arriving at your total insurance needs, be sure to give due consideration to the coverage made available to you by the U.S. government. I recommend that you first estimate what you require in the way of protection for you and your family. Then estimate the amount that is furnished by Social Security. Next, determine the insurance coverage you have from commercial sources plus other investments. If the total of Social Security, insurance, and savings fails to meet your requirements, you should secure additional protection.

*And down in fathoms many went, the
captain and the crew,
Down went the owners — greedy men
Whom hope of gain allured;
Oh, dry the starting tear for they were
heavily insured.*

—WILLIAM S. GILBERT

CAR, PROPERTY, HEALTH, AND LIABILITY INSURANCE

In July, 1977, my family lost everything in the flood that struck our hometown of Johnstown, Pennsylvania. I didn't have coverage on my car, and our home was destroyed. The furnishings were not insured. Mom and my sister were injured and had heavy hospital bills — again no insurance. We had higher priorities for our limited income and never thought another flood like 1899 would strike this area. We did get some help from the government but if my uncle hadn't given us money, I wouldn't be back in school. My family learned the hard way the importance of having adequate protection.

This comment by a student to members of my former class pointed up the importance of having appropriate insurance.

Most members of the work force can normally expect to have acquired a car, household property, and family responsibilities within a reasonable period. With these acquisitions comes the need for adequate protection. The importance of appropriate life insurance was discussed in Chapter 9. This chapter will investigate the other components of a sound insurance program. The number of dollars to be invested in insurance coverage will, of course, vary with the individual.

Special attention will be devoted to the area of car insurance and the high, sometimes prohibitive cost of automobile coverage for the young. We shall also investigate the areas of property and accident and health insurance, including Medicare, stressing the importance of liability coverage in most insurance areas.

NO-FAULT INSURANCE

"I will not be blackmailed by an industry" stated Governor Francis Sargent of Massachusetts on August 13, 1970, when he signed the no-fault insurance bill that, in effect, reduced auto premiums by 15 percent in his state. According to the governor, the $400 billion insurance industry had exerted enormous pressure to prevent passage of the bill. At the time, one young man from Boston was queried on TV about insurance costs. He said, "My premium would be about $1,000 a year on a new car, and I just can't afford those rates along with the monthly car payments."

The Massachusetts law requires third-party auto insurance for all drivers and makes it mandatory for insurance companies to pay the initial $2,000 in accident claims at once, regardless of which driver is at fault. The companies responded promptly to the no-fault bill. Three of the major firms stopped writing policies in the state. The governor indicated that he would have the state provide the coverage if the private companies failed to offer such protection.

This concern over various aspects of car insurance stimulated Congress to order a study by the Secretary of Transportation of the current system of liability protection. His recommendation — establish a federal no-fault insurance law.

In the eight years since Governor Sargent established no-fault insurance in Massachusetts, 16 states now have some form of this new concept. Furthermore, Congress has been in the process of authorizing a no-fault auto insurance bill since 1974. It was passed by the Senate in May 1974 but failed in the House. In subsequent sessions, it also did not pass. In 1977, President Carter supported no-fault legislation that would require all states and the District of Columbia to have no-fault programs that would meet U.S. Government standards. States not complying would be required to follow federal regulations. No-fault is not a panacea, but it should permit faster payments and perhaps rates will not climb as rapidly.

It is important to remember that even with a no-fault program you need other car insurance — liability coverage for bodily injury, property damage, and uninsured motorists — because although most states with no-fault restrict the right to sue, they do not eliminate it.

There is also considerable variation in the amount and type of coverage among the states. For example, Pennsylvania, Michigan, and New Jersey have unlimited compulsory no-fault in contrast to Massachusetts, Virginia, and South Dakota which have a $2,000 limit.

AUTO INSURANCE

Auto insurance permits a pooling of resources in order to transfer the burden of loss from an individual to a group that pays for this privilege. From a personal finance standpoint, your objective should be to make the minimum contribution for a policy with the maximum coverage. This requires shopping around for the best rates and by all means not accepting insurance proposals by an auto dealer without making valid comparisons. Young people are paying high rates today and should examine with care the types of companies available, coverage provided, and net premiums.

Types of Companies

There are two principal types of auto insurance companies — stock and mutual. A *stock company*, as the name implies, is owned by shareholders. Consequently, a portion of the profits generated by premiums go to owners of stock, in the form of cash dividends. A *mutual company* belongs to the policyholders and distributes its net earnings through premium rebates, which can amount to as much as 50 percent. In addition to the regular mutual company, there are also a few that are "assessable." They may, at times, provide maximum savings to their policyholders, but their rates can also exceed those of standard mutuals, when they have operating losses that require members to be assessed additional amounts. It is difficult to estimate annual payments to an assessable mutual, because their rates have been known to increase more than 100 percent in a given year.

Another type of auto insurance company deals with select membership. For example, the United Services Automobile Association restricts eligibility to certain military personnel. The Insurance Exchange of the Automobile Club of Southern California provides insurance only for members of its motor club.

Coverage Available

There are six major categories of insurance coverage — bodily-injury liability, property damage liability, medical payments, comprehensive (excluding collision), collision, and uninsured motorists. Let us look at each coverage, remembering that company terms vary; it is very important to read with care the fine print in a policy before buying it.

1. *Bodily injury liability* insurance pays for injury, sickness, or disease — including death resulting therefrom — to others, for which the insured may be legally liable. This includes damages for care and loss of services that may result from an accident involving the insured's automobile. It also protects the insured from claims or suits that are the result of an accident.

2. *Property damage liability* protects the insured from financial loss due to injury to, or destruction of, the property of others. This protection would include damage to other cars, homes, and buildings. It does not provide protection for destruction of your own car — only the property of others.

3. *Medical coverage* pays all reasonable expenses incurred from within one year from the date of accident for necessary medical, surgical, X-ray, and dental services. This coverage applies to the insured and his or her immediate family, whether they are riding in a car or walking. Passengers and guests are usually covered if riding in the insured's car, but this is subject to the terms of the policy.

4. *Comprehensive coverage* protects the policyholder against loss caused by other than collision. It includes breakage of glass and loss caused by missiles, falling objects, fire, theft, windstorm, hail, water, flood, larceny, and so on.

5. *Collision insurance* pays for loss to your own automobile or a nonowned vehicle and does not include other cars involved in an accident. This is the most expensive type for complete coverage, but the majority of contracts are written with a deductible clause. This means that the insurance company agrees to pay only for the amount of each loss in excess of the established deduction. Most deductible clauses provide that the insurer pays the actual cash value less $50, $100, $150, and up to $500.

6. *Uninsured motorist coverage* provides insurance protection for accidents caused by an uninsured motorist or a hit-and-run driver. It covers expenses resulting from bodily injury or death to the policyholder and resident members of his or her family (even as pedestrians). It also covers other persons occupying the holder's vehicle. Subject to the limits for uninsured motorists requested for a policy, the company will pay the amount that would normally be paid by the legally responsible party if insured. Check your state law. In New York, for example, coverage for uninsured motorists is required by law in limits of $10,000/$20,000 and is automatically included in all

liability policies. It applies to accidents which occur in New York. Some companies voluntarily provide such coverage for any accident which occurs outside the state involving an uninsured motorist or a hit-and-run driver.

Other special types of coverage may also be available, such as emergency road service.

Rates

Rates vary depending upon several factors. Most states are divided into a large number of territories for the purpose of determining rates. For example, a person living in Boston, Massachusetts, would pay twice as much for insurance as one living in a rural area like Hazleton, Iowa. Other considerations include the type of vehicle; its use; and the age, sex, occupation, and previous record of the driver.

Despite the continuing rise in insurance costs, you can find ways to save money. Drivers who are free of accidents and traffic violations for a set period may have their insurance reduced as much as 25 percent. A person who owns two cars should have them both insured in the same policy, as it may permit a 20 percent discount. Some students have Dad include their car in his policy. That is great if you can swing it. All insurance companies offer some means to save money and still have the necessary protection. Deductible insurance is one example.

An important point is to list your car properly. A vehicle used only for pleasure is insured much more cheaply than one required for business. Your car agent may overlook this point. Keep in mind that the more expensive the policy, the more money the agent receives in commission.

Driver's training is another way to have rates discounted. Most companies reduce premiums by 10 percent if the insured has had recent driver's training. Also, some companies are giving discounts for good students.

Companies

When you buy auto insurance, determine exactly what coverage you will need. Naturally, the overall cost of the policy is important, but selection of a fine company is paramount. In choosing a firm, check into its past history; reliability and financial stability have no substitutes. Some people have found out too late that their company did not possess the funds to pay its claims. In the past ten years, many companies accepting "high-risk" clients became insolvent, leaving over $500 million in unpaid claims.[1] A managerial approach to car insurance buying should include careful shopping for prices among top quality firms. In making price comparisons, it is helpful to use a chart similar to that shown in Table 10-1. By checking with care on prices charged by different insurance companies, you may be able to save up to 25 percent on premium payments.

Table 10-1. Car Insurance Rate Comparison Table.

	Annual Premium		
Coverage	*Company A*	*Company B*	*Company C*
Bodily injury liability			
Property damage liability			
Medical payments			
Comprehensive (excluding collision) and personal effects			
Collision			
Uninsured motorists			
Other			
Total annual premium			
Less estimated annual dividend			
Net annual premium			

It is important to check the financial rating of an insurance company prior to obtaining a policy. I recommend doing business with companies having the top financial rating from A. M. Best & Company (A^+). Be sure to obtain the current ratings because they do change.

Tale of Woe

My class discussions have elicited, almost without exception, sad experiences with respect to car insurance. Students are unanimous in the belief that protection is most needed during the learning years of driving—yet premiums are highest at this time, and "good" companies are apt to drop a young policyholder if he or she has one to two accidents. (An agency manager told me, "We do make exceptions, but what we shoot for are the best drivers that year after year

---

[1] These "high-risk" insurers have been called "excess-premium writers" or "surplus lines."

have no mishaps. If a young driver is in trouble but his father carries plenty of other insurance with us, we might go along with him one more time. You see, it's all dollars and cents with us.")

The students feel strongly that this attitude is unjust, because it forces them to turn to high-risk companies that charge exorbitant rates. Those who cannot obtain such premium money either give up driving or take the chance of operating a vehicle without coverage, thereby placing additional mental strain on the people involved and adding to the possibility of other accidents.

Driving, the students felt, improves with experience. Thus, more accidents should be expected from the younger age group. But to penalize youthful drivers so drastically, by revoking their insurance or making the rates exorbitant, seems unreasonable. Furthermore, the number of accidents a young person has should not be the governing criterion for revoking insurance. Other considerations should be weighed, such as the person at fault, the number of years of experience, and so on. It was also pointed out that the person who pays premiums for, say, 20 years without making a single claim against the company gets a bum deal. He or she does not get the next 10 years free but goes right on paying the rising annual rates. Thus, whether drivers are accident-prone or accident-free, the insurance companies get the best of the deal. A look at their buildings, salaries of executives, and financial holdings supports this position.

The courageous action of the Massachusetts governor in signing the no-fault insurance bill was applauded by the class, for they recognized that insurance firms have monumental financial resources for lobbying purposes at both the state and national levels.

It was suggested that youthful auto insurers band together in order to make their position understood and to obtain necessary auto insurance at fair rates.

The John Smith Case

One student's personal case presentation, with its concluding remarks, best expressed the class's attitude toward auto insurance companies.

Recently, three members of the "John Smith" family were involved in a serious accident in northern Illinois. The accident occurred at the intersection of two state routes. Despite a number of unanswered questions concerning the accident, the driver was charged by the State Highway Patrol for failing to yield the right-of-way. Consequently, Mr. Smith was responsible for all bodily injury and property damage at the scene of the accident. Of the three cars involved in the accident, two of them were "totaled." Three people were injured, fortunately none very seriously.

The worst news was yet to come. Less than 24 hours after the accident, Mr. Smith was informed by his insurance company that he was not covered. This was a real shock, since he had been paying premiums for six years. The insurance company claimed, however, that there was a policy lapse. Mr. Smith argued that he had a record of sending a check for the amount due. Somehow this check was lost, having never been received by the insurance company and therefore not cancelled.

The company stated it had informed Mr. Smith of his policy lapse, although he had received no notification. Neither of the two loan companies that financed the car was sent a lapse notice. Nevertheless, the insurance company claimed it had a record that proved that it did send such information.

To further complicate the situation, Mr. Smith was advised that the other car he owned was fully insured; that both cars were insured on separate policies; and the policy that lapsed was on the car involved in the accident.

The student relating this story summed it up:

This accident proved to be a very costly lesson. The insurance company did not possess the integrity Mr. Smith had expected. Equally important is the negligence of the agent involved. There was no reason for the two cars to have been insured on separate policies, as this is more expensive. A responsible agent would have made sure that both cars were insured on one policy to save money. Furthermore, after the company informed the agent of the lapse, he should have checked as to why Smith was paying on one policy and not the other.

As a result of this unfortunate situation, Smith now has insurance with a more reliable company, but the total cost of damages and possible lawsuits will still have to be paid for. It sure pays for the motorist to investigate a company and its history with care before he decides on an insurance policy. This is especially important concerning their payment of claims. Smith isn't the first person to have been taken by an insurance outfit and I doubt that he will be the last.

Accident Procedure

It is important to keep your "cool" if you have an accident. You may wish to give consideration to the following steps, recommended by one firm. Most companies furnish similar procedures, but some of us fail to read them. It is recommended that such instructions be kept handy in the glove compartment of your car.

1. Call an ambulance for anyone seriously injured.
2. Secure names and addresses of all persons in the other car, descriptions of cars, and license numbers.
3. Be sure to obtain names and addresses of all witnesses.
4. Measure any skid marks made by either vehicle.
5. *Do not admit responsibility* and make no statement regarding the accident except to authorized claims representatives and the police.
6. Comply with state laws by filing required Motor Vehicle Accident Report and send a copy to the Home Office.
7. *Do not disclose your policy limits to anyone.*
8. Immediately report the accident to law-enforcement officials and to your insurance company. Failure to do so may jeopardize your insurance protection and may result in loss of your driving privileges.[2]

OTHER INSURANCE NEEDS

There are many other kinds of insurance policies available to meet your needs. Let us look at the most common. Keep in mind that these will vary from company to company and that you can secure protection for almost any risk — provided you are willing to pay the price. Most firms are delighted to build an insurance program especially tailored for you. It helps to know first what your requirements are, and no one can judge that better than you.

Homeowner's Coverage

The homeowner's policy insures your home against fire, lightning, wind, hail, and many other perils. It is important to determine what these other perils include.

Comprehensive personal liability insurance (CPL) is included in the homeowner's policy. If you rent, the CPL can be obtained separately. This coverage provides protection should you or any member of your household be held legally liable for actions resulting in accidental injuries to others or accidental damage to the property of others. Coverage applies for personal and sports activities and is

---

[2] *Directory of Automobile Claims Representatives* (San Antonio: United Services Automobile Association, 1978).

effective both on and away from the premises and inside and outside the residence.

Following are some situations in which the CPL insurance would be effective:

1. A deliveryman or a guest is injured in your residence.
2. You accidentally injure someone while you are engaged in golf, hunting, or horseback riding.
3. One of your children injures a playmate with one of her or his toys.
4. Your pet bites someone.
5. A fire spreads from your property to the property of others.

The special medical payment clause and the property damage clause, which form an integral part of the CPL insurance, do not necessarily require legal liability to be effective. The insured's obligation may be moral rather than legal. Payment under these clauses may be authorized by the insurance company without resorting to a court trial.

Flood Insurance

We mentioned earlier in this chapter the financial loss to one family as a result of the Johnstown flood. Forty-six people died in the Johnstown area and property damage totaled 200 million dollars. However, this area was not alone in suffering heavy losses in recent years. The major flood devastation of Hurricane Camille in 1969 was in the area along the Gulf Coast, from just east of New Orleans to Mobile, Alabama. It was estimated to have caused $1.5 billion in damages, and 284 lives were reported lost. Among the tragedies resulting from Camille were the families who were paid almost nothing on property they had felt was appropriately insured; at least, the people had been paying good premiums each year for this purpose. A lady interviewed on TV said, "I received $272 on a property loss of $5,000. The agent informed me that almost all the loss was caused by flood, not wind, and I was not protected. He didn't mention this aspect when he sold me the policy."

Such a tragic financial loss was commonplace as an aftermath of Camille. As a result, the federal government took steps to alleviate such problems in the future. In mid-1970, the U.S. Department of Housing and Urban Development announced that 213 flood-prone American communities in 31 states are eligible for flood insurance. People in these areas may purchase insurance at federally subsidized premium rates. The maximum amounts range from $17,500 for single-family homes up to $30,000 for two- to four-family dwellings. Rates vary from 40 to 50 cents per $100 of insurance, depending on the value of the structure. Contents also may be insured up to $5,000, with rates of 50 to 60 cents per $100 of insurance. This insurance protection is available through local agencies. I was informed by an area agent that on a $17,500 single home, the premium would be $70 per year. To obtain $5,000 in personal-property coverage would cost $25.

The National Flood Insurance Act of 1968 states that "anyone who does not choose to buy flood insurance in a community which is eligible will not be able to get federal financial disaster aid for flood losses that occur after one year from the date his community became eligible to the extent that the loss would have been covered by flood insurance." It is wise to take advantage of this type of insurance if you live in a flood-prone region.

Comprehensive Personal Liability (CPL) Policy

CPL protects your bank account in case of an accidental injury to another person or damage to another's property for which you are legally liable. It covers damages awarded by a court, and attorney's fees.

Boat Owner's Policy

The boat owner's policy provides "all risks" of physical-loss protection for inboard or outboard motorboats and sailboats, including motors, attached and unattached equipment, accessories, and boat trailers. The policy furnishes watercraft liability for bodily injury, property damage, and medical payments. The watercraft liability is written only in conjunction with the "all risks" of physical-loss coverage.

Personal-Property Policies

There are two types of coverage you may obtain with respect to your personal possessions. First, the basic personal property coverage protects against losses from fire, lightning, smoke, flood, earthquake, wind, explosion, certain transportation hazards, and other related threats to personal property. Under this coverage some companies paid for losses to personal property after Hurricane Camille. The second type of personal property policy protects against losses from such events as theft, burglary, larceny, holdup, riot, civil commotion, loss (including cash to $100), and breakage of gemstones. This protection, in combination with the basic, provides an "all-risk" floater protection.

For the past several years the ratio of loss indemnities to premiums has been steadily rising because of increased claims, particularly in urban areas. This rise is aggravated by the increased rate of inflation in replacement costs, particularly in the case of valuables, so heavily insured under this coverage. As a result, premiums are increasing each year. A number of wealthy people no longer wear their jewels; they keep them in the safe-deposit box as a form of investment and wear imitations.

Farm Owner's Policy

A farm owner's policy insures eligible farm buildings and farm personal property, as well as the farm residence. It includes theft coverage, farmer's comprehensive personal liability, and additional living-expense insurance in one complete package policy. If a farm fire policy is more suitable, it is possible to obtain such protection, and you may order liability coverage under a separate farmer's comprehensive personal liability policy.

Heath and Accident Policies

There are a variety of health and accident policies available. Some furnish extensive coverage, and others provide auxiliary protection.

A number of companies and government organizations offer group policies for health and/or accident. Whenever possible, it pays to take advantage of this protection. The rates are reasonable, and in some cases the organization pays for part of the cost.

If you enter the armed forces, you will find they have a splendid health program. Your dependents can use the regular military facilities, when available, or obtain the services of a civilian physician. Under the Uniformed Services Health Benefits Program, the patient is required to pay the first $50 of any medical expenses ($100 for a family) and after that pays only 20 percent of his or her annual medical costs, with the government picking up the remainder.

Another example of an organization policy is the all-risk group accident insurance program. This coverage affords protection supplemental to the benefits provided under a group life insurance plan, group disability plan, workmen's compensation, or the employee's private insurance program. This particular insurance protection provides 24-hour, 365-day coverage against accidents at work, at home, at play, and while traveling anywhere in the world. The cost is 52 cents per month per $10,000 of coverage.

There are a number of auxiliary health coverage plans. For example, you can obtain protection for the differential between the 80 percent military coverage (under the Uniformed Services Program) and your total medical expenses. Similar additional insurance can be secured for those under Medicare. My own view is that, generally, the high cost is not worth the limited added coverage. However, if you have no group-type health or accident protection, I think it is most important to obtain a good commercial policy such as those available from Blue Cross, Blue Shield, private medical groups, and insurance companies.

MEDICARE

Determining Eligibility

Medicare is a program of health insurance under Social Security set up to help millions of Americans age 65 and older, and many disabled people under 65, to pay the high cost of health care.[3] In order to determine properly your health insurance needs at age 65 or older, it is essential that you be familiar with the major provisions of Medicare. Although virtually all people 65 or older are eligible for Medicare benefits it also covers disabled people who have been getting Social Security for two years or more and people insured under Social Security who need dialysis treatment or a kidney transplant because of chronic kidney disease. Wives, husbands, or children of insured people may also be eligible if they need kidney dialysis or a transplant.

To find out whether or not you are entitled to Medicare, and to make sure that you get full Medicare protection starting with the month you reach age 65, check with your Social Security office two or three months before your sixty-fifth birthday. If you are not receiving monthly Social Security checks, you should be contacted by mail a few months before you are 65. If you are a disabled person who has been receiving Social Security disability benefits for two years or more, you will get hospital insurance automatically. You

[3] This section draws on *Your Medicare Handbook* and *A Brief Explanation of Medicare* (Washington, D.C.: U.S. Department of Health, Education and Welfare, current editions).

will receive information about Medicare in the mail and need do nothing now.

There are two parts to Medicare — hospital and medical insurance. The hospital insurance part of Medicare helps pay for the care you receive as a patient in a hospital and for certain follow-up care after you leave the hospital.

The medical insurance part of Medicare helps pay for your doctor's services, outpatient hospital services, and many other medical items and services not covered under hospital insurance.

Sources of Further Information

Call any Social Security office for more detailed information about Medicare or any other form of Social Security program. I recommend that you ask for a copy of *Your Medicare Handbook*. It provides information on the various aspects of Medicare, including how to submit medical insurance claims.

ACTION YOU CAN TAKE TO COPE WITH INFLATION
AND THE ENERGY SHORTAGE

Review all your insurance policies annually to determine if they now meet your requirements based on the current rate of inflation. For example, if your household furnishings have $10,000 coverage and it would cost you $20,000 to replace them, you may wish to pay the extra premium for added protection.

SUMMARY

A sound insurance program is desirable for anyone with valuable material possessions. But it should be considered only one requirement in the overall financial plan. The number of dollars invested in insurance will of necessity vary with each individual. Nevertheless, certain guidelines are submitted for consideration.

First, what areas warrant this financial protection? Most students can normally expect to have acquired, within a reasonable time after graduation, a car, some household property, and family responsibilities. Accordingly, in these situations adequate insurance policies should include fire, theft, health, auto, and personal property. (In addition, appropriate life insurance is essential, as mentioned in the preceding chapter.) There will also be a need for home insurance for those who decide to purchase a dwelling. This should include flood insurance as a must in designated areas.

In regard to car insurance, it is very important to have adequate protection, particularly for bodily-injury liability, in view of the high awards being rendered by the courts today. The difference in insurance cost between $10,000/$30,000 and $100,000/$300,000 bodily injury coverage is relatively small for the significant additional security. In contrast, I believe $100 deductible is sufficient for your own vehicle in the event of collision.

The high cost of car insurance for young people is worthy of investigation. It is recognized that young people have a greater probability of car accidents according to actuarial tables and should pay a higher rate. Nevertheless, in a number of cases these rates have become prohibitive. If the private insurance firms cannot meet the legitimate needs of any group in our society, we should seek alternative solutions that might make it a state and federal responsibility. A number of states have taken the important first step of passing no-fault auto insurance laws. Likewise, the National Flood Insurance Act of 1968 points up the potential of federal government assistance.

A number of other policies are available to meet a variety of individual requirements. Insurance companies offer such policies as Comprehensive Personal Liability (CPL), Boat Owner's Policy, and Farm Owner's Policy. And keep in mind that Medicare is a program of health insurance under Social Security. It has been created to help millions of Americans age 65 and older and many disabled people under 65 to pay the high cost of health care.

Bankers are just like anybody else, except richer.

—OGDEN NASH

BANKS, SAVINGS AND LOAN ASSOCIATIONS, CREDIT UNIONS, MONEY MARKET

CASH RESERVES

"How stupid of me! I was laid off as a result of the energy crisis. I had thought my job was secure — my company had given me a glowing story of my future with them — and I hadn't put aside any money for an emergency."

This sad tale of a recent graduate was echoed many times during 1976 when unemployment approached the 9 percent level and hit hard at both white-collar and blue-collar workers. The financial impact on some families was tragic. They were forced into heavy debt at very high interest costs. My friend put it well: "Never again will my family get caught short. My pay was damn good, but we didn't realize the need for cash reserves."

What is a cash reserve? It is money saved that you can obtain immediately in the event you need it. In this chapter we shall look at those sources through which you can effectively build up these cash reserves.

I use the word "effectively" because cash in a mattress does not provide an effective buildup, and money held in the safe-deposit box at the bank is not the answer. The box provides maximum safety,

183

since you can get those same dollars quickly; but this money draws no interest (income), and a fee is being paid for the use of the box. Furthermore, since the long-term is increasingly inflationary, the dollars in the safe-deposit box are *not* safe, in terms of assuring comparable buying power in the future; they are constantly declining in value.

If safety of principal is the first objective, there are better choices than hoarding dollars. These choices include banks, savings and loan associations, credit unions, and the money market. In each instance, you are putting your money to work. Benjamin Franklin said, "Money makes money, and the money that money makes, makes more money." To support his concept, he bequeathed $5,000 in 1791 to the citizens of Boston, with the understanding that it be allowed to accumulate interest for one hundred years. A century later, the $5,000 had increased to $311,000.

A method of measuring how rapidly your money grows at a given rate of interest is called the Rule of 72. It provides an approximation of how long it takes to double your money. Merely divide the rate of return into 72 and you obtain the number of years it will require to double your money at that rate. Savings at 4 percent double in 18 years (72 ÷ 4 = 18). In contrast, savings at 6 percent will be worth twice as much in 12 years. These figures pertain to interest compounded annually; if your bank compounds interest on savings accounts semiannually, quarterly, or daily, doubling your money will take a shorter period of time. This points up the value of making your money work hard for you.

BANKS

Banks furnish a variety of services. You must be familiar with them in order to use these services to your advantage. Banks, like other businesses, vary from strong financial institutions to those on the brink of bankruptcy. It is essential to select a well-established commercial bank that is a member of the Federal Deposit Insurance Corporation (FDIC). It may offer safe-deposit boxes, checking and savings accounts, certified checks, bank drafts, money orders, a variety of loans, trust and estate management, financial advice, coins and currency for public use, foreign-exchange information, U.S. Savings bonds, credit cards, and travel service. If you are moving to another community, your bank can provide a helpful letter of introduction.

Federal Deposit
Insurance Corporation

It is important for your bank to be a member of the FDIC because this means that each account up to $40,000 is insured. "The Federal Deposit Insurance Corporation insures only deposits in national and most state banks, including commercial and mutual savings banks. Insured banks are required to display the official FDIC sign at each teller's window or station."[1]

The FDIC protects bank depositors as follows:

Each bank approved for deposit insurance must meet high standards. Adherence to these standards is determined regularly through bank examinations by federal or state agencies. If, despite these precautions, an insured bank gets into financial difficulties and must be closed for purposes of liquidation, the Federal Deposit Insurance Corporation is on hand promptly with cash to protect the depositors. The Corporation usually begins payments to the depositors within ten days after the date of final closing.[2]

It is interesting to note that FDIC insures against only the closing of a bank. Its leaflet poses the question, "Does the insurance protection afforded by the Corporation extend to losses sustained by depositors in any fashion other than through the closing of an insured bank?" The response: "No."[3]

Member of the Federal
Reserve System

In selecting a bank, you want a financially sound institution that will not be forced to close its doors. In addition to the FDIC, I recommend it be a member of the Federal Reserve System (FRS).

The FRS was organized in 1913; the Federal Reserve Act itself stated that its purpose included "to establish a more effective supervision of banking in the United States. . . ." Much has been accomplished since that date to improve the banking environment. In 1978 nearly 6,000 banks were members. Top policy emanates from the

[1] *Your Insured Deposit*, (Washington, D.C.: Federal Deposit Insurance Corporation, 1979 edition), p. 2.

[2] Ibid.

[3] Ibid., p. 3.

Board of Governors of the Federal Reserve System in Washington, D.C. There are 12 Federal Reserve Banks under the Board's supervision.

Bank membership, obligations, and reserves are highlighted in a Federal Reserve publication:

> All national banks in the United States are required to be members of the System, while state banks are admitted to membership upon application if they meet certain requirements. On April 30, 1978, there were 14,689 commercial banks in the country, of which 5,682 were member banks. Although the member banks accounted for only 39 percent of the total number of commercial banks, they held approximately 72 percent of total commercial bank deposits.
>
> Member banks assume certain obligations. They become subject to numerous safeguarding provisions of the Federal Reserve Act, among which are those pertaining to affiliations with securities and investment companies, interlocking directorates, removal of directors and officers because of unsafe or unsound practices, payment of interest on deposits, and branch bank relations. State bank members are subject to examination and supervision by the Federal Reserve System.
>
> Member banks also must keep reserves, in cash or on deposit with their Reserve Bank, equal to certain proportions of their various types of deposits. They are also required to subscribe to the capital of the Federal Reserve Bank of their district in an amount equal to 6 percent of their capital and surplus.[4]

Checking Account

A checking account should be utilized in college and definitely upon taking your first job. It can be a valuable financial tool. Put to work properly, it can save you time and money. Ineffectively employed, it can be expensive and can cause embarrassment because of checks returned marked "Not Sufficient Funds." A regular checking account draws no interest. Therefore, it is desirable to keep it at a minimum consistent with monthly expenses. Whenever feasible, I suggest that your take-home pay be sent to the bank for deposit to your checking account.

A minimum balance should be maintained in order to preclude service charges. After one of my lectures to a municipal government

[4] Ibid., p. 4.

society, the wife of a member told me she was paying 15 cents a check on an average balance of $50 per month. This lady said that each month she cashed approximately ten checks that averaged $5 each. Her charge for this service was $1.50 per month. Thus, she was paying 36 percent a year for the privilege of having this small account. By maintaining a minimum monthly balance, she could have eliminated this service charge. One bank cashes up to ten checks free of charge, as long as a minimum balance of $100 is maintained at any time during the month. On the assumption that the $100 could be invested at 5 percent, the lady in question would save 31 percent annually by keeping a minimum balance in a checking account with this bank.

Shop around to find a well-established bank that will give you the best deal. For example, in contrast to the bank that allows up to ten checks per month free with a minimum balance of $100, another institution may require $700 minimum for a comparable number of checks. If you have already established an account at a bank, be sure to ask them if they will offer you free checking services that are competitive with those of other banks in your area. In our city, several banks cash an unlimited number of checks at no charge, with a $300 minimum balance. My bank had a $1,000 minimum, and I asked the branch manager why he wasn't competitive. He replied, "You didn't ask. We didn't announce it, but to be competitive I can give you the same $300 minimum."

Effective January 1, 1974, Congress authorized two states (Massachusetts and New Hampshire) to offer interest-bearing checking accounts. The federal banking agencies set a 5 percent rate ceiling on these accounts, known as "negotiable orders of withdrawal" (NOW) accounts. The success of the NOW program resulted in all states being authorized to pay interest on a checking account effective June 1, 1978. The way it works is that an individual opens both a checking and savings account with a bank of his or her choice. The bank automatically transfers a set amount from the savings account whenever the checking account doesn't have a sufficient balance to pay any check due. The hitch in this new program, from a depositor viewpoint, is that the bank may make a sizable charge for each transfer. Therefore, it may be more economical to have a regular checking account and put your savings to work at the highest rate of return.

Savings Account

The second area in which banks provide a means to build an effective cash reserve is through a variety of savings plans. In recent years commercial banks' passbook rates varied from 5 to 5½ percent, depending on the type of account and the locality. However, in 1974 banks issued generous certificates of deposit (CDs) on large amounts. CDs of six-month duration were quoted at 12 percent in amounts of $100,000 or more. Money rates fell markedly in the following four years but in April 1979 top rates paid by major banks had risen to 10.2 percent. Six months later this rate increased to nearly 14 percent. In contrast, smaller certificates of six-year duration remained stabilized during the 1974–1979 period and were available with a $1,000 minimum. Commercial banks were permitted to pay up to 7½ percent on them if they were held for six years. And effective June 1978 commercial banks were authorized to pay 7¾ percent on CDs (minimum $1,000) if held for eight years. In addition they could issue short-term certificates (minimum $10,000) at the going rate for Treasury bills.

It is apparent from the high short-term rates in 1974, that the large investor had an opportunity to make a lot of money. For a short time, in 1973, it looked as if the monetary authorities were going to give people with limited funds a fair break in the money market. At that time the Federal Reserve Board, Federal Deposit Insurance Corporation, and Federal Home Loan Bank Board permitted thrift institutions and commercial banks to remove all ceilings on CDs with a face value of at least $1,000 falling due in not less than four years. This act gave people of limited means an opportunity to buy CDs at yields from 8 to 10 percent. They invested hundreds of millions of dollars, primarily by withdrawing funds from conventional savings banks and savings and loan accounts. But this fair deal was too good to survive. In 1974, Congress ordered the setting of interest-rate limits. This again points up the need for a powerful lobbying force in Washington that looks to the interest of the consumer.

Banks are delighted to open a savings account for you. Normally you must start with a $5 minimum deposit. Interest on accounts is usually paid quarterly or semiannually. You may make withdrawals as needed, but those made before due dates usually lose all interest.

The regular passbook interest rate for commercial banks in our community at this writing is 5 percent. There is a Gold Star Pass Book account that pays 5½ percent, but it carries definite restrictions to go along with the extra ½ percent, including, among others, a minimum initial deposit of at least $100. Read a copy of the rules before making your decision as to a regular or a special account. Savings banks are authorized to pay ¼ percent more than commercial banks on all types of deposits.

Most banks have Christmas-savings plans. But check carefully;

such a plan may be great for the bank but miserable for you. They spend a lot of money advertising the advantage of saving weekly so you will have a nice nest egg for Christmas shopping; one bank even offers a tiny cookbook for such a saver. But such a plan often pays *no interest*. However, recently some banks have begun to pay the going rate of bank interest on Christmas savings plans.

I stated that usually there is no charge for having money in a savings account. There are exceptions. For instance, a Midwest bank, located within walking distance of a university, has a large percentage of student accounts. Students were wisely using their savings accounts like checking accounts by making small withdrawals to meet their expenses. For this reason, the local bank put a 25 cent charge on all savings account withdrawals numbering over six in any one interest period. In some schools, such action could provide serious protests. As you can see, such a charge could result in a high interest charge in relation to the amount deposited.

SAVINGS AND LOAN ASSOCIATIONS

Purpose

Savings and loan (S&L) associations are privately owned financial organizations administrated by a board of directors. They provide loans for repair, construction, purchasing, or financing of homes and other real estate. In Louisiana, the state-chartered companies are called "homestead associations." Other names used include building associations, building and loan associations, savings associations, and cooperative banks.

S&L associations generate their money from depositors who establish share accounts. They use these funds mainly to make loans secured by home mortgages. These associations also invest a small amount of their funds in other areas such as U.S. government and agency obligations, loans on savings accounts, Federal Home Loan Bank stock, and GNMA and FHLMC investments. I asked one manager if his association earned interest on money deposited with local banks. He said, "No, but prior to issuing our semiannual statements, we like to beef this figure up. It makes good window dressing for our customers. You can rest assured we reduce it the next day to have it earning interest in some investment."

Charter

Savings and loan associations are chartered under federal and state laws. The Federal Home Loan Bank Board is the chartering agent for the U.S. government. Before granting a charter, the board, by law, passes upon (1) the character and responsibility of the applicant group, (2) the need for such an institution in the community to be served, (3) the probability of its usefulness and success, and (4) the effect of a new association on existing institutions of a similar nature.[5]

State associations are chartered by state banking commissioners who are usually guided by the same standards as those applied by the Federal Home Loan Bank Board.

Insurance

Savings and loan associations are insured by the Federal Savings and Loan Insurance Corporation (FSLIC). The FSLIC provides insurance on each savings account up to $40,000 in all federally chartered savings associations and in state-chartered associations that apply and qualify for membership. A majority of S&L's are members.

The FSLIC has a splendid record in paying insurance claims when an institution is declared in default. However, it attempts to arrange for the absorption of a failing institution by a strong one nearby so that accounts can be transferred intact.

People placing funds with associations are legally shareholders and are purchasing savings shares. An S&L may, if withdrawal requests exceed available funds, require a 30-day notice. If, after 30 days, the S&L is still unable to meet demands, it may institute a rotation plan of repayment. Under this system, withdrawal requests are numbered and filed in the order received. If a shareholder in a federal association has invested $1,000 or less, she (or he) is paid off when her request is reached; if her request is more than $1,000, she is paid $1,000 when her number is reached. Her request is repeated until all requests are fully met or until the association is declared in default. When it is declared in default and closed, the insurer usually begins payment of shareholders within 10 days. Rotation rules for state-licensed associations vary.

If an S&L is a member of the Federal Home Loan Bank System, it can borrow up to 50 percent of its total savings balance from a Home Loan Bank to meet an emergency. Most S&L associations are

[5] Federal Home Loan Bank Board, *Rules and Regulations for the Federal Savings and Loan System* (Washington, D.C.: the Bank Board, 1978).

Table 11-1. Savings Plans Available by a Number of Savings and Loan Associations, 1979.

Type of Account	Description of Savings Plans[a]	Rate Per Annum[b]
Regular Passbook	$10.00 minimum. Add or withdraw any amount at any time without penalty, after money has been invested 10 days. This is the favorite account of most savers. Earn on a "day in to day out" basis.	5.25% 5.39%
Telephone Transfer Account	$1,500 minimum. This is a regular passbook account with the added convenience of being able to transfer funds to or from your checking account in a minimum amount of $500. Transactions made in person may be made in any amount.	5.25% 5.39%
Full-paid Certificate	Save in $100 units. A negotiable certificate which should be safeguarded against accidental loss. Investments must remain in account until end of earnings distribution period to earn at stated rate.	5.25%
90-day Notice Account	$100 minimum. Withdrawals may be made only during the 10 days following the end of each quarterly period or by providing a written 90-day advance notice.	5.75% 5.91%
Bonus Account	$1,000 (minimum) earn at 5.25% per annum. After 90 days, receive bonus at rate of ½% per annum. Withdraw between quarterly interest period and earn 5.25% rate to date of withdrawal. Additional deposits to this account not permitted. No interest earned if funds withdrawn during first 90-day period.	5.25% Bonus ½%
Single-Payment Certificate	$1,000 (minimum). Issued to mature in 1 year, but less than 30 months. Automatically renewable if not notified. $1,000 (minimum). Issued to mature in 2½ years, but less than 4 years. Automatically renewable if not notified. $1,000 (minimum). Issued to mature in 4 years, but less than 6 years. Automatically renewable if not notified. $1,000 (minimum). Issued to mature in 6 years but less than 8 years. Automatically renewable if not notified. $1,000 (minimum). Issued to mature in 8 years but less than 10. Automatically renewable if not notified.	6.50% 6.72% 6.75% 6.98% 7.50% 7.79% 7.75% 8.06% 8.00% 8.33%
Money-Market Certificate	$10,000 minimum. The return on this certificate will be the average yield of 26 week Treasury Bills. Issued to mature in 26 weeks. Automatically renewable if not notified.	
Keogh Plan	Retirement plan for self-employed persons.	
IRA Plan	Retirement plan for employed persons whose company offers no retirement benefit.	

[a]Savings plans will vary so obtain current facts about the plan that interests you.
[b]Rate per annum will vary slightly among associations based on whether interest is compounded daily, weekly, etc. Check before you invest.

"mutual" organizations, so called because the shareholders have voting rights and theoretically own the capital of the institution. A number of associations are capital-stock, or "guarantee," associations. This means that in addition to the savings shares there is another class of stock, the holders of which own the association's equity.

Dividends

There is no limit under federal law, or under the statutes of most states, that restricts dividend rates for associations. Over the years, S&L's have paid slightly higher returns on savings than banks have. At the present time, most associations offer a variety of plans, with rates ranging from 5¼ to 8 percent plus variable rates on money market certificates (see Table 11-1). The passbook type of account normally does more than 50 percent of the business; an S&L official explained to me why the passbook is popular. He said, "A customer came to me yesterday with $5,000 and wanted a higher return than the passbook rate. But after I explained all the ramifications and penalties, she said, 'Oh, that's too complicated. I'll stay with the passbook.'" The S&L manager was delighted that she took the lower rate. Associations locally are charging 9 to 10 percent on mortgages, so the 2 to 5 percent spread permits a healthy profit, since S&L deposits are almost entirely loaned out in high-yielding mortgages.

CREDIT UNIONS

Purpose

A credit union may be viewed as a cooperative organization. It is comprised of a group of people who pool their money to make loans to each other. Members receive interest on their savings based upon revenues derived primarily from loans. These loans are normally of short duration. They are consumer-oriented loans for such purposes as cars, furniture, medical debts, appliances, and emergencies. "The principal goals of a credit union are to provide members with a good return on savings and a source from which they can borrow at reasonable rates of interest."[6]

Credit unions operate under a federal charter and supervision. Membership in each union is limited to a particular segment of the population, such as military personnel at an air base, employees of a

[6] *Pentagon Federal Credit Union News*, April 1970, p. 1.

university, a manufacturing group or government agency, or an association or trade union. At annual meetings the members select from within their group the people to manage it — the directors, the credit committee, and the supervisory committee.

Background

Credit unions were first established in the United States before World War I. The Credit Union National Extension Bureau was created in 1921 to provide the legislative, organizational, and operational services that fostered their growth. In 1934 the Credit Union National Association superseded the bureau. The same year, Congress passed the Federal Credit Union Act (amended in 1959), which spelled out standards and requirements, including annual verification of the records.

By 1978, there were over 23,000 credit unions in the United States, with 34 million members and $46 billion in assets. They ranged in size from fewer than 100 members to over 430,000.[7] The typical credit union had 1,000 members and $2 million in assets. There were more than $36 billion in loans outstanding in the United States in 1978.

Approximately one-half the credit unions are chartered under state laws, with the others under federal jurisdiction. Credit unions have been among the fastest growing institutions in recent years. They were organized originally to extend short-term credit at reasonable rates of interest to their members. Over the years their operations have expanded to include credit for real estate, consumer durable goods, and Thrifty Credit Loan Service as a means of paying monthly bills. A number have acquired the characteristics of a commercial operation instead of a voluntary mutual-aid group.

The National Credit Union Administration, in 1974 authorized credit unions to offer their members share-draft accounts. These share drafts are, in fact, interest-bearing checking accounts.

In 1977 a law was passed that permits federally chartered credit unions to make 30-year mortgage loans as well as 12-year improvement loans. Prior to 1977, some state-chartered credit unions had made longer term mortgage loans. Some large credit unions employ full-time professionals, with practices patterned after commercial lenders but with low rates on loans and a fair return on savings. However, the typical credit union is still small and has little expertise or professional staff.

[7] National Credit Union Administration, Washington, D.C.

Voting Shares

Savings shares are in $5 units; lesser amounts deposited are applied to the purchase of a share. A majority of the capital is available for loans to shareholders. When I checked on one association, 82 percent of its savings were on loan to its members.[8] Each member, irrespective of his or her holdings in the credit union, is entitled to one vote in the annual election of the board of directors and its committees. Most laws provide that dividends shall not exceed 7 percent. In some associations free insurance is provided for the amount of the savings, with a limit varying from $1,000 to $5,000. Thus, if a member dies and has savings of $1,000, his or her beneficiary would receive $2,000.

Safety

The Bureau of Federal Credit Unions, Department of Health, Education and Welfare, supervises credit union operation under federal charter, and in most states, the state banking commission supervises the credit union under state charter.

Loans to officers, directors, and members of committees are limited to the value of their shares in the organization. Further, such persons may not act as endorsers for borrowers. The accounting records of credit unions are subject to regular examination by government authorities. Protection is also offered the members by surety-bond requirements for those who handle money. Most state laws provide for a ceiling on loans to members. Under the federal law, interest on credit union loans may never exceed 1 percent per month on the unpaid balance, which is 12 percent on an annual percentage rate. Associations will normally vary from 9 to 12 percent in their annual charges.

The safety of savings in a credit union is dependent upon its loan policy, its management, the strength of the employer, and the general economy. There is federal or state supervision of credit unions, but not to the same degree as with S&L institutions or banks, and they often do not have the same expertise in management as other savings institutions. However, members of credit unions may also have their share accounts insured up to $40,000 by an FDIC type of agency.[9]

[8] Navy Federal Credit Union as of December 31, 1977.

[9] The Credit Union Share Insurance Bill became law on October 19, 1970. The law (Public Law 91-468) provides for the insurance of members' share accounts up to $40,000 in the event an insured credit union becomes insolvent for any reason.

Withdrawal of savings from a credit union constitutes a repurchase by the union of shares in the organization. Shares are not transferable to others; they are bought back by the union as funds are available. If no funds are available, the shareholder must wait his or her turn for repayment. Credit unions maintain certain cash and government bonds for the purpose of meeting ordinary withdrawals. They also use new savings and repayments on loans. They do not, however, have secondary sources to fall back upon in the event that these normal sources are insufficient.

MONEY MARKET

The money market is composed of short-term securities. The major categories include U.S. Treasury bills, select U.S. government agency issues, banker's acceptances, and commercial paper. "The money market may be thought of as a group of submarkets, one for each kind of security. No one rate of return prevails in the national money market. The rates of return on various money-market instruments do move in a trend and in harmony, however. Because market rises differ and because liquidity differs, yields also vary."[10] Money rates are quoted daily in the *Wall Street Journal* and in 1978 they averaged 2 to 4 percent higher than the commercial-bank passbook rate.

Here is the market in which savings and loan associations, banks, and credit unions invest a portion of their money. It is a very active market and the securities are normally easy to buy and sell, either at the initial issuance or in the secondary market.

This is an ideal place to invest cash reserves as you acquire sizable funds available for investment. The drawback to money-market investment is that it requires a large sum of money in most cases.

Treasury Bills

Treasury bills are issued on a discount basis, under competitive bidding, with maturities not exceeding one year from the date of issue when the face amount is payable. The most common periods are three-month, six-month, and one-year issues. If you wish to purchase these bills at original issue, you can do so at Federal Reserve Banks and branches. Bids are invited weekly for the three-month and six-month bills, and monthly for the one-year bills. Small purchases are

[10] *Financing a Trillion-Dollar Economy*, MLPFS pamphlet, September 1969, p. 23.

accepted at the average of accepted competitive tenders. Treasury bills are bearer securities, currently issued in denominations of $10,000, $50,000, $100,000, $500,000, and $1 million. Within the same series, exchanges are permitted for other authorized denominations.[11]

"The rich get richer and the poor get nothing" was never truer than when the Treasury Department raised the minimum bill denomination in February 1970 from $1,000 to $10,000. It took the action after small investors, in increasing numbers, found that this money-market medium provided a 2 percent better return than the savings media. The Treasury's publicity release, in presenting its reasons for the change, quoted the Secretary of Housing and Urban Development, George Romney, as follows:

> The outflow of savings from Savings and Loan Associations, Mutual Savings Banks, and other thrift institutions has aggravated the shortage of mortgage funds and contributed to a serious decline in housing production. To avoid a serious, growing housing shortage, it is essential that we discourage the outflow of funds from mortgage lending institutions. This Treasury action should substantially improve our housing outlook.[12]

There was no suggestion made that large investors and corporations should, conversely, transfer a portion of their Treasury bill investments into these thrift institutions — a process that could solve the problem without depriving the small investor of his or her opportunity for greater profit.

The Treasury also cited the increased costs in handling "the extraordinarily large volume of small transactions in short-term Treasury bills." Of course, the Treasury issues small-denomination U.S. Savings bonds (Series E) ranging from $18.75 to $7,500, and it does not complain about their size — perhaps because the interest rate was only 5 percent in lieu of nearly 7 percent when the change was made. The Treasury release stated that the small investor is subject to "sizable charges" in buying Treasury bills from "dealers, banks, and brokers." This is not necessarily true because in every city where there is a Federal Reserve Bank or branch an investor can go and purchase newly issued bills at no cost.

---

[11] Primary source for this background information is *United States Securities Available to Investors*, Department of the Treasury Fiscal Service, Bureau of the Public Debt, Washington, D.C., 1978.

[12] Last paragraph in a press release by the Treasury Department, February 26, 1970.

Bankers' Acceptances

An acceptance is a time draft that a bank has promised to honor at maturity. Bankers' acceptances are used in the import export business. The bank substitutes its own credit for that of an importer. Here is an example of how an acceptance is created.[13]

John Doe, a New York importer, wants to buy bananas from José Paz, a Honduras exporter. Mr. Doe asks his bank (First National City) to issue a letter of credit in favor of Mr. Paz. The letter of credit includes shipment details, terms, and amount for which Mr. Paz may draw a time draft on the bank. John Doe promises to pay First National at maturity of the draft (upon receipt of the bananas in New York). First National looks to Mr. Doe for payment under the terms of their agreement. However, Mr. Paz, who is the drawer of the draft, remains contingently liable for the life of the transaction (six months or less). José Paz discounts his draft at his Honduras bank, which has been notified of the letter-of-credit agreement by the First National City Bank. The shipping documents and draft are forwarded by the Honduras bank to First National. Upon its receipt in New York, the draft is stamped "accepted" and signed by a bank official. The draft, now an acceptance, has become an irrevocable obligation of First National. Normally, the bank in Honduras will discount the acceptance. First National may then sell the acceptance to a dealer.

Acceptances are a very safe form of investment. There is no record of an investor's ever having sustained a principal loss on an acceptance of a U.S. bank. Acceptances are usually considered second only to U.S. government issues in safety, and on a par with certificates of deposit.

Bankers' acceptances are issued on a discount basis and may be purchased through a bond dealer. They come in denominations of from $25,000 to $1 million and are issued to mature in 180 days or less.

Commercial Paper

Commercial paper (CP) consists of short-term negotiable promissory notes issued by large corporations for periods up to 270 days.[14] These

[13] Source for this material is "Bankers' Acceptances for the Institutional Investor," Merrill Lynch, Pierce, Fenner & Smith, Inc., Government Securities Division, Liberty Plaza, New York, N.Y. 10005.

[14] Source for this material is "Commercial Paper: an Expanding Market for the Institutional Investor," Merrill Lynch, Pierce, Fenner & Smith, Inc., Government Securities Division, Money Market Securities Department, 1 Liberty Plaza, New York, N.Y. 10005.

notes are normally available in amounts ranging from $100,000 to $1 million. A few dealers sell smaller amounts. Corporations such as GMAC place their own paper and may sell amounts as small as $25,000.

There are three CP ratings: prime, desirable, and satisfactory. Paper that is rated prime represents the largest percentage outstanding. Commercial paper is a general obligation of the issuing corporation. Its status as to payment priority, with respect to other fixed-income obligations, in the event of bankruptcy, has not been clarified.

Commercial paper is sold either by direct placement — by a few major finance companies — or through dealers. Dealers underwrite the commercial paper of several hundred industrial corporations and finance companies. Four factors effect the CP rate: conditions of the money market, anticipated rates, comparative yields with other money-market instruments, and dealer inventories.

Commercial paper is sold on a discount basis, like bills and acceptances. Yields may be quoted in either fractions or decimal increments. The discount can be computed as follows:

$$\text{Discount} = \text{Face amount} \times \text{Rate} \times \frac{\text{Days to maturity}}{360}$$

There is normally a slightly higher yield from commercial paper than from bankers' acceptances and Treasury bills but it can be less safe. I recommend buying only the top, prime category. The bankruptcy of the Penn Central Transportation Company, in 1970, left a number of people and institutions holding their commercial paper.

A POINT OF VIEW

Before closing the subject of money markets and savings institutions, I would like to caution you concerning consumer protection. Some savings institutions are not responsive to customer demands. For example, savings and loan associations have so-called shareholders. However, these people really have no voice in management. I asked an association manager why no proxies were ever issued. He replied, "We find it best to leave them at the office. It saves a lot of headaches. If a shareholder asks for one, we give it to him, although few ask for them. But if the proxies were mailed, it would result in inquiries. Our eleven-man board keeps tight control."

"What about seeing your earnings statement?" I asked.

"This is not possible, because it would divulge our secrets. After all, we have thirty-nine local associations. It might also raise questions about the money we spent for advertising. You know, in this tight money market we have to spend a lot. Some associations have given away radios and silver dollars. I believe a New York bank offered TV sets."

Savings and loan associations, credit unions, and banks should divulge the same information as do corporations listed on the New York Stock Exchange. Furthermore, members of associations and credit unions should have an important voice in management decisions, and bank depositors should be able to influence decisions of managers. Unfortunately, there is little regard for the views of the people who supply the funds for all these financial institutions. As a means of having the views of the little depositor or shareholder heard, I strongly recommend that the shareholder be represented by at least two directors on every board, and that the highlights of these board meetings be made available for all interested parties.

The voice of consumer protest should also be heard in the money-market area. There is no valid excuse for Treasury bills not being available in the $1,000 denomination. Likewise, there could be small-lot transactions of commercial paper, bankers' acceptances, and certificates of deposit. I asked a senior partner of a large brokerage firm, "Would it be feasible to deal in lesser amounts of money-market securities?" His reply: "Yes, I will look into it." A follow-up found nothing accomplished.

At a recent congressional hearing a senator pointed out that only the powerful protests made an impact. The security-minded little investors should unite behind a Nader-type leader to give them a better deal in areas of the money market.

ACTIONS YOU CAN TAKE TO COPE WITH INFLATION AND THE ENERGY SHORTAGE

1. Annually review your savings in banks, savings and loan associations, credit unions, and the money market to determine if you are earning the highest return based on your requirements. For example, if you won't need the money in your 5 percent passbook account for six years, you may wish to obtain a higher return by transferring it to a longer-term certificate.

2. Review your holdings annually to determine the rate of return

that you are receiving and compare it with the loss in value of the dollar because of inflation. Determine if your cash reserves can be reduced and this difference placed in investments that are keeping pace with or exceeding the rate of inflation.

SUMMARY

Cash reserves can be acquired by placing your funds initially in selected financial institutions and later in the money market.

It is important to select banks, savings and loan associations, and credit unions that have a fine track record. There is no substitute for long-term success in the way of growth, profit, and sound management. But most important, how is the organization currently doing, and what can be expected in the future, based on present observations? Answering this requires your frequent reappraisal of the institutions where you have invested your cash reserves.

Although banks and savings and loans may be insured, you do not want to be involved in one that closes or defaults. Likewise, in the money market, you do not wish to buy commercial paper from a corporation that may not meet its commitments. Penn Central also caught astute buyers of their commercial paper.

No one has a corner on the investment brain market. There is no simple or foolproof answer to financial management. Therefore, I stress the importance of diversification — that is, distributing available funds into a variety of sound investments. After you meet insurance requirements, cash reserves should be the first line of dollar defense in the development of a diversified portfolio. The cash reserve should be established in the following sequence: (1) checking account; (2) bank savings account, savings and loan association, or credit union.

In regard to the checking account, the required minimum balance should be maintained to avoid the monthly service charge. After acquisition of a minimum-balance checking account, investment in interest-bearing savings accounts is then wise. Funds currently placed in commercial savings accounts receive a fair rate of interest under present monetary conditions. For example, banks of excellent repute are paying 5 percent on savings deposits, and well-established savings and loan associations have an interest rate of 5¼ percent.

The banks referred to in this discussion have the bulk of their funds in a variety of conservative loans and investments; savings and loan associations normally have most of their money invested in real estate loans. Therefore, both banks and savings and loan associations may require a waiting period before withdrawal of savings accounts.

Interest on savings may not be credited to an account unless funds remain until the end of the established payment periods. For example, if interest is paid on January 1 and July 1 of each year, and the depositor invested $500 in a savings account on January 25 and withdrew it on June 20 of the same year, he would receive back only the $500 deposited. However, an increasing number of savings institutions are paying interest from day of deposit to day of withdrawal.

The interest rate paid by various banks and savings and loan associations varies a good deal, so it is best to determine where you can get the greatest return on your savings — with the realization that the first consideration is the caliber of the institution itself.

The amount to be placed in the cash reserve depends on individual requirements and will fluctuate. Normally, I suggest that this reserve comprise four months' salary. If adequate funds are not available, an emergency may necessitate borrowing or making credit purchases at high rates of interest. People with securities, other than cash-reserve holdings, can sell them to meet these needs, but the necessity to do so may not happen at the best time and may result in substantial loss. The amount of reserve could be lowered for someone who has no family requirements or heavy expenditures; but a larger amount may be needed by someone with a large family, a home purchase plan, and other responsibilities.

The purpose of a cash reserve is to provide funds when you need them. Find out the restrictions that may be imposed in the event you want the money immediately. Above all, do not sacrifice safety of principal for a small differential in interest. Place your savings in first-quality credit unions and institutions that are properly insured, and in sound financial condition, and have a long record of successful management.

After you have acquired the initial cash reserve, consider government bonds, which are outlined in the next chapter. As your savings grow, you may wish to move into the money market, which offers a fine return and safety. My preference is for Treasury bills, in view of their prime safety factor; and normally there isn't too much difference in yield between bills and other money-market securities.

Take Stock in America — Buy Bonds.
— U.S. TREASURY

BONDS

Between 1970 and 1979, the bond market provided high interest rates to investors. A prime reason was the impact of inflation; people would buy bonds if they received a good current yield to compensate for their being paid back with cheaper dollars at maturity. Bonds continue to provide a good return.

DEFINITION

What is a bond? It may be defined as a certificate of indebtedness on which the issuing agency promises to pay the holder a precise sum, including an established rate of interest at times specified in the agreement.

In the case of corporate obligations, the bondholder has a higher priority claim against the corporation than does the stockholder. This applies to both the receipt of income and the return of principal in the event of bankruptcy. If a corporation earns only enough in a particular year to pay bondholders, and it has no surplus or other available sources to obtain funds, the stockholders receive nothing. But in prosperous years, bondholders continue to receive only the

202

established rate of interest, while stockholders, as owners, may share in the high earnings through larger dividends.

However, the fact that bondholders precede stockholders in payment is not the most significant criterion for investors. In the 1930s, during the Depression, a great many companies failed to pay either bond interest or dividends, although many other corporations met all their obligations. From the investor's point of view, therefore, it is desirable to select those issues that have proved they can weather periods of economic adversity. Bonds in this category are more likely to be issued by the U.S. government and its agencies, first-rate municipalities, and well-established companies that have excellent management and long records of financial solvency. Let us look first at the federal government issues.

U.S. GOVERNMENT SECURITIES

The federal government has two general classes of interest-bearing public issues: (1) nonmarketable, nonnegotiable securities and (2) marketable, negotiable securities.[1]

Nonmarketable Securities

Nonmarketable, nonnegotiable securities issued are U.S. Savings bonds of Series E and H. The bonds are dated as of the first day of the month in which they are purchased, are issued only in registered form, and are payable only to the registered owners during their lifetime. The bonds may not be used as collateral for loans. To compensate for their nonnegotiability, these securities are not subject to market fluctuations. Neither are they callable for redemption before their extended maturity dates; however, at the option of the owners, the bonds are redeemable before maturity or extended maturity, as the case may be, in accordance with their terms at fixed redemption values.

Series E Bonds
Series E bonds are appreciation-type bonds issued on a discount basis. Purchase prices, maturity prices, and denominations are as follows:

---

[1] Primary source for the information on U.S. government securities is *United States Securities Available to Investors* (Washington, D.C.: Department of the Treasury, Fiscal Service, Bureau of the Debt, 1978).

Purchase Price	Maturity Price[a]
$ 18.75	$ 25.20
37.50	50.40
56.25	75.60
75.00	100.80
150.00	201.60
375.00	504.00
750.00	1,008.00
7,500.00	10,080.00

[a]This maturity price applies to those bonds bearing issue dates beginning December 1, 1973. For specific details on redemption values of Series E bonds, refer to a current *Federal Register,* pamphlet published by the Department of the Treasury.

The bonds mature five years from issue date, but they may be redeemed at any time after two months from issue date at fixed redemption values. No interest as such is paid; but the periodic increase in redemption value over the issue price, paid only on redemption, represents interest. When the bonds are held to maturity, the yield or investment return is equivalent to interest at the rate of 6½ percent per annum, compounded semiannually. If they are redeemed before maturity, the yield is less. Therefore, you should normally invest in Series E bonds only when you plan to hold them until maturity.

The bonds may be registered in the names of natural persons — whether adults or minors — in single-ownership, co-ownership, or beneficiary forms, and in single-ownership form in the names of fiduciaries and private and public organizations, but they may not be registered in the names of commercial banks in their own right. Series E bonds are subject to an annual limitation of $10,000 (face amount) for each owner.

They may be purchased at banks generally, or by mail at any Federal Reserve Bank or branch, or at the Office of the Treasurer of the United States, Securities Division, Washington, D.C. 20220. Purchase applications must be accompanied by payment in full.

Series H Bonds
Series H bonds are ten-year current-income bonds, issued at par in denominations of $500, $1,000, $5,000, and $10,000. They are redeemable at par at the owner's option after six months from issue date, except during the calendar month preceding an interest-payment date. Interest is paid semiannually by check, in varying amounts based on a graduated scale fixed to produce a return of about 6½ percent per annum, compounded semiannually, if the bonds are held to maturity.

Series H bonds may be registered in the same forms as Series E bonds and may be purchased from the same sources. They are subject to an annual limitation of $10,000 for each owner, but the limitation does not apply to Series H bonds acquired through exchange of Series E bonds.

Thus, an owner of, say, $10,000 in Series E bonds may replace them with an equivalent amount of the Series H.

Marketable Securities

Treasury bonds and notes are issued from time to time, pursuant to public offerings, through the Federal Reserve Banks as fiscal agents of the United States and by the Office of the Treasurer of the United States, Securities Division, Washington, D.C. 20220. They can also be obtained through your stockbroker or bank, but there is normally a fee for this service. All your securities are available in bearer form, are transferable, and may be sold in the market. Ordinarily, they may be used as collateral for loans.

Marketable securities are issued in series, each series having similar terms and conditions. Generally, bonds are issues of long term and notes of medium term. Bonds and notes bear interest.

Bearer securities, the ownership of which is not recorded, are payable to bearer, with the title passing by delivery without endorsement and without notice to the Treasury. Coupons for interest attached to bearer bonds and notes must be detached and presented for payment when interest is due.

Bonds and most issues of notes are also available in registered form; that is, the names and addresses of the owners are recorded. Interest on these is paid by check drawn to the order of the owner of record on the Treasury's books. Registered securities may be transferred by assignment executed by the registered owner or his or her authorized representative.

Treasury Bonds

Treasury bonds of each series have a fixed maturity, usually more than five years from date of issue, when the principal amount becomes payable. When so provided in the offering circulars, bonds may be called for redemption before maturity at the option of the United States, on and after specified dates, on four months' notice.

Bonds bear interest at fixed rates, payable semiannually. Interest ceases when the principal amount becomes payable, whether at maturity or an earlier call date. Denominations of recent series are $500, $1,000, $5,000, $10,000, $100,000 and $1 million. Within the same series, bonds may be exchanged as follows: (1) for other authorized denominations, (2) bearer for registered bonds, and (3) registered for bearer bonds.

Treasury Notes

Treasury notes of each series have a fixed maturity of between one and seven years from date of issue, when the principal amount becomes payable. They bear interest at fixed rates, payable semiannually. Denominations are $1,000, $5,000, $10,000, $100,000, $1 million, $100 million, and $500 million. Within the same series, exchanges are authorized (1) for other authorized denominations, (2) bearer for registered notes, and (3) registered for bearer notes.

Purchase of Marketable Securities

From the Treasury

Marketable bonds and notes may be purchased directly from the Treasury only on the occasion of a public offering. Subscriptions, subject to allotment, may be made at Federal Reserve Banks and branches, and at the Office of the Treasurer of the United States, Securities Division, Washington, D.C. 20220, at such times. Banks and brokerage firms will handle subscriptions for customers, but they do make a charge for this service, whereas no charge is made at the Federal Reserve Banks and branches.

If you are interested in subscribing for any future issue of any class of securities, you can get information from a Federal Reserve Bank or branch or from the bond specialists in a brokerage firm. Financial sections of newspapers and your local bank usually have this information, too.

In the Market

After their original issue Treasury bonds and notes may be purchased in the market, at prevailing market prices. Anyone interested in purchasing them should consult a broker, bank, or dealer in these securities. Requests for information on marketable issues may be addressed to any Federal Reserve Bank or branch, or to the Commissioner of the Public Debt, Department of the Treasury, Washington, D.C. 20226.

Tax Status

Income derived from Treasury bonds, notes, and savings bonds is subject to income tax. For purposes of federal taxation, any increase in the value of savings bonds — the difference between the price paid and the redemption value received, whether at or before maturity or final maturity — is considered to be interest.

All securities are subject to estate, inheritance, gift, or other excise taxes, whether federal or state, but are exempt from all other taxation by any state, any possession of the United States, or any local taxing authority.

Observations on U.S. Government Securities

In my opinion, the safest bond purchase is an investment with the U.S. government, particularly in view of the improved features on Series E and H savings bonds. The latest Series E bonds mature in five years, and if held to maturity, they yield 6½ percent.

Interest on them does not have to be reported in a tax return until they are cashed or at the time of final maturity, whichever is earlier. So a person who wishes to retire at the ripe old age of 38 could begin a Series E program at age 33 and save an appreciable amount in federal income taxes by cashing them in and paying the tax after retirement, when his (or her) income is reduced. Or if he is not yet ready for retirement when the bonds mature, he can, instead of redeeming them for cash, exchange them for an equivalent amount of Series H bonds, and the tax on the accumulated interest will be deferred until the H bonds are redeemed.

However, the Series E bondholder does have the privilege of reporting the accrued interest earlier. If this is done, the entire amount to date has to be shown in the current tax return, and each return thereafter must list the annual gain for that year.

Series H bonds currently provide a return of 6½ percent when held to the full ten-year maturity. If it should be necessary to cash them during the first few years after purchase, a lower rate of interest is received. The H series is well suited to people who want a periodic income, as its holders receive interest payments by check every six months.

Series E and H Savings bonds also have such features as these: ease in converting to cash; assured rate of return; guaranteed redemption values; replacement by the Treasury for any bonds lost, stolen, mutilated, or destroyed; and the ease of purchasing E bonds through monthly payroll-deduction plans.

In view of the advantages to buying savings bonds, I am frequently asked why this form of investment is not included as a "cash reserve." There are several reasons. They qualify from the standpoint of safety of principal, but you cannot obtain your principal during the first two months after purchase, and this may be just the time you are hit with an emergency. These bonds also cannot be used for collateral. Another disadvantage is the lower interest rate in the early years; if funds are needed for an emergency during that time, a savings account would normally provide a higher yield. This is the primary drawback of Series E and H bonds — their low return in relation to other savings media, a problem that has existed since their initial issuance at 2.9 percent in 1941. A 6½ percent return in 1979 did not even keep pace with inflation that year.

The danger in purchasing bonds other than Series E and H, including negotiable government issues, is the daily fluctuation based on interest rates. It could happen that when cash is needed, the bonds could be disposed of only at less than the original cost. As an illustration, U.S. Treasury bonds (Series December 15, 2½ 72/67) were initially sold at par in November 1945 to provide a yield of 2½ percent. Each $1,000 bond has sold as high as $1,065.31 (1946) and as low as $849.60 (1970). In 1971 the 72/67 series was selling for $966.00, to yield 4.7 percent at maturity. This series matured December 15, 1972, but could have been called at the option of the U.S. Treasury on or after December 15, 1967.

It is significant that a call for redemption must be made at par, plus accrued interest. The Treasury is required to give four months' notice before taking such action. Normally, the call for redemption is made at the most opportune time for the government. With prime interest rates much higher than 2½ percent during the period 1967–1972, it was obviously wise for the government not to make payment until maturity on the series of December 15, 2½ 72/67.

U.S. Savings bonds can be bought at any time at no extra cost to the buyer. Negotiable government bonds, except at the time of issuance, do cost the purchaser a fee. The cost involves two factors: the brokerage commission, and the spread between the bid and the asked price. This spread is quoted in thirty-seconds of a point and currently approximates one point. Nineteen years ago, the spread on the longest-term governments was only 8/32, but costs have risen on all investment transactions. If possible, buy new issues of negotiable bonds and notes to avoid the commission, which can amount to $1,000 on long-term bond transactions involving amounts of $100,000.

The bid and asked prices of Treasury bonds and notes are listed daily in the financial section of major newspapers. Currently, these marketable securities pay up to 100 percent higher return than U.S. Savings bonds during this era of high interest rates. There is also the appreciation potential on these bonds, in the event that interest rates fall in the years ahead.

A number of U.S. Treasury bonds selling below par today offer a feature that is important to estate planning. Under certain conditions, they may be redeemed at par, plus accrued interest, for the purpose of applying the proceeds to the payment of federal estate taxes. For those interested in further details, I suggest contacting the Treasury Department.

It is advantageous to have your negotiable government issues in registered form, that is, in your name. This measure reduces the risk of loss or theft.

GOVERNMENT AGENCIES
AND IBRDS

In addition to securities of the U.S. government, there are also debt issues of agencies that have federal government participation. These obligations generally provide a slightly higher interest return to the holder. They are also a very safe purchase from the standpoint of return of principal at maturity and payment of interest on due dates. Since 1965 the number of these securities has increased considerably, owing to the expanded role of the various agencies and their need for additional money.

The securities have been well accepted in the marketplace. They play an important role in the nation's economy by providing significant sources of funds for worthy projects. The best known agencies issuing them are the Bank for Cooperatives, Federal Home Loan Banks, Federal Intermediate Credit Banks (FIC), Federal Land Banks, Federal National Mortgage Association, and International Bank for Reconstruction and Development (IBRD; World Bank).[2] These organizations are able to attract funds at a return only slightly higher than that of U.S. government issues.

These agency issues are fine for banks and other organizations that employ bond experts to determine which yields are best for their portfolios. However, for most individuals, I recommend staying with a simple program that includes Treasury bonds and/or notes. The rate differential is normally so small that it is not worth the extra effort required to evaluate yields.

---

[2] For further information on government agencies and IBRD, read *Handbook of Securities of the United States Government and Federal Agencies and Related Money Market Instruments* (Boston: The First Boston Corporation, 1978).

Other Agencies

There are a number of other agencies clothed with a public interest that issue debt instruments. They include the Commodity Credit Corporation (CCC), Department of Housing and Urban Development, Federal Housing Administration, Export-Import Bank of Washington, Farmers Home Administration, Inter-American Development Bank, Merchant Marine, and Tennessee Valley Authority.

The sophisticated investor may be interested in securities of a relatively new public agency. The Government National Mortgage Association (GNMA) was established in 1968 to assume certain functions of the Federal National Mortgage Association. A primary objective of the GNMA is to assist in the financing of more housing by making real estate mortgage investments attractive to all types of investors. It accomplishes this objective by guaranteeing bonds, participation certificates, and pass-through securities. This guarantee is backed by the full faith and credit of the U.S. government. the GNMA has complete authority to borrow from the U.S. Treasury to meet its obligations under the guarantee.

Of the three types of securities guaranteed by the GNMA, the pass-through securities have been the best received. They represent a share in a pool of FHA and/or VA mortgages. An issuer, usually a mortgage banker, will put together a minimum of $2 million of FHA-VA mortgages. The issuer will place them in the custody of a bank and, through the GNMA, issue a pass-through security.

Purchasers of these GNMA pass-through securities receive monthly payments of principal and interest. The average life of these investments is 12 years; the maximum maturity would be 30 years. The high rate of interest for such a safe investment has drawn a good number of astute institutional and private investors. Yield has varied between 6½ and 9½ percent during the past years. Before you purchase these securities, I suggest you confer with your banker or broker and become more familiar with the subject.

STATE AND MUNICIPAL SECURITIES

State and municipal bonds — known collectively as "municipals" — are obligations issued by states, cities, school districts, housing and port authorities, and other political subdivisions to raise money for a variety of projects.

General-obligation bonds are secured by the full faith and credit of the issuing state or municipality, and all the community's tax resources are pledged to the repayment of the obligation.

Limited- and *special-tax bonds* are secured by a partial or limited pledge of the issuer's taxing power (the first two cents of a cigarette tax, for example).

Revenue bonds are secured by revenues from the operation of a specific project, such as a water or electric system or a toll road.

Public-housing-authority bonds are primarily secured by the rentals of individual housing projects. If these rents are not sufficient to cover indebtedness, the public-housing authority each year makes up any deficit with funds granted by Congress.

Agency bonds may be secured by charges for services an agency renders. For example, a state may create an agency to provide water and sewerage services or build a bridge and impose a toll. Agency bonds may also be general obligations.

Lease-secured bonds are secured by a pledge of money sufficient to cover principal and interest by an organization other than the issuer to guarantee payment.

Quality Ratings

Two services, Moody's and Standard & Poor's analyze and rate state and municipal bond issues. Ratings on thousands of municipals can be found in Standard & Poor's *Bond Guide*, arranged alphabetically by states, and indicating whether the bonds are state bonds, general obligations, or revenue bonds.

Standard & Poor's has seven ratings, from the top quality (AAA-prime) down to those in default (D). Moody's has a somewhat similar rating system with eight classifications, ranging from Aaa down to C.

General Observations

Bonds should be purchased for safety, and I recommend only the AA rating or higher. Municipals are advantageous for those in the higher tax brackets, a matter we shall discuss shortly.

Daily prices of municipals are more difficult to come by than those of corporates or governments, although the *Wall Street Journal* does report the coupon, maturity, bid, and asked prices of a few active tax-exempt revenue bonds issued by toll roads and other public authorities. Your stockbroker can give you current bid and asked prices on various municipal issues and information on new issues.

Bonds issued by American and foreign corporations come in a variety of forms and range from those of the highest quality to the extremely risky. The capitalization of corporations may be composed primarily of bonds or consist of a small bond issue and the remainder in common stock. The bond may have a sweetener and be convertible into stock. The company may be newly organized or have been in business 100 years. The bonds may be sold over-the-counter or on a major exchange. It may be easy to dispose of them or almost impossible to find a buyer. Therefore, it is most important to have the necessary facts before making a purchase.

Because of the complexity of the corporate-bond market, the potential buyer should be familiar with bond ratings. For example, Standard & Poor's grades corporate bonds in seven classifications, ranging from the highest grade (AAA) to bonds in default (D). The safer the bond, the less interest you can expect to receive.

Standard & Poor's *Bond Guide* provides pertinent information about U.S. government, corporate, and foreign bonds. The facts on corporates include interest rate, due dates, ratings, eligibility, legality, form of bond, call price, price range for three current years, yield to maturity, principal business of the corporation, underwriting information, outstanding debt, financial position, ratio of debt to net property, overall earnings, and interim earnings.

Convertibles

A convertible bond is one that may be exchanged for a certain number of shares of stock. A bond with this "exchange" sweetener may be issued at a lower rate of interest than would a normal bond. It may also be the only way the company can market its issue.

Convertibles permit investors to participate in the appreciation potential of common stock, but with relatively less risk. In the event that the price of stock declines, support may be provided by the bond yield. The appreciation potential of a convertible is determined primarily by the price of the common stock for which it may be exchanged. The built-in safety of a convertible in a declining stock market is based on its status as a debt obligation of the corporation with a fixed interest rate. The relation between the price of a convertible and the value of the number of shares for which it can be exchanged usually determines how closely the price of the convertible will follow the price action of the common stock.

As a general rule, appreciation prospects are long term if the premium over conversion value is substantial. If the price of the common stock should decline, the convertible is supported by the yield; the price is unlikely to fall below that of nonconvertible senior securities of the same quality.

The risk of call should be taken into consideration before investing in convertible securities. A corporation usually issues convertible bonds with the intention of effecting their conversion into common stock. Therefore, the convertible securities are unlikely to be called before the common stock is selling at a price that provides the investor with equal value in the exchange.

In mid-1978 the combination of declining stock prices and increasing interest rates deprived convertible bonds of their two primary price supports. Lower stock prices resulted in lower conversion values, and high interest rates depressed estimated investment values, or the theoretical price floor. As a result, many good-quality convertibles of sound companies were selling at reasonable prices. For example, let us assume the convertible bond X initially sold at par ($1,000 per bond) to provide a 6 percent yield. It can be converted into two shares of X common stock until June 30, 1986. If the common-stock shares are selling at $500 or below, there is no advantage to the conversion feature. However, if X common stock moves to $1,000, X bonds should appreciate to $2,000. In contrast, if the stock declines to $50 and interest rates for this type of bond rise to 9 percent, the 6 percent X bond will sell well below par.

Observation
A stock should be considered for income and/or growth, but I believe that it is better to select a bond for its features of safety and fair interest return. Convertible bonds are an attempt to combine features of each, but they do not provide the best of either.

YIELD TO MATURITY

It is helpful to understand what *yield to maturity* is all about as it relates to the bonds discussed in this chapter.[3] Bond tables have been prepared to inform you of the exact yield to maturity for various coupons and can be seen at a brokerage firm or bank. A complex

[3] In the next chapter, *current yield* is presented as it applies primarily to the stock market. However, it is also pertinent to bonds, and you may wish to read about it on pages 219 and 220 after finishing this material on yield to maturity.

formula is utilized for the precise determination of yield to maturity. However, an approximation can be made by utilizing the following formula:

$$\text{Yield to maturity} = \frac{\text{Annual bond interest} + \dfrac{\text{Discount}}{\text{Years to maturity}} \left(\text{or} - \dfrac{\text{Premium}}{\text{Years to maturity}} \right)}{\dfrac{\text{Purchase price} + \text{Redemption price}}{2}}$$

Let us apply this formula. First, let us assume you made a purchase of a 4 percent $1,000 bond issued on February 15, 1980 for $1,010 and it has four years remaining until maturity. The $10 premium disappears during this period because you will only receive $1,000 in 1984. Here is how to arrive at the approximation:

Annual bond interest = $40
Premium = $10
Years to maturity = 4
Purchase price = $1010
Redemption price = $1000

$$\frac{\$40 - \$10/4}{(\$1,010 + \$1,000)/2} = \frac{\$37.50}{\$1,005} = 3.7\% \text{ Yield to maturity}$$

Thus the yield to maturity approximates 3.7 percent. It is less than the 4 percent coupon because you paid a $10 premium on $1,000 bond at time of purchase.

Now let us take an example of a high interest era and assume the bond is bought for $800 on February 15, 1980.

Annual bond interest = $40
Discount = $200
Years to maturity = 4
Purchase price = $800
Redemption price = $1,000

$$\frac{\$40 + \$200/4}{(\$800 + \$1000)/2} = \frac{\$90}{\$900} = 10\% \text{ Yield to maturity}$$

Thus the yield zooms to 10 percent if you bought the 4 percent bond for $800 four years prior to maturity. It pays to look at various bond issues in order to determine yields to maturity. Good buys in discount bonds are possible in terms of both high interest and a reduced capital-gains tax on redemption.

ACTIONS YOU CAN TAKE TO COPE WITH INFLATION
AND THE ENERGY SHORTAGE

1. Review your bond holdings annually and determine if your tax bracket would make it desirable to sell some of your taxable bonds and buy municipals.

2. If you have savings bonds, determine the yield and see if you can't obtain a higher rate in other U.S. government issues.

SUMMARY

A criticism leveled against bonds is that they have failed to keep pace with inflation, that dollars invested in fixed-income securities in recent years do not have comparable buying power today. This cannot be denied. However, it must be remembered that violent fluctuations have occurred in other types of investments, such as real estate and stocks. Compare the losses in property values and corporate stocks with government bonds for the ten-year period ending in 1932. At that time, the person with government securities was in a far more favorable financial position than one with stock and property holdings. And the person who in 1979 invested money in short-term Treasury issues received a much higher yield than the stockholder did.

What about the future? Based upon what has happened in the past, we cannot forecast the years ahead with certainty. We do know that our society has never been able to eliminate cyclical fluctuations. Accordingly, the wise investor acquires various holdings in order to have adequate protection. Highest-quality bonds furnish a strong pillar in building a diversified investment program. Although I do not believe bonds generally should be thought of as a cash reserve, I recommend that marketable government bonds be included in an investment portfolio. If held to maturity, they provide good income coupled with unexcelled safety of principal. Furthermore, at today's prices, all long-term Treasury issues are selling under par and therefore have a certain growth potential. For example, the 1993–1998 series (7 percent) can currently be bought at about 34 percent below redemption value. In the meantime, if lower interest rates and the cheaper money era should return, this would raise their market price. Of course, the converse is also possible. If interest rates should rise above present levels, then the price of the bonds would decline further. Nevertheless, a purchaser could be assured of receiving $1,000 by 1998 for a $660 investment now, and during the intervening years the holder would be earning nearly 12 percent on his or her investment. The growth portion of such an investment is also subject to the lower capital gains tax.

Municipal bonds may be a desirable purchase as you move up the economic ladder. Interest paid on these bonds is exempt from the federal income tax, and most states exempt interest on bonds of their own state from state taxes. The wisdom of an investment in municipals would depend upon the tax bracket of the person concerned. I normally recommend their purchase for those whose bracket is 36 percent or higher. Let us assume that a person is in the 36 percent group. If she (or he) bought a $1,000 municipal yielding 6 percent, it would provide her with an after-tax income of $60 a year. In contrast, a comparable corporate bond might offer a 9 percent yield, but the federal income tax bite would leave her with only $57.60. The couple filing jointly who has a net taxable income, for example, of $20,200 and buys a 5 percent nontaxable bond need only obtain more than 6.94 percent on a corporate issue to have a higher net return. However, the couple with a net taxable income of $215,400, or more, must find a corporate bond earning more than 16.67 percent. It is apparent the higher your income, the more important it is to consider tax-exempt bonds. Whether it would be beneficial in your particular case could be determined readily by consultation with your broker.

There are a great many other types of bonds available today. Many excellent corporate issues of high quality provide both safety and good income. For example, in 1979 several AAA issues were offered to provide a yield of nearly 14 percent. Also available at that time were some lower-rated bonds with higher interest rates; however, there are greater risks involved in this more speculative type of investment. People should buy bonds primarily for safety of principal and a fair income. The simplest and easiest way for the college graduate to do this is systematically to buy U.S. Savings bonds through a monthly allotment and, once a sizable number are accumulated, to convert them (on maturity) into negotiable U.S. Treasury issues, thus permitting a higher yield and a limited growth potential.

Timing for bond purchases, as for other investments, is very important. It is foolish to buy long-term Treasury bonds when interest rates are low. Conversely, it is wise to buy them when yields are high.

What portion of savings should be placed in government bonds? I have recommended that the equivalent of four months' salary be used as the norm for a cash reserve. After this, I suggest that an additional sum equal to the cash reserve be placed in U.S. Savings bonds. Upon completion of the cash reserve and savings bond goals, capital (up to $10,000) should be divided equally among Treasury bonds, stocks, real estate, and other investments. Once the savings bonds reach maturity, they should be converted to Treasury bonds.

Men have been swindled by other men on many occasions. The autumn of 1929 was, perhaps, the first occasion when men succeeded on a large scale in swindling themselves.

—JOHN KENNETH GALBRAITH

THE STOCK MARKET

MAGIC STOCKS

"How can I make a fast buck in the stock market?"

"Can you give me the names of some good penny stocks?"

"I bought 1,000 shares of a new computer-service company that the salesman said should double in price soon—should I buy more?"

"A friend said his stock paid a 20 percent cash dividend over the years. Is this true?"

"Look at those go-go stocks that were purchased by the new breed of investment managers! Where can I find issues like National Student Marketing and Panacolor?"

Questions like this were being asked by some of my friends and clients prior to the sharp stock market decline that bottomed in May 1970. Panacolor fell from $22.00 per share to $1.75; Student Marketing from $32.50 to $2.00. Other drastic losses occurred in "magic stocks" that, according to some salespeople, were going to make instant wealth. Stockbrokers earned up to $150,000 per annum in the 1967–1969 era, but precious few investors who put their hard-earned dollars into go-go issues in 1968 had anything to show but very heavy losses a few months later. Between 1973 and 1974 the

218

blue chips of the stock market suffered a sharp decline of 45 percent, but a group of highly speculative issues declined more than 90 percent in dollar value. Equity Funding Corporation sold mutual funds and insurance during this time. Prior to the disclosure of massive fraud in its insurance operations, in 1973, the stock sold as high as $37.25 per share. A short time later it had no value.

EMPHASIS ON QUALITY

There is no sure road to sudden riches in the purchase of shares in unique situations pushed by high-pressure agents. For every success story in this type of venture, there are thousands of disappointments and heartaches. It is important to question why you are being singled out to buy an unusual opportunity. Is it friendship or a chance for the solicitor to make a good profit at your expense? Salespeople receive sizable commissions for completing transactions on these "bargains."

Our discussion in previous chapters has emphasized the desirability of making quality investments in all areas and doing business with a firm that is well established in the community and has a record of successful management. This applies to the purchase of bonds and stocks as well as household appliances, clothing, home, and car.

Furthermore, securities should not be bought without adequate background and understanding of the problems confronting the investor. It is entirely possible to establish a satisfactory investment program by making your primary concerns a fair return on your money and growth in consonance with the economic development of our nation. But you run into difficulties when you try to beat the averages.

For example, many top-rated stocks today are returning little, if any, more than 6 percent in yield. Do not expect a 12 percent return on stock of the same quality — this yield involves far greater risk. A fine growth stock may produce *no* yield. But so do some very poor issues. Therefore, appropriate analysis is called for.

HOW TO COMPUTE YIELD

Yield is computed by taking the annual dividend (or interest) paid and dividing it by the current market price. For example, if a stock pays a $1.20 annual dividend and is selling today at $24 per share, its yield is 5 percent. The same method of computing current yield applies to interest on savings accounts or bonds. A bank paying $5.25 per year on each $100 invested gives the investor a yield of 5¼ percent. A $1,000 corporate bond paying $40 per year and currently purchased in the open market at $500 yields 8 percent. By determining the yield before purchase, you have a measure of comparative values related to the income objective.

We must realize that buying and selling securities is done in a free market. That is, the person who sells probably does so because he or she thinks the price of the stock is going down; whereas the person who buys is of the opinion that it is going up. Recognize that there are people more skilled than you who look for special situations and bargain issues. *Do not* try to compete with them. If the "experts" — followed by the crowd — believed a stock's 12 percent yield was a good buy, they would have bought it themselves. The effect of heavy demand for a security is to raise its price, with the resultant lower yield.

However, yield on your stocks should be your last concern. Stock dividends, after you deduct $100 in any one year, are taxable on the same basis as your other income. Therefore, even if your tax bracket is as low as 19 percent (and it probably will not be, if you are in a position to buy stocks), a 5 percent yield will actually give you only about 4 percent.

For this reason, it is very seldom wise for a person who is under retirement age to buy income stocks. Growth stocks are far more likely to bring you to your million-dollar goal.

STOCKHOLDER RELATIONSHIP

What is a share of stock? It is a part ownership in a corporation, and it is represented by a stock certificate. As an owner, the shareholder receives dividends only after all other obligations against the corporation are paid. There are two principal classes of stock — preferred and common. *Preferred*, as the name implies, normally has priority over common stock in the payment of dividends and assets. Preferred shareholders usually receive a stated dividend rate. However, there are participating preferred issues available that, under specified conditions, are eligible for dividends above the stated rate. A corporation may have more than one class of preferred stock, such as preferred and prior-preferred stock. The prior preferred has priority as to the distribution of dividends and assets over either the preferred or the common. There is also convertible preferred, stock which can be converted into common stock.

The most widely used method of capitalization is through issuance of *common stock*. Shareholders of common have a right to dividends subordinate to holders of all other stock in the corporation and are not limited to any fixed rate of return. Thus, in prosperous earning periods common stockholders may receive a high yield on their investment, whereas in poor earning periods they may receive nothing. On the other hand, growth companies like Xerox and IBM provide small yields regardless of earnings because they plow profit back into their corporations in lieu of paying out higher dividends. Owners of IBM and Xerox stock sacrifice dividend return for increases in the market value of their issues. This is a common characteristic of all growth companies.

COSTS – ORGANIZED EXCHANGES

A student recently related his experience in regard to the high cost of buying and selling small amounts of stock. He had purchased one share of a company listed on the New York Stock Exchange. A short time later, the bank threatened to repossess his car unless a payment was made promptly, and he was forced to sell the stock at the same price. His costs were as follows:

Purchase price for one share	$56.00	
Commission paid[a]	+15.00	
Total cost		$71.00
Selling price	$56.00	
Commission paid	−15.00	
	$41.00	
N.Y. State tax	− 0.03	
	$40.97	
Amount received from sale		40.97
Net loss		$30.03

[a]The commission that brokerage firms may charge per order on an amount involving less than $100 is as mutually agreed between the firm and the client.

The student lost $30.03, or approximately 54 percent of the price of the stock, and he received no dividend during the two-month period he owned it. This loss was due entirely to commissions and other fees involved in buying and selling the share; there was no decline in the price of his stock. He had also been required to pay $12\frac{1}{2}$ cents more than the market price when he made the purchase, and he received 12½ cents less than the market when he sold. This differential is because odd-lot purchases (less than 100 shares) are made for ⅛ point more in shares selling for more than ⁵⁄₃₂. Thus, the student paid $56.00 a share when the round-lot (100 shares or more) buyer was paying $55.88, and he sold at $56.00, versus $56.13 for the round-lot transaction.

In the class discussion that followed the student's presentation, there was general agreement on the following:

1. Do not buy stock unless you can afford it. Preferably be out of debt.
2. Buy stock in sufficient quantities so that the commission is only a small percentage of the total investment. The long-range goal should be to make round-lot transactions.
3. Be sure to figure all costs before making a purchase or sale.

Fixed Commission Rates

Table 13-1 presents the commission rates charged by brokers for transactions on the New York Stock Exchange prior to May 1, 1975. This information can give you a basis for comparing current negotiated rates with the old fixed commissions.

Table 13-1. Minimum New York and American Stock Exchange Commission Rates Prior to May 1, 1975.

Money Involved in the Order	Minimum Commission
On 100-Share Orders and Odd-Lot Orders	
$ 100–but under $ 800	2.0% plus $ 6.40
$ 800–but under $2,500	1.3% plus $12.00
$2,500–and above	0.9% plus $22.00
Odd Lot − $2 Less	
On Multiple Round-Lot Orders	
$ 100–but under $ 2,500	1.3% plus $ 12.00
$ 2,500–but under $20,000	0.9% plus $ 22.00
$20,000–but under $30,000	0.6% plus $ 82.00
$30,000–to and including $300,000	0.4% plus $142.00
Plus (for Each Round Lot)	
First to tenth round lot	$6 per round lot
Eleventh round lot and above	$4 per round lot

Plus: On any order involving an amount not in excess of $5,000, the commission computed in accordance with the foregoing provisions was increased by 10%, and on any order involving an amount in excess of $5,000, the commission computed in accordance with such provisions was increased by 15% and then 8%.

In actual practice, the commission charge for bond transaction is usually around $5.00 per $1,000 bond, with some discounts for large-quantity orders.

Negotiated Rates

On May 1, 1975, fixed commissions on exchanges were eliminated. What brought about this change? In recent years there had been criticism about the fixed commission rates established by the various organized exchanges. Since all firms charged the same price, this precluded the customers shopping around. A breakthrough occurred in 1968, when it was decreed that commissions on large orders ($300,000 and over) could be negotiated. After considerable study, the Securities Exchange Commission (SEC) ordered that fixed rates be eliminated by the May 1975 date regardless of the amount involved. As a first step, on April 1, 1974, the SEC authorized brokerage firms to establish their own commission rates on transactions of $2,000 or less. As a result, some firms lowered their commissions and others raised them. Merrill Lynch, Pierce, Fenner, & Smith, for example, lowered its rates by 16.7 percent to 29.5 percent. However, by accepting the lower prices under this special plan, the customer forfeited certain benefits. Merrill Lynch required such investors to buy at the current market price and pay for their purchases at the time the order was placed. The dollars given to Merrill Lynch determined the number of shares to be purchased — including fractional amounts. The firm kept the securities in its possession; however, if you, the customer, desired certificates for the full shares, it would mail them to you at a prevailing charge. If you wanted those services formerly offered for the $2,000-or-under purchase, Merrill Lynch provided them at the established commission rates effective prior to May 1, 1975 (Table 13-1).

The move to negotiated rates has, in general, resulted in higher costs for the small investors and reduced rates for institutionalized buyers. Although it is possible in some cases for the small investor to obtain a lower commission charge it requires astute shopping. Investors should obtain all the necessary facts about costs and benefits before selecting a brokerage firm. For example, if you only want the broker to buy your stock and ship the certificate to you, be sure this is understood. Obtain a copy of the current posted rates. It pays to take your time in order not to be taken.

Over-the-Counter Costs

The cost on over-the-counter stocks is more difficult to compute. For example, a recent bid price on Affiliated Bank Shares was 25½ and the asked price 26½. So if you had bought Affiliated it might have cost you $26.50 per share. If you had sold it, you might have received $25.50. Thus, on a 100-share transaction, there would be a

$100 differential, or nearly a 4 percent loss. This is a higher commission than if you made a similar transaction on a major exchange. However, over-the-counter prices appearing in financial sections of newspapers are representative quotations supplied by the National Association of Security Dealers through NASDAQ, its automated system for reporting quotes. Prices don't include retail markup, markdown or commission.

Therefore, it is very important to find out the actual costs when buying and selling over-the-counter stocks. Some brokers charge a commission in addition to the spread between the bid and asked prices. Others price the over-the-counter stock at a greater spread than is listed in the papers. Shop around to get the best deal.

Normally, you pay a good bit more commission on over-the-counter transactions than on the major exchanges. Also, you do not normally have as active a market; so if you wish to sell in a hurry, you may have trouble trying to find a buyer at a fair price.

HOW TO READ THE FINANCIAL SECTION

There is an abundance of factual material about stocks to be found in the financial sections of the major newspapers. An understanding of this material can be helpful in arriving at your selection of appropriate stocks. There are approximately 2,000 stocks listed on the New York Stock Exchange (NYSE). Nevertheless, each day a small number account for most of the sales. If you want a ready market for the sale of your securities, it is advantageous to buy an issue with a large number of common shares that are actively traded on a major exchange.

Let us examine the information available in the financial sections of major newspapers on each individual NYSE issue. American Airlines, for example, would read as follows:

New York Stock Exchange
April 5, 1979

| 52 Weeks | | | | | | | | | |
High	Low Stocks	Div.	Yield %	P E Ratio	Sales (100s)	High	Low	Close	Net Chg.
19¾	9½ AmAir	.40	3.0	3	331	13¼	13⅛	13⅛	-¼

Note that the high and low for American Airlines during the 52-week period varied between $9\frac{1}{2}$ and $19\frac{3}{4}$. Imagine having bought 100 shares at the high and sold them at the low. Your loss, including commissions, would be over 50 percent.

The amount of the dividend is listed immediately after the name of the company. We see that American Airlines is paying a 40-cent dividend in 1979. There were 33,100 shares of American Airlines traded on April 5, 1979. The price earnings ratio (P-E ratio) was listed as 3. The low price for the day was $13\frac{1}{8}$ ($13.13 per share) and the highest price per share was $13.25. The closing transaction was at $13\frac{1}{8}$. The stock had closed at $13\frac{3}{8}$ on April 4; therefore, there was $-\frac{1}{4}$ net change from the previous day's close. The yield in percent is also provided for each stock. For American Airlines, the figure listed is 3.0.

Similar information can be found on issues traded on the American Stock Exchange. There is also a list of transactions on other exchanges: Boston, Midwest, Pacific, Philadelphia, Montreal, and Toronto. Individual stock information presented for "Other Markets" is less complete than that for the two biggest exchanges: "Other Markets" furnishes only sales, high, low, close, and change. Furthermore, stocks that are also listed on other exchanges do not appear in this compilation; there are a number of corporations that list their stock on several exchanges.

Of all the markets, the over-the-counter market carries the largest number of corporate issues. Major newspapers list daily transactions of the more active companies. Information on select foreign securities may be found daily in some financial sections. The sales, net change, bid, and asked prices are furnished.

INVESTMENT LITERATURE

John Stillman, founder of a department-store chain and an eminently successful financier, has said, "Hard work is the price of stock market success; few are willing to pay the price." Hard work, in the form of studying investment literature over a reasonable period of time, is a helpful tool in improving your monetary position. There are many financial periodicals and books currently being published to satisfy a wide variety of interests. They are prepared in order to meet the needs of people who have funds available for investment purposes.

I have mentioned that securities should not be bought without adequate background and understanding of the problems confronting the investor. Selected texts and periodicals will provide much of this necessary information. The extra time spent in reading the literature should result in a more favorable financial return on hard-saved dollars. Much of this data is available in university and public libraries, as well as in brokerage houses. Some investment firms have a reading room for perusal of current financial literature. And it must be current, because changes occur rapidly, and outmoded writings can be detrimental. Keep up to date by staying abreast of political, economic, social, and military events that have an impact on the stock market. An extensive list of financial literature is provided in the Appendix.

BROKERAGE FIRMS

Once you have acquired an adequate background on securities and have accumulated the necessary funds, you must decide where to buy your stocks and bonds. There are many brokerage houses available for this purpose. It is desirable to select a well-established firm, conveniently located, that has achieved a fine reputation based upon integrity, profitability, good service, and growth, and large enough to provide a variety of services. It pays to be familiar with these services in order to make use of them.

I am frequently asked, "Are they interested in my business? I have very limited funds to invest." My experience has indicated that some firms are helpful to the client with little money as well as to those with sizable funds. Others, at least in recent years, have not been too kind to the small investor. The better firms not only are glad to see the small investor, but also will stress the need for such protection as an emergency cash reserve before buying stocks. Brokers within the same firm vary to a marked degree in age and temperament. It is a good idea to select a person with whom you can communicate well, and do not hesitate to change if you are dissatisfied. If you encounter any really disagreeable situation, inform the home office and the local manager.

There are many free services obtainable from various brokerage firms. Research facilities are often large, and detailed recommendations to fit your needs can be obtained from their home offices. As I mentioned previously, a library stocked with excellent financial publications is frequently available. Surveys can often be secured either on individual corporations, on particular industries, or of a general nature. In certain cases pamphlets relating to understanding financial statements and stock market terminology may be provided.

In most instances your securities can be held by the brokerage house, and it will send you the dividends or let them accumulate as desired. For the young graduate who may join a large corporation and be subject to frequent transfers, the privilege of leaving securities with the broker may interest you. There are onerous details involved in the collection of bond interest, stock dividends, transfers, redemptions, purchases and sales, and so on. If funds are allowed to remain with certain companies and to be reinvested, minimal interest may be paid — except in states where this is prohibited.

A word of caution about leaving your funds and securities with a brokerage firm. My advice is to have interest and dividends sent to you upon payment by the firms concerned. It is ridiculous to let the broker use your money when he or she would have to pay 15 percent or more elsewhere. And be sure the securities are registered in your name. A number of firms have failed in recent years. Some clients lost money and had great difficulty obtaining their securities. This loss occurred in spite of a federal statute in 1970, creating a Securities Investor Protection Corporation (SIPC) that protects investors holdings up to $50,000.[1]

I believe it is helpful to visit various establishments and find out what each firm has to offer. The Yellow Pages in the telephone book will indicate the brokers available in your community. Select the institution that best meets your requirements.

AVERAGES AND INDEXES

How is the stock market doing? The answer to this question will vary, depending upon what basic information is used. The stock market, in the broadest sense, is composed of the thousands of companies that have made their stock available to the public, and a complete listing of them would take in the New York, American, Midwest, Pacific, Boston, and Philadelphia exchanges, various foreign exchanges, and the many unlisted equities bought and sold in over-the-counter transactions. It would be extremely difficult to use all corporate stocks in determining what happens in the marketplace as a result of the multitude of daily purchases and sales. Therefore, limited numbers are used for the purpose of providing an answer to the question, "How is the market doing?"

---

[1] Some brokerage firms provide additional surety insurance policy protection for each investor's securities and have a special policy against robbery, fire, or natural disaster.

There are numerous statistical compilations that are prepared by various concerns to arrive at an answer. The advent of the computer age has made it possible to compute daily the average price of all stocks listed on the New York Stock Exchange. Other well-known stock averages are those of Standard & Poor's and the American Stock Exchange. There are also indicators for over-the-counter issues, prepared by the National Association of Securities Dealers.[2] One of my classes, with the assistance of the university computer, developed an index for over-the-counter issues in the New Orleans area.

The four Dow Jones Stock Averages[3] are the best known of these market computations. The *composite* average consists of all the stocks in the three individual averages — *industrials, transportation,* and *utilities* — each comprising large and well-established companies. Table 13-2 lists the 65 "blue chip" giants of American industry currently making up the Dow Jones Averages (DJA). The most popular of the four averages is the industrial category, whose origin may be traced back to 1896.[4]

The daily Dow Jones Industrial Average (DJIA) was at first computed by adding up the current market prices of all of the stocks and dividing the aggregate by the number of corporations. Let us assume that at the close of business on a particular day in 1897, the share values totaled $600. This figure would have been divided by 12 (the number of companies in the Dow Jones Industrial Average at that time), for an average market price of $50. If this figure had been $49 the day before, it could be said the market was up for the day.

Over the years, the number of corporations comprising the industrial average was increased to its present total of 30.[5] To permit

[2] The over-the-counter index has the short title of NASDAQ (National Association of Securities Dealers Automated Quotations).

[3] The Dow Jones index includes, in addition to the four stock averages, six bond averages.

[4] Charles H. Dow, the originator of the DJA, presented his initial stock average on July 3, 1884, in a brief financial bulletin, entitled *Customer's Afternoon Letter.* It was composed of 11 stocks and 9 of this group were railroad companies. The list was modified considerably between 1884 and 1896 to include more industrial issues. The Dow Jones Industrials first appeared on a daily basis, in October 1896, in the *Wall Street Journal.* Mr. Dow also devised the Dow Theory at this time. He hypothesized that the performance of the market was predictable and his theory could determine market trends as a result of compiling daily averages of selected stocks.

[5] The present industrial average actually includes 29 industrials and one utility, American Telephone and Telegraph (see Table 13-2). AT&T was substituted for IBM in 1939. If IBM had remained in the DJIA, this average would have been considerably higher over the past 40 years and reached 1,000 in 1961 instead of 1972. IBM returned to the DJIA along with Merck on June 29, 1979, replacing Chrysler and Esmark. This was the first major change in the Dow Jones Industrials in 20 years.

Table 13-2. Stocks Used in the Dow Jones Averages.

Industrials (30)

Allied Chemical	General Foods	Owens-Illinois
Aluminum Co.	General Motors	Procter & Gamble
American Brands	Goodyear	Sears, Roebuck
American Can	INCO	Standard Oil of
American Telephone	International Business	California
& Telegraph	Machines Corporation	Texaco
Bethlehem Steel	International Harvester	Union Carbide
du Pont	International Paper	United Technologies
Eastman Kodak	Johns-Manville	U.S. Steel
Exxon	Merck & Co.	Westinghouse Electric
General Electric	Minnesota Mining	Woolworth
	& Manufacturing	

Transportation (20)

American Airlines	Missouri Pacific Corporation	Seaboard Coast Line
Burlington North	Norfolk & Western	Southern Pacific
Canadian Pacific	Northwest Airlines	Southern Railway
Chessie System	Pan American World	Transway International
Consolidated Freightways	Airways	Trans World Airline
Eastern Airlines	St. Louis-San Francisco	UAL Inc.
McLean Trucking	Railway	Union Pacific Corporation
	Santa Fe Industrials	

Utilities (15)

American Electric Power	Detroit Edison	Peoples Gas
Cleveland Electric Ill.	Houston Industrial	Philadelphia Electric
Columbia Gas System	Niagara Mohawk Power	Public Service Electricity
Commonwealth Edison	Pacific Gas & Electric	& Gas
Consolidated Edison	Panhandle Eastern Power	Southern California
Consolidated Natural Gas	& Light	Edison

appropriate comparisons, it has been essential to make frequent adjustments in the divisor as the result of stock splits and stock dividends. The divisor now stands at 1.474.[6]

The DJIA is actually an unweighted arithmetic mean. The

[6] A problem with the Dow Jones Industrial Average is that a slight change in actual prices of its 30 stocks results in a large change in the DJIA. This is due to the fact that the divisor continues to be reduced in size with each stock split and stock dividend. Thus, a 25-cent rise (¼ point) in the price of its stocks would be reflected in a movement of 5 points in the DJIA (assuming the divisor of approximately 1.5). It is important to remember that the DJIA presents an overview of how the market is doing as measured by daily trading. It does not reflect either the true dollar value of corporate stocks or the actual dollar increase or decrease.

formula utilized to compute the daily average is as follows:

$$\frac{\Sigma P}{D} = DJIA$$

where

Σ = Sum
P = Price of each stock comprising the DJIA
D = Current DJIA divisor.

On May 27, 1977 (see Table 13-3) the formula provided the following answer:

$$DJIA = \frac{1,324.875}{1.474} = 898.83$$

The unweighted approach results in more importance being given to higher-priced issues in the DJIA. Likewise, a stock with the greatest market value (current price times number of shares outstanding) is given the same weight as one with the smallest number of shares in the DJIA.

The DJIA reached 1,052 in early 1973, establishing an all-time peak. Figure 13-1 portrays the yearly price movements of the DJIA since its inception in 1896. Note that in 1929 it peaked at 381 and then followed with a low of 41 in 1932. The chart indicates that, as of April 1979, the 30 industrials were 21 times above their Depression bottom of 1932 and had risen 300 points since the low in 1974. However, the investor who bought the DJIA stocks at 1,052, in 1973, would have lost money if he or she sold after that date. For example, in 1974 the DJIA slumped to 578 and has not risen since above 1,015. Since 1965 the DJIA has had a lateral movement with considerable variation in price as apparent from an examination of Figure 13-1. These marked fluctuations show that timing is important in the purchase and sale of securities.

Figure 13-1 points up the remarkable technological progress made in the United States since the DJIA was first reported on a daily basis. The mass production of cars, airplanes, radios, TV, computers, nuclear equipment, and space flights have all occurred within the memory of some individuals living today. The United States has also been involved in five wars since the DJIA's inception. And the stock market has not reacted well in wartime, as is apparent from Figure 13-1. In contrast, peaceful periods have seen remarkable

Table 13-3. Dow Jones Industrials (How to Compute the DJIA).

Corporation	Market Price as of May 27, 1977
Allied Chemical	$ 46.500
Aluminum Company of America	56.000
American Brands	46.000
American Can	40.000
American Telephone & Telegraph	63.000
Bethlehem Steel	32.875
Chrysler	16.625
du Pont	119.000
Eastman Kodak	56.000
Esmark Inc.	51.125
Exxon	54.500
General Electric	32.375
General Foods	66.625
General Motors	19.375
Goodyear	27.125
INCO	36.750
International Harvester	51.250
International Paper	34.500
Johns-Manville	47.500
Minnesota Mining & Manufacturing	27.625
Owens-Illinois	31.500
Procter & Gamble	74.500
Sears Roebuck	55.250
Standard Oil of California	41.375
Texaco	26.250
Union Carbide	50.375
United Technologies	37.500
U.S. Steel	41.875
Westinghouse Electric	19.750
Woolworth	21.750
Total	$1,324.875

$$\text{DJIA } (5/27/77) = \frac{1,324.875}{1.474} = 898.83$$

rises as well as the worst depression. Vietnam, Watergate, soaring inflation, and the energy crisis have been major factors in the lateral movements of the market since 1965.

But regardless of how the averages move, there are extensive disparities in the progress of individual issues. Although there have been substitutions made over the years in the composition of the DJIA, it is possible to make comparisons among those in the group today. Some have had limited advances since 1932, while others have

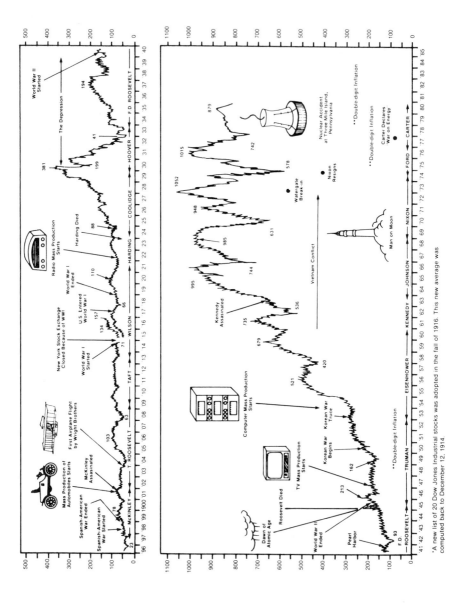

Figure 13-1. The Yearly Price Movement of the Dow Jones Industrials, 1896–1979.

*A new list of 20 Dow Jones Industrial stocks was adopted in the fall of 1916. This new average was computed back to December 12, 1914.

232

increased manyfold. And there are the same differences in corporate issues during periods of economic uncertainty. For example, between 1975 and 1979, Westinghouse ranged from 25 to 13 and Eastman Kodak fluctuated between $120\frac{1}{4}$ and $41\frac{1}{8}$.

The changing fortunes of American corporations is obvious from a look at the composition of the Dow Jones Industrials since 1896 (Table 13-4). It emphasizes the importance of frequent checking on your financial holdings to ascertain if they are appropriate for today and the foreseeable future.

The DJIA is composed of the so-called blue chips — it includes

Table 13-4. Stocks Used in Previous Dow Jones Industrial Averages.

1896 (12)	1916[a] (20)	1928 (30)
American Cotton Oil	American Beet Sugar	Allied Chemical
American Sugar	American Can	American Can
American Tobacco	American Car & Foundry	American Smelting
Chicago Gas	American Locomotive	American Sugar
Distilling & Cattle Feeding	American Smelting	American Tobacco B
General Electric	American Telephone & Telegraph	Atlantic Refining
Laclede Gas	Anaconda Copper	Bethlehem Steel
National Lead	Baldwin Locomotive	Chrysler
North American	Central Leather	General Electric
Tennessee Coal & Iron	General Electric	General Motors
U.S. Leather Pfd.	Goodrich	General Railway Signal
U.S. Rubber	Republic Iron & Steel	Goodrich
	Studebaker	International Harvester
	Texas Company	International Nickel
	U.S. Rubber	Mack Trucks
	U.S. Steel	Nash Motors
	Utah Copper	North American
	Westinghouse	Paramount Publix
	Western Union	Postum, Inc.
		Radio Corp.
		Sears Roebuck
		Standard Oil (NJ)
		Texas Corporation
		Texas Gulf Sulphur
		Union Carbide
		U.S. Steel
		Victor Talking Machine
		Westinghouse Electric
		Woolworth
		Wright Aeronautical

[a]This new list of 20 Dow Jones Industrial stocks first appeared in 1916 but was computed back to December 12, 1914.

major United States corporations. Other averages may show a somewhat divergent picture from time to time, owing to their composition, weighting of shares outstanding, and method of arriving at a divisor. Some other averages embrace much larger numbers of stocks, and several contain some of the smaller companies.

Standard & Poor's composite index has a much broader base than the DJIA. S&P comprises 500 issues (400 industrials, 20 transportations, 40 utilities, and 40 financial institutions). Its companies appear on the various exchanges with a few traded over-the-counter. In contrast to the Dow's sole reliance on the daily price of individual stocks (unweighted average), Standard & Poor's is weighted by taking into consideration the number of shares outstanding of each corporation. The daily market price of each issue is multiplied by the number of shares to obtain the total value of all 500 issues. This figure is divided by the market value of all S&P stocks during the period 1941–1943. The answer is then multiplied by 10.[7]

The New York Stock Exchange Composite Index comprises all of the stocks on that exchange and is computed daily. The index is based on a value of 50, which was the approximate price of NYSE issues on December 31, 1965. The NYSE has four other indexes — Industrials, Utilities, Transportation, and Finance.

The over-the-counter (OTC) market has seven indexes to reflect daily price movements. They include the following: Composite, Industrials, Banks, Insurance, Other Finance, Transportation, and Utilities. The composite index of NASDAQ (National Association of Security Dealers Automated Quotations) comprises about 2,400 OTC companies. The index is based on a value of 100 which was the approximate price of the selected OTC issues on February 5, 1971.

The DJIA, however, continues as the most popular index and is found most frequently in various publications. It is helpful for the investor to have a general picture of how the market is doing. Although it will vary from average to average, the *secular trend* gives the same picture — a rising price with in-between ups and downs. More important to the investor is the vast difference in what happens to particular corporations. The market in general may decline over a period of time while individual securities are experiencing a remarkable advance.

---

[7] The Dow averages are unweighted arithmetic means. Standard & Poor's are weighted arithmetic means. A further refinement is by Value Line's (VL) weighted geometric mean, which is used to determine its seven averages. Price fluctuations are weighted equally in the VLA by use of ratios.

AN INVESTMENT STRATEGY

As a potential investor, you are interested in finding the appropriate securities for your portfolio. I recommend that you keep your securities program as simple as possible, since the layperson seldom has the time or background necessary to develop a complex portfolio. Therefore, I believe that only common stock should be purchased. Preferred issues have some features of both bonds and stocks, but in my opinion they lack the best qualities of either. They are not as safe as U.S. Treasury bonds and do not offer the dividends or growth potential found in common stock.

As you recall, I believe an investment portfolio should be developed in orderly progression. Previous chapters have presented three areas: (1) checking account; (2) savings account in a bank, credit union, or savings and loan association; and (3) U.S. Savings bonds and negotiable U.S. government securities. The fourth link in the financial chain is common stock in growth corporations.

I cannot stress too emphatically the importance of buying quality securities through a highly *respected brokerage firm*. A wealthy lady in California found her broker "churning" her large stockholdings — that is, buying and selling frequently to make himself good commissions. In the meantime, the value of her rapidly changing portfolio was going down while the stock market was rising, and her original holdings were doing very well. She finally went to court and won back the money her stockbroker had squandered. But how many people are in a position to take legal action? Therefore, it is wise to give the same care to stock market selections that you do to other important matters.

First, keep current on financial material by reading literature written by financial authorities. Second, select a brokerage firm that has an excellent reputation and a fine research department, and that meets your requirements. Third, before buying, secure factual data about the company and take the time to analyze them. This analysis should also take into consideration the potential for a major disaster. An investment in a nuclear plant, for example, has potential for causing greater damage than a company making tennis balls. General Public Utilities fell sharply after the company's accident at its nuclear power facility in Pennsylvania. You will spend less time on money matters than your peers do if you have a logical program. Fourth, do not be rushed into closing a deal. Give it the same careful attention you accord any significant expenditure, such as buying a car or a home.

If you do not wish to go through the four steps described above, then utilize the services of an outstanding investment advisory service.

ACTIONS YOU CAN TAKE TO COPE WITH INFLATION AND THE ENERGY SHORTAGE

1. Plot on Figure 13-1 your estimate of how the Dow Jones Industrial Average will perform between now and 1985. Does your estimate indicate that the stock market will be a good investment after taking into consideration inflation and taxes during this time?

2. Examine corporations in energy-conservation fields. These might include manufacturers and retailers in such areas as insulation, solar energy, temperature controls, and new methods to conserve fuel for planes, cars, and buildings.

SUMMARY

A share of stock reflects an ownership interest in a corporation and it is represented by a stock certificate. As an owner, the shareholder receives dividends only after all other obligations against the corporation are paid. Likewise, in the event of bankruptcy, or liquidation, the stockholders receive payment only after all creditors are paid.

In view of the greater risk in buying stocks, in contrast to bonds, it pays to invest your money in quality growth issues of companies that have a proven reputation over a long period of time. There is no sure road to sudden riches by buying shares of magic stocks. For every success story in this type of venture there are thousands of failures.

In arriving at your decision as to which stock is appropriate it is helpful to be familiar with how to compute yield. By determining yield before purchasing stock, you can obtain a measure of comparative value among stocks of interest to you. Yield is determined by taking the annual dividend paid and dividing it by the current market price.

Securities should not be bought without adequate background and understanding of the problems confronting the investor. Selected books and periodicals will provide helpful information. Much of this data is available in public libraries as well as in brokerage houses.

Once you have acquired adequate background on securities,

and accumulated the necessary funds, you must decide where to buy your securities. There are many brokerage houses available for this purpose. It is desirable to select a well-established firm, conveniently located, that has achieved a fine reputation based upon integrity, profitability, good service, growth and is large enough to provide a variety of services. Nevertheless, there are considerable differences in fees charged by quality brokers.

Fixed commissions on exchanges were eliminated effective May 1, 1975. The move to negotiated rates has, in general, resulted in higher costs for the small investor and reduced rates for institutional buyers. Today, prior to making a stock transaction, it is essential to shop around to determine what is the best deal for you.

Keep your securities program as simple as possible. Buy quality issues through a highly respected brokerage firm. If you do not wish to manage your own investment portfolio then utilize the services of an outstanding investment advisory service.

How is the stock market doing? The answer to this question will vary, depending upon what basic information is used. However, the most popular market indicator is the Dow Jones Industrial Average (DJIA), whose origin may be traced back to 1896. The present DJIA contains thirty large and well-established U.S. corporations.

REAL ESTATE

Land is a precious commodity, and the continuing increase in world population will make it more precious in the years to come. With more and more people occupying a relatively constant supply of land,[1] this type of property will obviously become more and more scarce.

California, for instance, currently has 20 million people and this number is expected to double in the next 30 years. In Hawaii it is very difficult to obtain ownership of a piece of land; such property is normally available only on a lease basis. A number of foreign countries have also adopted this policy.

Land prices in the United States over the past 57 years reflect a sizable increase in value. In 1922, land in this country was valued at $93.9 billion, in contrast to over $1.8 trillion in 1979. This chapter will look at real estate as it pertains to personal finance; that is, how it can fit into your investment program.

Real estate, according to Webster's Dictionary, is "land and its . . . buildings . . . its improvements and its natural assets (as

---

[1] "Relatively" because there are means of increasing land utilization by taking arid or swampy areas and making them habitable; fill can make shallow waters usable; buildings can be made taller to accommodate more people.

minerals, crops, waters) and with the inclusion of . . . rights that follow ownership of land. . . ."

Three aspects of real estate will be presented as potential investments: land, property, and organizations established for such purposes as financing and owning land as well as improving it.

LAND

We have all heard tales of remarkable profits being made by buying land at a bargain and selling it for many times the original cost. These success stories make good reading. However, there is also the other side of the coin. Like the stock market, land values fluctuate with the times. In some areas they are now as much as 400 times what they were 20 years ago. In contrast, many people made land investments near military bases and NASA facilities that recently closed down, and they lost money. Such disasters as earthquakes and slides can also cause bankruptcy in heavily financed land. Hurricane Camille devastated the Mississippi Gulf Coast area in 1969 and ruined several land developers and a number of people holding sites. The 1971 earthquake in the Los Angeles area proved costly to purchasers of real estate. The energy shortage has caused land values to decline sharply in certain localities. The Johnstown flood of 1977 lowered land values markedly in sections of that community. And scandals in Arizona land sales resulted in some people losing 100 percent of their original investments. The nuclear accident, in 1979, at Metropolitan Edison Company's Three Mile Island Nuclear Plant No. 2, caused an initial decline in property values near the plant site. Only time will tell what the long-term impact will be on property values in the vicinity of this Pennsylvania site and of other nuclear plants. But it is fair to assume that a nuclear plant next door will not normally be a plus factor in regard to home valuation.

One way to make money in land is to buy it on the outskirts of a dynamic growth area before the general public realizes what is taking place. Such an approach adopts the adage, "Buy it by the acre and sell it by the lot," and requires much hard work in the way of market research. Consideration must be given to the potential movement of city folks to suburban areas, the direction in which the city will grow and what new industries or other developments will make the land appreciate. For example, a new university that acquired 15,000 students in 16 years had a decidedly favorable effect on land values in the vicinity.

As with love and war, it would appear that all is fair in seeking out information on actions that will have an impact on land. By being informed, the astute buyer can take advantage of a change before prices rise. You may know that a state's population will double by the year 2000 — but the trick is to find out *where* in the state the primary growth will occur. Some cities may triple in size and others decline. Then, too, you must pinpoint that section of the community where the big boom will take place.

When you are in the market for a piece of land in a certain area, learn as much as you can about the future of that area. Read the newspaper ads to check out prices. Take a hard look at the available sites. You should also ask brokers about the land area you are interested in buying. A check at the county seat can also be advantageous. The county clerk can furnish information as to who owns the property that you wish to purchase. This will permit direct contacts and avoid brokers' commissions. You may also uncover people who can't meet their taxes and might be willing to sell at a reasonable figure. When it comes to closing the deal, be a tough bargainer. You can expect the seller to be equally astute in seeking a fair price.

The purchase of land is made on a different basis from that of property. You cannot obtain long-term loans from mortgage companies. The seller may, however, agree to take a mortgage. The land contract is another means of financing the transaction. It is comparable to buying on time such merchandise as furniture or a car. The seller retains title until payment has been completed.

Borrowing money can be expensive, and there are also other considerations. In determining if a site is a good buy, it is important that you compute all costs. Let us take an example of a piece of land purchased for $10,000, held for five years, and sold for $20,000 (Table 14-1).

Table 14-1. Land Investment.

Cost	
Initial land cost	$10,000[a]
Mortgage interest at 9%	4,500
Taxes	1,500
Maintenance (grass cutting)	200
Sales commission, 10%	2,000
Total cost after 5 years	$18,200
Profit	
Land sale price	$20,000
Total costs	18,200
Profit before taxes	$ 1,800

[a]The assumption is made that the principal is not repaid until after the land is sold.

The average annual profit amounts to $360 ($1,800 ÷ 5), or 3.6 percent on the original investment; however, by the end of five years the cost has increased to $18,200, and therefore the return is actually less than 2 percent per year on the *total* investment. In contrast, if you put the $10,000 to work in a safe investment like U.S. Treasury notes or bills, you could earn from $600 to $800 a year. And this annual return would increase with each passing year if you invested that additional $8,200 over a five-year period.

It is apparent that making a profit on land requires a sizable appreciation over the years. Tax costs, maintenance, and interest expense must be checked with care prior to purchase, and it also helps to eliminate the sales commission. The rate at which you can borrow money is a key determinant of whether such an investment will be worthy of your money and time. In periods of high interest, it would not pay unless you are able to obtain a 20 to 25 percent annual appreciation in the land.

PROPERTY

In Chapter 8 we spoke of housing from the viewpoint of a place to live. Now I would like to discuss property as a source of income or capital gains. It may help if you review the material presented in Chapter 8 because the same basic approach is taken in regard to selecting housing for investment purposes. Such factors as location, construction, loan rate, and market conditions must be taken into consideration. The question of whether to buy or build is also important. It would appear that you can normally do better, from an investment standpoint, by building a house or small apartment yourself.[2]

First let us consider the leasing of a home. You must determine what return you will receive in contrast to placing your money elsewhere — although this should not be the sole criterion because there is an advantage to diversifying your investments. Property is one more bastion in your financial fortification.

What can you expect to earn on your property? A normal monthly income may approximate 1 percent of the property cost, and somewhat more if you built the house yourself. But other factors could make it exceed the norm. It is a good idea to provide a 25 percent margin in your computations. Thus, on an $80,000 house, the

[2]Larger commercial properties should not be considered until you have experience in smaller real estate ventures.

income should approximate $800 a month; but in some situations you might receive $600 and in other cases $1,000.

A prominent builder, Mr. Hanover Hamllits, rents to foreign dignitaries working in local legations. He receives approximately 20 percent above the going rate from this clientele. They take fine care of his properties, and as a result he has moved from selling his homes on completion to renting whenever he finds such individuals. He also finds that the rate of return on the original investment increases each year that he holds the property because he raises rents periodically and at a faster rate than the costs of maintenance and taxes rise. At the end of eight years, or sooner if the market is favorable, he sells each house.

Let us look at Mr. Hamllits' income and expenses from a federal income tax perspective to see how he computes his annual earnings (Table 14-2).

His fourth house cost him $80,000 to build in 1979. He paid $10,000 for the land and borrowed the remainder at 9 percent, making a five-year loan with principal to be paid at the end of the fifth year. It is apparent that the high interest rate in 1979 would take the major bite of expenses, amounting to $6,300 annually.

Hamllits finished the house in December 1979, and rented it to a consul-general on January 1, 1980. The going rate was $800 a month, but he obtained $960. His property tax was $800 and he expected this to increase the next year. Insurance was currently $320, but this also was due to rise. Labor costs forced him to do much of the maintenance himself, but he still spent $560. Depreciation was initially written off at 5 percent. Rent collection and other supervision would have cost him $576 a year, so he decided to handle this himself.

Table 14-2. Income and Expenses, Hamllits House No. 4 January 1 to December 31, 1980.

Income:		$11,520
Expenses:		
Interest (9%)	$6,300	
Property taxes	800	
Insurance	320	
Maintenance	560	
Depreciation	3,500	
Supervision	0	11,480
Net profit before taxes		$ 40
Federal taxes (50% bracket)		20
Net profit after taxes		$ 20

Hamllits House No. 4 reported a profit before taxes of $40. However, actual overflow of funds in relation to income presents a different picture. No payout is made for the $3,500 in depreciation: so from a funds-flow standpoint, Mr. Hamllits spent $7,980 and thus had a cash balance of $3,540. This gave him a return of over 35 percent on his $10,000 investment. (Even if he were to rent the property at $800 per month, his return would approximate 16 percent.) However, he paid only $20 in federal income tax, thanks to his depreciation write-off. Furthermore, by building a quality home, he can anticipate appreciation each year and on its eventual sale, a healthy profit.

Significant Property Considerations

There are several factors that should be studied with care in regard to property. We indicated Mr. Hamllits's concern with a funds-flow analysis. But he also made good use of leverage.

Leverage
This subject is also presented in our discussion on stocks and commodities. It results from borrowing money at a given rate of interest and using it to obtain a higher return. The leverage factor in real estate permits the investor to utilize small initial equity. Hamllits used $10,000 of his own money to buy the land and borrowed $70,000. Some people borrow 95 to 100 percent of the property cost. Mr. Hamllits obtained a 5-year loan, but it is possible to secure 25- to 30-year mortgages. A loan that can be assumed for a long period may be highly advantageous in view of the long-term inflationary trend because it permits repayment of principal in lower cost dollars. (Hamllits had a sweet deal in which he did not have to repay any of his principal until maturity.)

The significance of leverage is more pronounced on property than on securities, because of increasing realty values. Let us illustrate this advantage:

1. A $4,500 investment may obtain the use of $90,000 in property. Thus a 5 percent equity has 95 percent leverage.
2. The rent is determined by the property valuation. In this case a normal return would be $900 per month.
3. Depreciation is allowed on the total cost of the building.
4. All increases in rent and appreciation accrue to the owner.

Leverage, however, is a two-edged sword. If rents are not forthcoming and no other source of income is available, it can result in a forced sale or bankruptcy.

Diversification

The higher the leverage, the larger is the risk. This is great with a winner but can wipe you out with inadequate resources. An investment program that includes several properties in various localities reduces risk. If a person has only one rental property and it becomes vacant, there is a total loss of income. Payments on principal, upkeep, taxes, and insurance must be met from other sources. As the number of sound rentals increases, the chance of total income loss is reduced. Furthermore, each additional lease contributes to greater income for meeting expenditures. This permits flexibility in securing cash to pay fixed expenses on vacancies. In the event of a recession the buildup of equity also offers an owner greater opportunity to refinance his or her mortgages as a reduction in fixed monthly payments.

From a diversification viewpoint, there is also a distinct advantage to owning a modest four-unit apartment rather than an expensive home. The chances of all apartments in a well-situated building being unoccupied are remote, whereas a high-priced home can remain vacant for a long time unless bargain rentals are provided.

Appraisal

Before purchasing any real estate, it is essential to have an appraisal made in order to get an estimate of its current value. You can go to a professional appraiser for this purpose and obtain the view of local real estate brokers. But you should also be familiar with the factors determining property values. Points to consider include:

1. *Location.* Rentals should be looked at in regard to proximity to schools, churches, shopping, and adequate transportation. Consider the adequacy of police and fire protection, as well as the relationship to other properties in that locality. To make a valid comparison requires weighting each factor equitably. No two buildings will be exactly alike, and this is what makes a decision difficult.
2. *Condition.* Age and physical condition should be studied with care. It would be unfair to compare a poorly maintained building with well-kept property. Normally, the newer building will enjoy higher rents and lower operating costs.
3. *Allowances.* On income property allowance must be made for income lost as a result of vacancies and periodic turnover. Repairs, redecorating, and other renovation may be required before property is acceptable to new tenants. There are also losses due to occupants who may be willfully destructive or present bad checks, and cost you plenty in legal expenses

and other headaches. These losses will be reduced with experience. But it always pays to make a thorough appraisal — including an investigation of a potential lessee.

Income Sources
Properties create profits from two sources: rentals and appreciation. Income may be estimated based upon returns from comparable housing in the area, but property appreciation is more difficult. Income accrues from current monthly cash payments and reduction in principal. In contrast, a capital gain is not obtained until the unit is sold.

Depreciation is deductible yearly for federal income tax purposes. From a tax standpoint, it is considered a partial return on the basic cost of the housing. In reality, it is income, because property increases in value faster than the deterioration of the structure.[3] The fact that depreciation is tax deductible makes it especially attractive to people in higher tax brackets. On a profitable sale of property, the maximum tax is 25 percent of the capital gain.

Energy Shortage
Since the formal announcement of the energy crisis, in October 1973, it has been a new ball game in real estate. Suburban values have declined in a number of locations, and urban property has risen in price. It is imperative that any property investment be analyzed with respect to the energy shortage. A real estate authority expressed his views as follows:

The impact of a sustained energy crisis on the continuing need for new housing will inevitably bring about basic changes in the type and location of residential construction. For the ailing central cities, it could mean a revival of construction with both families and business returning to a more central location where utilities are in some cases now underutilized as a result of earlier urban erosion and where the facilities for common carrier transportation exist.

It is new housing, especially single-family units, that will experience major changes if the current energy crisis becomes a long-term fact of life.

---

[3] From a technical standpoint, depreciation cannot be considered a partial return on the basic cost of housing. If the value of the property increases and the depreciation schedule is not adjusted accordingly, the property owner is erroneously overstating his wealth.

Regional coordination of all construction, so often praised in theory, will become a necessity to balance the demand for space against the available supply of fuel, gas, and electricity. Moreover, the new housing that is built on land closer to the central city will cost more because of the increase in the cost of land.

Under these circumstances, single-family homes on individual plots may simply become impractical, since the additional cost of materials and labor would tend to price such housing out of its market. This could lead to a wide-scale revival of duplex and row housing, which was the solution to urban housing needs as early as a century ago. Indeed, the construction of townhouse condominiums in many parts of the country in recent years may well portend this trend.[4]

FIRMS SPECIALIZING IN
REAL ESTATE

The remarkable growth of companies specializing in real estate may be attributed to a recognition by astute financiers of the profit potential in this area. There have been three choices available to investors in recent years — syndicates, trusts, and companies.

Real Estate Trusts

Real estate investment trusts (REITs) began to gain popularity in the early 1960s when they were permitted to qualify as real estate investment trusts in accordance with the Internal Revenue Code. In order to qualify as business trusts, they must pay out to the shareholders annually at least 90 percent of their taxable income, thus avoiding federal income tax. This 90-percent-or-greater distribution does not include capital gains, which may be dispensed at the pleasure of the management (trustees).

The purpose of these trusts is to provide individuals with an opportunity to invest in various real estate holdings. Hubbard Real Estate Investments, for example, was formed in 1969 and invests primarily in operating properties leased to major corporations. Hubbard is listed on the New York Stock Exchange and has over 4 million shares outstanding, with diversified assets of nearly $94 million.

---

[4] Emanuel M. Brotman, chairman of the board and president of J. I. Kislak Mortgage Co., "Housing Changes to Come," the New Orleans *Times Picayune*, December 16, 1973, Sec. 3. p. 15.

Its stockholders number over 10,000. Hubbard can also distribute to shareholders funds paid out of appreciation; these are tax free.

A drawback to dealing with REITs is the sizable counseling charge involved. Hubbard's advisor receives an annual fee, based on a percentage of the trust's gross income, that has been equal to 4 percent of the gross income of the trust, reduced to the extent the advisor receives fees or additional compensation from others in connection with the sale of properties to the trust. You will have to determine for yourself if you can do a better job by direct investment in property. Considering a fee that is 4 percent of gross income (plus other costs), I believe you can beat the trusts. Another drawback to REITs is the potential sharp loss in price when property values decline in a recession and interest rates climb markedly.

In 1974 real estate investment trusts and real estate companies, experienced very hard times. A number of REITs went bankrupt. Others found the prices of their stock had declined sharply. Hubbard, for example ranged from $9\frac{1}{8}$ to $19\frac{5}{8}$, in 1974, as compared to 20 to $25\frac{1}{2}$ in 1971. Kaufman and Broad went from the $38\frac{1}{4}$–$52\frac{1}{4}$ spread in 1972 to $2\frac{1}{4}$–$14\frac{3}{4}$ in 1974.

Why the sharp decline in 1974? The high cost of borrowing money, the housing recession, and defaults by some leasees were surely contributing factors. But by April 1975, things were on the mend for a number of REITs. By April 1979, Hubbard had recovered from a low of $9\frac{1}{8}$ to $18\frac{1}{2}$ and Kaufman and Broad was selling at $9\frac{1}{8}$ — more than four times its earlier low. Availability of money and the real estate boom have been prime factors.

Real Estate Companies

A number of corporations have been organized to deal primarily in real estate. They may be listed on the various exchanges and their assets are sizable. For example, Transnation Development Corporation was formed in June 1969, with $62 million in assets.

There are many other companies that specialize in various aspects of real estate. For example, Kaufman and Broad, organized in 1965, is a large independent builder of homes in the United States. By using mass-production techniques, it has supplied homes to the large middle-income group. It now has housing developments in Chicago, Detroit, Los Angeles, New York, San Francisco, and Paris. There are also diversified companies, construction firms, and local development organizations.

From an investor's viewpoint, an investment in a real estate company normally permits excellent marketability. The company's sizable holdings also provide safety through diversification. In analyzing income and expense statements, it is essential to look at the cash flow. Transnation, for example, listed $1,927,421 in depreciation. If this amount were added to their income, before federal income taxes, it would produce an increase of 68 percent.

There is a prime distinction, from an investor's perspective, between a trust and a realty company. The former pays out its yearly income to shareholders and avoids taxes. This normally provides recipients with a favorable yield. A realty company is taxed on its income but may plow back a majority of the after-tax earnings to further growth. Therefore, its yield may be lower than that of the trust, but the potential rise in its stock price may be greater.

Real Estate Syndicates

Another approach to indirect investment in property could be through a syndicate. This medium was in vogue during the Eisenhower era. Much like the trust, it permitted the individual with limited capital to obtain an equity in real estate holdings. However, in the syndicate he or she became a limited partner in a specialized real estate project. The managers were supposedly individuals with professional real estate experience who pooled funds for investment in income-producing property. The rewards to individual investors came from high tax-free return.

The syndicate would write off depreciation rapidly, and yields might reach 10 percent in the early years. However, unsound property investments resulted in some syndicates paying low yields. There were also exorbitant fees charged by certain firms for their professional management guidance. The lack of any plan to buy back investments of limited partners and few regulatory checks further militated against this investment. The Securities and Exchange Commission had no control over the activities of these syndicates because they were exclusively intrastate operations. Syndicates had their day but are no longer popular and those in existence are relatively small.

LOW-INCOME PROPERTY

The profits are large for those renting property to low-income families. Some of the wealthiest families and institutions in America have made their fortunes by this means. Maintenance is minimal and the people living in these slums do not know how to go about making complaints. Slum landlords make money by deferring maintenance. They are in fact taking income from tenants in the form of capital accretion.

One student made a pilot study of slum ownership in New Orleans. He called it "a classic confrontation between economic self-interest and the moral code of the individual."[5] The report indicated that owners in one section included a theological seminary, a church, and some prominent citizens; but the largest single landowner was a professional slum speculator. He was prominent in civic affairs and a one-time member of the Citizens' Committee for Better Housing, from which he had been forced to resign when a fire destroyed one of his dwellings. "The Fire Department investigation found the structure was in flagrant violation of the city fire, electrical, and housing ordinances."[6]

You may wish to consider this form of investment for your portfolio. The financial rewards are high — but I believe there are some more desirable ways to make a fair return on your money, and you may sleep better with other forms of investment. Furthermore, the docility of the slum occupant is less prevalent than in years gone by. A social consciousness is awakening in America, and the risks for the slumlord are on the rise — not only because of demands for property improvement but also in the form of threats against life and limb.

TIMING IS IMPORTANT

Real estate has been a splendid investment since the depression era of the 1930s. Timing, however, is important — as it is for all investments. The following story was related to me by a successful real estate broker during a recent visit to southern Florida.

I have been buying and selling real estate in the Miami area for over fifty years. I am concerned about the present high prices. Lots that sold for $15,500 two months ago are currently priced at $17,000. A lot that I sold for $3,000 in 1968 was bought for $18,000 last week. I just sold a modest, three-bedroom, two-bath home for $58,000. It was purchased for $18,000 nine years earlier. This recalls memories of a bygone era. My father bought a four-bedroom, two-bath home on 17th Street in Miami for $25,000 in 1922. He sold it for $55,000 three years later. And then bought a comparable-sized house on North Bay Road in Miami Beach for $90,000. This was at the peak of the Florida real estate boom. The crash followed, and he tried for

[5] Taylor E. Clear, "Private Property and Public Responsibilities," unpublished term paper at LSUNO, p. 16.
[6] Ibid.

years to sell it at what he considered a fair price. Finally, in 1935, he sold it for $13,000. He then built a magnificent home on two lots on Alton Road that had five bedrooms, five-and-one-half baths, servants quarters, two-car garage, and the finest appointments — cost $49,300. Remember, this was the Depression! Dad sold that house in 1947 for $51,500. In 1964 it was sold for $33,500. Last week, it sold again for $103,000. I would caution a potential real estate investor to answer this question: "Is the price I have to pay today too high?"

ACTIONS YOU CAN TAKE TO COPE WITH INFLATION AND THE ENERGY SHORTAGE

1. Annually review your investment portfolio and determine the amount of money (on a percentage basis) that you have in real estate. After studying the current real estate market in your community, decide if you should have more or less of your funds in properties in order to better cope with inflation.

2. Compare annually the rise or fall in the value of your real estate holdings with the Consumer Price Index.

SUMMARY

There are three ways you may invest in real estate: through the purchase of raw land, of property, or of an indirect equity through trusts and companies specializing in realty ventures. After your portfolio contains cash reserves, bonds, and stocks, give serious consideration to the inclusion of real estate. But do not buy at the peak of a real estate boom.

Land investments require a substantial annual appreciation to make them profitable. If you plan to build a house or apartment, you can cut costs markedly and acquire a built-in capital gain by undertaking the construction yourself.

A prime advantage to owning property for rental purposes is the tax break in regard to depreciation. Trusts also afford the shareholder a tax advantage; however, these indirect investments cost you a middleman's fee, which should be avoided wherever feasible.

Real estate requires more patience in order to maximize profits than do other forms of investment. Time is on the side of young people, who can capitalize on this advantage.

INCOME TAX

A major barrier to acquiring a sizable fortune today is the heavy tax burden, and it is safe to assume that taxes will increase during your lifetime. The social problems facing our nation are enormous. Pollution, decay of inner cities, inadequate educational facilities, the energy shortage, and racial discrimination are only a few of the areas in which citizens are demanding that the government take action. And the solution of these problems requires a great deal of money.

Revenue to meet these needs comes primarily from a multitude of taxes. They may be included in the price of food, clothing, and other items, as is the sales tax, or raised through assessment on property. The major source of revenue, however, is the federal income tax. A number of states and some cities also levy a tax on income but take a much smaller bite of your dollar.

In view of the fact that the federal tax is the one that will be of greatest concern to you, this chapter will devote primary attention to this topic.

AVOID, NOT EVADE, TAXES

Today's heavy tax load makes it essential that you avoid taxes wherever possible. But *never* must you *evade* taxes. There is a very great

distinction between the two. You want to pay what is due and legal —
but not a penny more. Randolph W. Thrower, former commissioner
of internal revenue, made this statement in a special message to taxpayers: "It is our hope that the new [federal income tax forms]
will . . . encourage you to take full advantage of the tax benefits the
law provides."[1]

It is your after-tax dollars that count, so you should learn ways
of minimizing your payments. If you expect to attain that million-
dollar objective, or even a much lesser goal, it is mandatory to avoid
taxes wherever possible. Later in this chapter, we will list income
specifically exempt from taxation, according to the Internal Revenue
Service (IRS).

INCOME TAX BACKGROUND

Let us first look briefly at the history of the federal income tax. The
Sixteenth Amendment to the Constitution, passed in 1913, authorized the U.S. government to "lay and collect taxes on incomes, from
whatever source desired." The first permanent individual income tax
in the United States became effective on March 1, 1913. The rates
were modest initially, but today the tax is much increased. Table
15-1 shows the difference in after-tax income for a single person at
various times between 1912 and 1979.

Table 15-1.

Year	Taxable Income	Remaining after Taxes
1912	$10,000	$10,000
1915	10,000	9,930
1929	10,000	9,910
1942	10,000	8,412
1952	10,000	7,044
1962	10,000	7,360
1979	10,000	7,910

In 1913, less than 1 percent of the people of the United States
paid an income tax. The rate was graduated from 1 percent on the
first $20,000 of taxable income to 7 percent on the excess over
$500,000. Today, a single person's rate ranges from 14 percent on

---

[1] Federal income tax forms, Department of the Treasury, 1969, p. 1.

amounts between $2,301 and $3,400 to 70 percent above $108,300, and 75 percent of all income earners pay an income tax. Of the 90 million taxpayers, the majority are eligible to file on either a simple one-page form (1040A) or the first two pages of Form 1040. Over $208 billion was collected in 1979 — about $2,300 per return. The number of audits currently performed by the IRS approximates 21 per 1000 returns.

The importance of the budget process was emphasized in the third chapter. How much of your budget will be spent for taxes? It may be a larger percentage than you realize. You should, therefore, understand your income tax laws and take advantage of every tax-saving possibility.

TAX REFORM ACT OF 1976
AND TAX REVENUE ACT OF 1978

A review of income tax laws over the past 65 years indicates that changes have been frequent. And you can be sure there will be continuing modifications in the future. Therefore it is important to read with care the instructions accompanying the annual federal income tax forms. For example, in 1976, a letter from the commissioner of internal revenue pointed up major changes that occurred as a result of a 1976 law. The commissioner's letter said in part:

> The 1976 Tax Reform Act may affect your taxes substantially. An expanded and simplified credit for the elderly has replaced the old retirement income credit. A credit for child care expenses is available to all eligible taxpayers, whether or not they itemize deductions. On the other hand, the former exclusion for sick pay has been replaced by a more restrictive disability income exclusion.
>
> Completing your return this year could be more difficult. This year all taxpayers, whether or not they itemize their deductions and regardless of the size of their income, will need to compute taxable income. . . . Also, last year's simple credit for personal exemptions has been replaced by a larger, but more complex, general tax credit.[2]

---

[2] *1976 Federal Income Tax Forms,* Internal Revenue Service, Department of the Treasury, 1977, p. 1.

Six important provisions of the Tax Reform Act became effective after 1976:

1. *Capital gains and losses.* In 1977, property had to be held for more than 9 months to receive long-term capital gain or loss treatment. The holding period went to 12 months in 1978.

2. *Capital losses.* The net capital loss that may reduce ordinary income was increased from $1,000 to $2,000 in 1977 and to $3,000 in 1978.

3. *Moving Expenses.* For 1977 the minimum distance requirement for business-related moves was reduced from 50 to 35 miles. The maximum deduction for house hunting trips, temporary quarters, selling and purchasing expenses, etc., increased from $2,500 to $3,000.

4. *Sale of residence by the elderly.* The base amount to be considered in the election to exclude gain on the sale of a residence by an individual aged 65 or older increased from $20,000 to $35,000 in 1977.

5. *Alimony.* For 1977 alimony was an adjustment to gross income rather than an itemized deduction. Thus a person may claim the standard deduction in addition to deducting alimony.

6. *Dependency exemption for divorced parents.* For 1977 the rule allowing a dependency exemption to a noncustodial parent who provides $1,200 or more support for the child (or children) was changed to require $1,200 support for each child.

President Carter hoped to simplify our federal income tax forms. As part of his tax reform package he proposed to provide direct tax credits in lieu of personal exemptions. But in the Tax Revenue Act of 1978, Congress made only the following major modifications:

1. *Energy credits.* If you had certain energy saving expenditures for your residence after April 19, 1977, you might have taken a credit on your 1978 Form 1040. The credit was allowed for expenditures for items such as storm windows and insulation. Form 5695, Energy Credits, told you which expenses qualify and how to figure the credit.

2. *Capital gains.* The amount of long-term capital gain that can be excluded was increased from 50 percent to 60 percent effective November 1, 1978.

3. *Sale of personal residence.* For sales after July 26, 1978, individuals 55 and over are allowed a one-time exclusion of up to $100,000 of profit on the sale of their personal residence. This replaces the provision that allowed individuals 65 and over to exclude all of the

profit on the sale of their residence if the sale price was less than $35,000.

In addition to the modifications above in the federal income tax for *1978*, the Tax Revenue Act also made the following major changes effective for the tax year *1979:*

1. Personal exemption for each taxpayer and each dependent was increased from $750 to $1,000.

2. The general tax credit of $180 per taxpayer was eliminated.

3. Tax brackets were expanded so that taxpayers generally paid a lesser rate on similar amounts of income. For example, in 1978, a married taxpayer filing jointly and earning $19,200, was taxed at a 25 percent rate on the amount over $15,200. But in 1979 a couple filing jointly and earning $19,200 were taxed at a 24 percent rate on the amount over $16,000.

4. The standard deduction (presently called zero bracket) was increased as follows:

Filing Status	Standard Deduction	
	1978	*1979*
Married taxpayers filing jointly	$3,200	$3,400
Married taxpayers filing separately	$1,600	$1,700
Single taxpayers	$2,200	$2,300

In the meantime, it is important to be familiar with the current forms, as the basic format has remained substantially the same in recent years.

WHO MUST FILE AN INCOME TAX RETURN

Every citizen of the United States and every resident alien, adult or minor, who receives more than a specified amount of income in one year must file an individual income tax return (Form 1040A or Form 1040). Table 15-2 shows who must file a return.

The IRS mails forms and schedules, whenever practicable, to taxpayers based upon what they filed the preceding year. The IRS prepared two forms in 1979 for the submission of income tax information — Form 1040A and Form 1040.

Table 15-2. Who Must File a Return.

File a return if you are:	And your income is at least:
Single (legally separated, divorced, or married living apart from your spouse for the entire year with dependent child) and:	
You are under 65	$3,300
You are 65 or older	4,300
A person who can be claimed as a dependent on his or her parents' return, and have taxable dividends, interest, or other unearned income of $1,000 or more	1,000
Married filing jointly, living with your spouse at the end of 1979 (or at date of death of spouse), and:	
Both of you are under 65	5,400
One of you is 65 or older	6,400
Both of you are 65 or older	7,400
Married filing separately or married but not living with your spouse at the end of 1979	1,000
A person entitled to exclude income from sources within U.S. possessions	1,000
A qualifying widow(er) with dependent child and:	
You are under 65	4,400
You are 65 or older	5,400
(A qualifying widow(er) who is required to file *must* use Form 1040).	

Source: 1979 Instructions for Form 1040, IRS pamphlet, p. 4.

Form 1040A may be used if all of your income tax was from wages, salaries, tips, other employee compensation, and not more than $400 is from dividends or $400 from interest, and you do not itemize deductions.[3]

Form 1040A is not difficult to complete. You must list all wages, salaries, tips, other employee compensation, dividends, and interest income. Then total them up. You can now proceed, if you like, to take advantage of the IRS's generosity and let it figure your

[3] Each taxpayer must decide if he or she wishes to itemize deductions or not. Work out the results for itemization as against the standard deduction. If you are single and earn over $15,000, you may have a smaller taxable income if you itemize your deductions because of the $2,000 limit on the standard deduction ($3,200 for married and head of household). If you itemize deductions, it is most important that you keep detailed records. The *Internal Revenue Service will not accept approximations.* Some people find that it is possible to save by using the standard deduction one year and itemizing the next. In the year they are using the standard deduction, they wait to pay their charitable contributions, medical costs, and so on, until the first of the following year.

taxes due. Sign your return, and if appropriate, attach copy B of Form W-2.[4]

Now let us turn to the more complex Form 1040, which may include a number of attached schedules in addition to the main form. Taxpayers receive a Form 1040 package that may include not only Form 1040 — U.S. Individual Income Tax Return — but also a number of the following: Schedules A and B for itemized deductions and dividend and interest income; Schedule C, for profit (or loss) from a business or profession (sole proprietorship); Schedule D, for capital gains and losses; Schedule E and R, for supplemental-income and retirement-income credit computation; Schedule F, for income from farming; Schedule G, for income averaging; and Schedule SE, for reporting net earnings from self-employment. If you wish to correct your income tax return you should obtain Form 1040X (Amended U.S. Individual Income Tax Return). In addition, Form 1040-ES, for making estimated tax payments, is mailed separately to those who require it. If you do not receive any required form or schedule, you can obtain it from an IRS office or at many banks and post offices. Forms can also be obtained by filling out an order form provided by the IRS. Once a person is on record for paying taxes, the IRS will send him or her the necessary forms each year.

PREPARING YOUR RETURN

People tend to gripe about how difficult it is to make out a tax return, particularly after the recent revisions in the tax forms. Although some complaint is justified, I believe that most people can file their own returns. A majority of the 90 million taxpayers are eligible to use either the 1040A form or the first two pages of the standard 1040 form. If you prepare your own form from the start, it becomes relatively easy to continue doing so through the years as the task becomes more complex. Furthermore, many taxpayers can have the IRS compute their tax for them after they themselves have filled in certain information.

You can, of course, pay to have your tax returns prepared by "experts." In our community alone listings of companies offering this service take up half a page in the telephone directory. But why pay someone else to do a job which anyone with a reasonable amount

[4] Wage and Tax Statements provided by your employer. Only your employer can issue your W-2 or correct it. If you are unable to secure Form W-2 contact an Internal Revenue Service office.

of intelligence, fairly uncomplicated sources of income, and up-to-date records of income and expenditures should be able to do? Besides, no one is as familiar with your financial affairs as you are. If you should have a problem, write, call, or visit the IRS, and you will receive the answer free. This IRS service was highlighted by a recent commissioner of internal revenue, Donald C. Alexander. He said: "Call us toll free for answers to your federal tax questions. . . . To help us provide courteous responses and accurate information IRS supervisors occasionally monitor calls. No record is made of the taxpayer's name, address or Social Security number except when taxpayers request, and a follow-up telephone call must be made." Mr. Alexander also made this important point: "If you decide to have someone else help you, be sure to select a qualified person."[5]

One last tip — begin your tabulations early (in February, if possible) so that you do not get caught in a last-minute rush.

HOW TO PREPARE A RETURN — A SAMPLE CASE

Tom and Tricia Tee Tamllits were out of college just a year and believed that by working together on their income tax they could save time and money. They had been working in New Orleans since January 1978. Early in February 1979 they went to their bank to pick up the 1978 federal income tax forms.

After reading the IRS material carefully, they assembled the necessary records to complete Form 1040 and the appropriate schedules. Tom and Tricia were glad to see that the IRS provides an extra copy of each form, permitting them to make a duplicate copy of everything submitted. They tackled Form 1040 (Figure 15-1) by first filling out their names, address, Social Security numbers,[6] and occupation. Tricia and her husband decided not to designate $1 each of their taxes for the Presidential Election Campaign Fund; therefore, they checked the "No" boxes. They next checked their filing status as married filing a joint return. This entitled them to two exemptions (6a, 6b, 7).

---

[5] Source: IRS Instructions for Form 1040.

[6] If you do not have a number, file Application Form SS-5 with the local office of the Social Security Administration. If you do not receive your number prior to filing your return, enter "Applied For" in the space provided for the number.

Form **1040**	Department of the Treasury—Internal Revenue Service **U.S. Individual Income Tax Return** 19**78**	

For Privacy Act Notice, see page 3 of Instructions. | For the year January 1–December 31, 1978, or other tax year beginning _____ , 1978, ending _____ , 19 ____

Use IRS label. Other-wise, please print or type.	Your first name and initial (if joint return, also give spouse's name and initial) _Tom T. and Tricia T._ Last name _Tamllits_	Your social security number 000 ¦ 00 ¦ 000
	Present home address (Number and street, including apartment number, or rural route) _121 Richton Avenue_	Spouse's social security no. 000 ¦ 00 ¦ 000
	City, town or post office, State and ZIP code _New Orleans, La. 70122_	Your occupation

Do you want $1 to go to the Presidential Election Campaign Fund?   Yes ☐   No ✓   **Note:** Checking Yes will not increase your tax or reduce your refund.
If joint return, does your spouse want $1 to go to this fund? . .   Yes ☐   No ✓   Spouse's occupation

Filing Status
Check only one box.

1	☐	Single
2	✓	Married filing joint return (even if only one had income)
3	☐	Married filing separate return. If spouse is also filing, give spouse's social security number in the space above and enter full name here ▶ _____
4	☐	Unmarried head of household. Enter qualifying name ▶ _____ See page 6 of Instructions.
5	☐	Qualifying widow(er) with dependent child (Year spouse died ▶ 19 ____). See page 6 of Instructions.

Exemptions
Always check the box labeled Yourself. Check other boxes if they apply.

6a	✓ Yourself	☐ 65 or over	☐ Blind	} Enter number of boxes checked on 6a and b ▶ 2
b	✓ Spouse	☐ 65 or over	☐ Blind	

c First names of your dependent children who lived with you ▶ _____   Enter number of children listed ▶

d Other dependents:

(1) Name	(2) Relationship	(3) Number of months lived in your home	(4) Did dependent have income of $750 or more?	(5) Did you provide more than one-half of dependent's support?

Enter number of other dependents ▶

Add numbers entered in boxes above ▶ 2

7 Total number of exemptions claimed . . . .

Income
Please attach Copy B of your Forms W–2 here.

If you do not have a W–2, see page 5 of Instructions.

Please attach check or money order here.

8	Wages, salaries, tips, and other employee compensation	8	22,000	00
9	Interest income (If over $400, attach Schedule B)	9	2,235	00
10a	Dividends (If over $400, attach Schedule B) _____ , 10b Exclusion _____			
10c	Subtract line 10b from line 10a	10c	225	00
11	State and local income tax refunds (does not apply unless refund is for year you itemized deductions)	11		
12	Alimony received	12		
13	Business income or (loss) (attach Schedule C)	13		
14	Capital gain or (loss) (attach Schedule D)	14	188	80
15	Taxable part of capital gain distributions not reported on Schedule D (see page 9 of Instructions) . .	15		
16	Net gain or (loss) from Supplemental Schedule of Gains and Losses (attach Form 4797)	16		
17	Fully taxable pensions and annuities not reported on Schedule E	17		
18	Pensions, annuities, rents, royalties, partnerships, estates or trusts, etc. (attach Schedule E)	18		
19	Farm income or (loss) (attach Schedule F)	19		
20	Other income (state nature and source—see page 10 of Instructions) ▶ _____	20		
21	Total income. Add lines 8, 9, and 10c through 20 . . . . ▶	21	24,648	80

Adjustments to Income

22	Moving expense (attach Form 3903)	22			
23	Employee business expenses (attach Form 2106) . .	23			
24	Payments to an IRA (see page 10 of Instructions)	24			
25	Payments to a Keogh (H.R. 10) retirement plan . . .	25			
26	Interest penalty due to early withdrawal of savings	26			
27	Alimony paid (see page 10 of Instructions)	27			
28	Total adjustments. Add lines 22 through 27 . . . . ▶	28	—0—	

Adjusted Gross Income

29	Subtract line 28 from line 21	29	24,648	80
30	Disability income exclusion (attach Form 2440)	30		
31	**Adjusted gross income.** Subtract line 30 from line 29. If this line is less than $8,000, see page 2 of Instructions. If you want IRS to figure your tax, see page 4 of Instructions. . . . . ▶	31	24,648	80

☆ U.S. GOVERNMENT PRINTING OFFICE 1978—O-263-305 58-040-1110   Form 1040 (1978)

Figure 15-1. The Tamllitses' Income Tax Return for 1978 (Form 1040). Source: Internal Revenue Service, Department of the Treasury.

Tax Compu- tation	32	Amount from line 31	32	24,648	80
	33	If you do not itemize deductions, enter zero . . . .⎫ If you itemize, complete Schedule A (Form 1040) and enter the amount from Schedule A, line 41 . . . .⎬	33	—0—	
		Caution: If you have unearned income and can be claimed as a dependent on your parent's return, check here ▶ ☐ and see page 11 of the Instructions. Also see page 11 of the Instructions if: • You are married filing a *separate return and your spouse itemizes* deductions, OR • You file Form 4563, OR • You are a dual-status alien.			
	34	Subtract line 33 from line 32. Use the amount on line 34 to find your tax from the Tax Tables, or to figure your tax on Schedule TC, Part I . . . . Use Schedule TC, Part I, and the Tax Rate Schedules ONLY if: • The amount on line 34 is more than $20,000 ($40,000 if you checked Filing Status Box 2 or 5), OR • You have more exemptions than those covered in the Tax Table for your filing status, OR • You use any of these forms to figure your tax: Schedule D, Schedule G, or Form 4726. Otherwise, you MUST use the Tax Tables to find your tax.	34	24,648	80
	35	Tax. Enter tax here and check if from ☐ Tax Tables or ☐ Schedule TC	35	4,179	00
	36	Additional taxes. (See page 11 of Instructions.) Enter total and check if from ☐ Form 4970,⎫ ☐ Form 4972, ☐ Form 5544, ☐ Form 5405, or ☐ Section 72(m)(5) penalty tax . . .⎬	36		
	37	**Total.** Add lines 35 and 36 . . . . ▶	37	4,179	00
Credits	38	Credit for contributions to candidates for public office . .	38		
	39	Credit for the elderly *(attach Schedules R&RP)*	39		
	40	Credit for child and dependent care expenses (attach Form 2441) .	40		
	41	Investment credit *(attach Form 3468)*	41		
	42	Foreign tax credit *(attach Form 1116)*	42		
	43	Work Incentive (WIN) Credit *(attach Form 4874)*	43		
	44	New jobs credit *(attach Form 5884)*	44		
	45	Residential energy credits (see page 12 of Instructions, attach Form 5695)	45		
	46	**Total credits.** Add lines 38 through 45	46		
	47	**Balance.** Subtract line 46 from line 37 and enter difference (but not less than zero) . ▶	47	4,179	00
Other Taxes	48	Self-employment tax *(attach Schedule SE)*	48		
	49	Minimum tax. Check here ▶ ☐ and attach Form 4625	49		
	50	Tax from recomputing prior-year investment credit *(attach Form 4255)*	50		
	51	Social security (FICA) tax on tip income not reported to employer *(attach Form 4137)* . .	51		
	52	Uncollected employee FICA and RRTA tax on tips *(from Form W-2)*	52		
	53	Tax on an IRA *(attach Form 5329)*	53		
	54	**Total tax.** Add lines 47 through 53 . . . . ▶	54	4,179	00
Payments Attach Forms W-2, W-2G, and W-2P to front.	55	Total Federal income tax withheld	55	2,998	28
	56	1978 estimated tax payments and credit from 1977 return .	56		
	57	Earned income credit. If line 31 is under $8,000, see page 2 of Instructions. If eligible, enter child's name ▶	57		
	58	Amount paid with Form 4868	58		
	59	Excess FICA and RRTA tax withheld (two or more employers)	59		
	60	Credit for Federal tax on special fuels and oils (attach Form 4136) .	60		
	61	Regulated Investment Company credit *(attach Form 2439)*	61		
	62	**Total.** Add lines 55 through 61 . . . . ▶	62	2,998	28
Refund or Due	63	If line 62 is larger than line 54, enter amount **OVERPAID** . . . . ▶	63		
	64	Amount of line 63 to be **REFUNDED TO YOU** . . . . ▶	64		
	65	Amount of line 63 to be credited on 1979 estimated tax . ▶	65		
	66	If line 54 is larger than line 62, enter **BALANCE DUE.** Attach check or money order for full amount payable to "Internal Revenue Service." Write your social security number on check or money order . . ▶ (Check ▶ ☐ if Form 2210 (2210F) is attached. See page 14 of instructions.) ▶ $	66	1,180	72

Under penalties of perjury, I declare that I have examined this return, including accompanying schedules and statements, and to the best of my knowledge and belief, it is true, correct, and complete. Declaration of preparer (other than taxpayer) is based on all information of which preparer has any knowledge.

Please Sign Here

▶ *Tom T. Tamllits*   4/5/79   ▶ *Tricia L. Tamllits*
Your signature   Date   Spouse's signature (if filing jointly, BOTH must sign even if only one had income)

Paid Preparer's Information	Preparer's signature ▶		Preparer's social security no.	Check if self-employed ▶ ☐
	Firm's name (or yours, if self-employed), address and ZIP code ▶		E.I. No. ▶	
			Date ▶	

Figure 15-1 (continued).

Reporting Salary

The Tamllitses' first dollar figure was entered on line 8 of their Form 1040. Tom and Tricia reported an income from "Wages, salaries, tips, and other employee compensation" of $22,000. Their only sources of funds in this category were their 1978 salaries from ABC and XYZ Corporations, respectively. In view of the fact that they had been placed on their companies' payroll as of January 1, 1978, they reported their compensation for the entire year. Tom and Tricia's employers had provided them with "Wage and Tax Statements" (Form W-2) in January 1979. These indicated that Tricia and Tom had wages paid subject to withholding in 1978 for a combined total of $22,000; federal income tax withheld $2,998.28 and Social Security[7] tax withheld $1,331.00. In addition, Tom and Tricia worked in a state with its own income tax, which had also been deducted from their monthly salaries. The W-2 forms were furnished in triplicate because the originals were to be attached to Form 1040, the second copies to be used for filing state income tax returns, and the third to be retained for their own records.

Reporting Other Income

Now came the more difficult part—reporting their other income. Tom and his wife, Tricia, realized that it is obligatory to report all sources of income except those specifically exempted. Income that must be reported includes the following:

Wages, including employer supplemental unemployment benefits, salaries, bonuses, commissions, fees, and tips.

Dividends.

Earned income from sources outside the United States.

Earnings (interest) from savings and loan associations, mutual savings banks, credit unions, etc.

Interest on tax refunds.

Interest on bank deposits, bonds, notes.

Interest on U.S. Savings bonds.

Interest on arbitrage bonds issued after October 9, 1969, by state and local governments.

Profits from businesses and professions.

[7] The correct term is FICA, which stands for Federal Insurance Contributions Act.

Taxpayer's share of profits from partnerships and small business corporations.

Pensions, annuities, endowments, including lump-sum distributions.

Supplemental annuities under Railroad Retirement Act (but not regular Railroad Retirement Act benefits).

Profits from the sale or exchange of real estate, securities, or other property.

Sale of personal residence.

Rents and royalties.

Taxpayer's share of estate or trust income, including accumulation distribution from trusts.

Employer supplemental unemployment benefits.

Alimony, separate maintenance or support payments received from and deductible by a taxpayer's spouse or former spouse.

Prizes and awards (contests, raffles, etc.).

Refunds of state and local taxes (principal amounts) if they were deducted in a prior year and resulted in tax benefits.

Fees received for jury duty and precinct election-board duty.

Fees received by an executor, administrator, or director.

Embezzled or other illegal income.

Nontaxable income.

Tricia and Tom also checked with care to see what income was specifically tax exempt. Examples of income that should not be reported include:

Disability retirement payments and other benefits paid by the Veterans Administration.

Dividends on veterans' insurance.

Life insurance sums received at a person's death.

Workmen's compensation, insurance, damages, etc., for injury or sickness.

Interest on certain state and municipal bonds.

Federal Social Security benefits.

Gifts, money, or other property inherited by or willed to the taxpayer.

Insurance repayments that were more than the cost of the taxpayer's normal living expenses should he (or she) lose the use of his home because of fire or other casualty. Repayments of the amount spent by the taxpayer for normal living expenses must be reported as income.

Reporting Dividends and Interest

Only Tom was fortunate enough to have received outside income early in life. His parents had set aside IBM stock for his college education, but he had decided to live at home and attend the University of Southern California. When he graduated, his father gave him $35,000 that had not been required for his schooling. Tom had taken a course in personal finance and had proceeded to invest his nest egg in U.S. Treasury notes, quality stocks, and a cash reserve. Tricia had done it the hard way, working her way through school. She considered herself fortunate to be out of debt — she had no outside income.

The fact that Tom and Tricia had kept good records helped in posting the information on Schedule B of Form 1040 (Figure 15-2). Table 15-3 presents the format that the Tamllits used to record their dividends and interest. As you will note, Tom had stock in four corporations plus a no-load mutual fund. He correctly did not include the $10 capital gains distribution as a dividend. Therefore, he entered the figure of $325 on Form 1040, line 10a.[8] Next, on line 10b, Tom took advantage of the $100 dividend exclusion on his stock that the law authorizes.[9] Thus, on line 10c, he wrote $225. He and Tricia also decided to fill out Part II of Schedule B (Figure 15-2), although the IRS only required the submission of this part if the taxpayer received more than $400 in gross dividends.

Tom's interest income came from four sources, as recorded in Table 15-3.

1. Earnings from the QR Credit Union (5½ percent on $1,000)
2. ST Savings and Loan Association ($1,000 at 5 percent)
3. U.S. Treasury notes ($26,000 at 8 percent)
4. UV National Bank savings account ($1,000 at 5 percent)

Thus, his total interest income came to $2,235. He posted this amount on Schedule B, Part I (Figure 15-2), as well as entering $2,235 on Form 1040.

Reporting Sales or Exchange of Property

Tom reported a profit on his first round-trip stock transaction. He had bought 100 shares of WX Corporation at 18⅜ and sold it at 23⅛. The fact that it was held in his portfolio for more than one

---

[8] The Tamllits decided to round off all computations to whole dollars, which they were permitted to do in accordance with the IRS instructions. They eliminated amounts less than 50 cents and increased any amounts from 50 through 99 cents to the next higher dollar.

[9] If you file a joint return, the law allows you and your spouse to exclude up to $200. However, neither can use any part of the $100 exclusion not used by the other. Tom planned to put the stock in joint ownership so next year they could take the $200 deduction.

Name(s) as shown on Form 1040 (Do not enter name and social security number if shown on other side)	Your social security number
Tom T. and Tricia T. Tamllits	*000 00 000*

Part I Interest Income				**Part II** Dividend Income		
1 If you received more than **$400** in interest, Complete Part I. Please see page 8 of the instructions to find out what interest to report. Then answer the questions in Part III, below. If you received interest as a nominee for another, or you received or paid accrued interest on securities transferred between interest payment dates, please see page 18 of the instructions.				**3** If you received more than **$400** in gross dividends (including capital gain distributions) and other distributions on stock, complete Part II. Please see page 9 of the instructions. Write (H), (W), (J), for stock held by husband, wife, or jointly. Then answer the questions in Part III, below. If you received dividends as a nominee for another, please see page 18 of the instructions.		
Name of payer		Amount		Name of payer		Amount
QR Credit Union		*55*	*00*	*ABC Co. (H)*		*80* *00*
ST Savings & Loan Assn.		*50*	*00*	*DEF Co. (H)*		*110* *00*
8% U.S. Treasury Note		*2080*	*00*	*GHI Co. (H)*		*20* *00*
UV National Bank		*50*	*00*	*KLM Co. (H)*		*90* *00*
				NOP Fund. - Div. (H)		*15* *00*
				NOP Fund. -Cap. Gain (H)		*10* *00*
						15 *00*
						10 *00*

2 Total interest income. Enter here and on Form 1040, line 9	*2235*	*00*	**Part II total**	*335*	*00*

Part III Foreign Accounts and Foreign Trusts

If you are required to list interest in Part I or dividends in Part II, OR if you had a foreign account or were a grantor of, or a transferor to a foreign trust, you must answer both questions in Part III. Please see page 18 of the instructions.

	Yes	No
A Did you, at any time during the taxable year, have an interest in or signature or other authority over a bank, securities, or other financial account in a foreign country (see page 18 of instructions)? . . .		✓
B Were you the grantor of, or transferor to, a foreign trust during any taxable year, which foreign trust was in being during the current taxable year, whether or not you have any beneficial interest in such trust? . . If "Yes," you may be required to file Forms 3520, 3520–A, or 926.		✓

4 Total of line 3		
5 Capital gain distributions. Enter here and on Schedule D, line 7. See Note below . . .	*10* *00*	
6 Nontaxable distributions		
7 Total (add lines 5 and 6)	*–10* *00*	
8 Dividends before exclusion (subtract line 7 from line 4). Enter here and on Form 1040, line 10a	*325* *00*	

B

Note: If you received capital gain distributions and do not need Schedule D to report any other gains or losses or to compute the alternative tax, do not file that schedule. Instead, enter the taxable part of capital gain distributions on Form 1040, line 15.

☆ U.S. GOVERNMENT PRINTING OFFICE : 1978—O-263-311 58-040-1110

Figure 15-2. The Tamllitses' Dividend and Interest Income for 1978 (Schedule B, Form 1040). Source: Internal Revenue Service, Department of the Treasury.

year permitted him to report it as a long-term capital gain in Schedule D, line 6 (Figure 15-3). This meant that his tax on the profit would be 60 percent smaller than if he had held the shares one year or less.

The capital gain of $10 from his 100 shares of the NOP Fund is listed in line 6, Figure 15-3. The capital gains of such regulated investment companies are all long term, regardless of how long the recipient may have owned stock in the fund.

Tom's total net gain (line 13) amounted to $472, as indicated in Part II, Schedule D. He posted this total to Part III, lines 14, 16, 17, and 18. He then entered 60 percent of line 18 on lines 19 and 22. Next, Tom subtracted line 22 from 14 and entered the amount of $188.80 on line 14, Form 1040. Then Tom and Tricia computed their total income (line 21), which added up to $24,648.80.

Table 15-3. Worksheet Used by Tom Tamllits to Record His Yearly Dividends and Interest.

	1978 Estimate (as of 1/1/78)	1/1–3/31	4/1–6/30	7/1–9/30	10/1–12/31	Total
	Dividends Received in 1978					
Stock						
ABC Co.	$ 80.00	$20.00	$ 20.00	$20.00	$ 20.00	$ 80.00
DEF Co.	100.00	25.00	25.00	25.00	35.00	110.00
GHI Co.	40.00	10.00	10.00	10.00		30.00
KLM Co.	80.00	22.50	22.50	22.50	22.50	90.00
NOP Fund (no-load)	15.00	3.50	3.50	3.50	4.50	15.00
	$ 315.00	$81.00	$ 81.00	$81.00	$ 82.00	$ 325.00
NOP Fund (cap. gain)	$ 8.00				$ 10.00	$ 10.00
	Interest Received in 1978					
QR Credit Union	$ 48.00	$12.00	$ 12.00	$15.50	$ 15.50	$ 55.00
ST Savings & Loan Assn	50.00	12.50	12.50	12.50	12.50	50.00
8% U.S. Treasury Note	2,080.00		1,040.00		1,040.00	2,080.00
UV National Bank	50.00	12.50	12.50	12.50	12.50	50.00
	$2,228.00	$37.00	$1,077.00	$40.50	$1,080.50	$2,235.00

Capital Gains and Losses
(Examples of property to be reported on this Schedule are gains and losses on stocks, bonds, and similar investments, and gains (but not losses) on personal assets such as a home or jewelry.)
▶ Attach to Form 1040.   ▶ See Instructions for Schedule D (Form 1040.)

1978

Name(s) as shown on Form 1040	Your social security number
Tom T. and Tricia T. Tamllits	000 00 000

Part I   Short-term Capital Gains and Losses—Assets Held One Year or Less   D

a. Kind of property and description (Example, 100 shares of "Z" Co.)	b. Date acquired (Mo., day, yr.)	c. Date sold (Mo., day, yr.)	d. Gross sales price less expense of sale	e. Cost or other basis, as adjusted (see instructions page 19)	f. Gain or (loss) from all sales during entire tax year (d less e)	g. Enter gain or (loss) from sales after 10/31/78
1						

2 Enter your share of net short-term gain or (loss) from partnerships and fiduciaries **2**
3 Enter net gain or (loss), combine lines 1 and 2 . . . . **3**
4 Short-term capital loss carryover attributable to years beginning after 1969 (see Instructions page 19) . . . . **4** ( )
5 Net short-term gain or (loss), combine lines 3 and 4, column (f) **5**

Part II   Long-term Capital Gains and Losses—Assets Held More Than One Year

6						
Security—100 sk WX Corp	*Dec. 15, 1977*	*Dec. 21, 1978*	*2,350.⁰⁰*	*1,888.⁰⁰*		*426 ⁰⁰*

7 Capital gain distributions . . . . **7** | *10 ⁰⁰*
8 Enter gain, if applicable, from Form 4797, line 6(a)(1) (see Instructions page 19) **8**
9 Enter your share of net long-term gain or (loss) from partnerships and fiduciaries **9**
10 Enter your share of net long-term gain from small business corporations (Subchapter S) **10**
11 Net gain or (loss), combine lines 6 through 10 . . . . **11** | *472 ⁰⁰*
12 Long-term capital loss carryover attributable to years beginning after 1969 (see Instructions page 19) . . . . **12** ( )
13 Net long-term gain or (loss), combine lines 11 and 12, column (f) . . . . . **13** *472 ⁰⁰*

NOTE: *If you have capital loss carryovers from years beginning before 1970, do not complete Parts III, IV, or VI. See Form 4798 instead.*

Part III   Computation of Capital Gain Deduction
(Complete this part only if line 14 shows a gain)

14 Combine lines 5 and 13, column (f), and enter here. If result is zero or a loss, do not complete the rest of this part. Instead skip to Part IV, line 24 on page 2. . . . . **14**
15 Enter line 13, column (f) or line 14, whichever is smaller. If zero or a loss, enter zero and skip to line 23 . **15**
16 If line 11, column (g) is a gain, combine lines 3 and 11, column (g), and enter here. If this line or line 11, column (g) shows a loss or zero, enter a zero and skip to line 20 . . . . **16**
17 Enter line 11, column (g) or line 16, whichever is smaller **17**
18 Enter line 15 or line 17, whichever is smaller **18**
19 Enter 60% of amount on line 18 . . . . **19**
20 Subtract line 18 from line 15 . . . . **20**
21 Enter 50% of amount on line 20 . . . . **21**
22 Add line 19 and line 21. This is your capital gain deduction **22**
23 Subtract line 22 from line 14. Enter this amount on Form 1040, line 14 . . . . **23**

Figure 15-3. The Tamllitses' Capital Gains, 1978 (Schedule D, Form 1040). Source: Internal Revenue Service, Department of the Treasury.

Schedules A&B—Itemized Deductions AND
(Form 1040)
Interest and Dividend Income
Department of the Treasury
Internal Revenue Service
▶ Attach to Form 1040. ▶ See Instructions for Schedules A and B (Form 1040).

1978

Name(s) as shown on Form 1040

Tom T. and Tricia T. Tamllits

Your social security number

000 : 00 : 000

Schedule A—Itemized Deductions (Schedule B is on back)

Medical and Dental Expenses (not paid by insurance or otherwise) (See page 15 of Instructions.)

1 One-half (but not more than $150) of insurance premiums you paid for medical care. (Be sure to include in line 10 below.) . ▶	120	00
2 Medicine and drugs	39	00
3 Enter 1% of Form 1040, line 31 . . .	246	00
4 Subtract line 3 from line 2. If line 3 is more than line 2, enter zero	—0—	
5 Balance of insurance premiums for medical care not entered on line 1 . . .	120	00
6 Other medical and dental expenses:		
a Doctors, dentists, nurses, etc. . . .	161	00
b Hospitals		
c Other (itemize—include hearing aids, dentures, eyeglasses, transportation, etc.) ▶	47	00
7 Total (add lines 4 through 6c)	328	00
8 Enter 3% of Form 1040, line 31 . . .	740	00
9 Subtract line 8 from line 7. If line 8 is more than line 7, enter zero	—0—	
10 Total medical and dental expenses (add lines 1 and 9). Enter here and on line 33 . ▶	120	00

Taxes (See page 15 of Instructions.)

11 State and local income	362	00
12 Real estate		
13 State and local gasoline (see gas tax tables) .		
14 General sales (see sales tax tables) . .	324	00
15 Personal property		
16 Other (itemize) ▶		
17 Total taxes (add lines 11 through 16). Enter here and on line 34 . . . . ▶	686	00

Interest Expense (See page 16 of Instructions.)

18 a Home mortgage		
b Credit and charge cards		
19 Other (itemize) ▶		
20 Total interest expense (add lines 18a through 19). Enter here and on line 35 ▶		

Contributions (See page 17 of Instructions.)

21 a Cash contributions for which you have receipts, cancelled checks or other written evidence	700	00
b Other cash contributions (show who you gave to and how much you gave) ▶		
22 Other than cash (see page 17 of instructions for required statement)		
23 Carryover from prior years		
24 Total contributions (add lines 21a through 23). Enter here and on line 36 . . ▶	700	00

Casualty or Theft Loss(es) (See page 17 of Instructions.)

25 Loss before insurance reimbursement .		
26 Insurance reimbursement		
27 Subtract line 26 from line 25. If line 26 is more than line 25, enter zero . . .		
28 Enter $100 or amount on line 27, whichever is smaller		
29 Total casualty or theft loss(es) (subtract line 28 from line 27). Enter here and on line 37 . ▶		

Miscellaneous Deductions (See page 17 of Instructions.)

30 Union dues		
31 Other (itemize) ▶		
32 Total miscellaneous deductions (add lines 30 and 31). Enter here and on line 38 ▶		

Summary of Itemized Deductions
(See page 18 of Instructions.)

A

33 Total medical and dental—from line 10 .	120	00
34 Total taxes—from line 17	686	00
35 Total interest—from line 20		
36 Total contributions—from line 24 . . .	700	00
37 Total casualty or theft loss(es)—from line 29 .		
38 Total miscellaneous—from line 32 . .		
39 Total deductions (add lines 33 through 38) ▶	1,506	00
40 If you checked Form 1040, Filing Status box: 2 or 5, enter $3,200 1 or 4, enter $2,200 3, enter $1,600	3200	00
41 Subtract line 40 from line 39. Enter here and on Form 1040, line 33. (If line 40 is more than line 39, enter zero and see "You Must Itemize Deductions" on page 11 of the Instructions.) . . . . . ▶		

Figure 15-4 The Tamllitses' Itemized Deductions, 1978 (Schedule A, Form 1040). Source: Internal Revenue Service, Department of the Treasury.

267

Itemizing Deductions

Tricia and Tom knew that their itemized deductions would not equal the standard $3,200 deduction.[10] They had some subtractions but could not take advantage of the two areas that provided the largest potential: interest on home mortgage payments and taxes on real estate. Since they had no car, there were no deductions for gasoline taxes or interest paid on an auto loan. However, they considered it good practice to fill out the appropriate form, for eventually it could mean a sizable saving.

Their computations on itemized expenses were listed in Schedule A (Figure 15-4). The total figure amounted to $1,506 (line 39, Schedule A), in contrast to the $3,200 standard deduction (line 40).

Computing Taxes Due

The Tamllits were now ready to determine the sum due the U.S. government. They used the Tax Computation section of Form 1040 to determine their taxes. First they listed their adjusted gross income from line 31, Form 1040. Then they turned to Tax Table B (Married Taxpayers Filing Joint Returns and Qualifying Widows and Widowers). Their tax came to $4,179.00 which they entered on lines 35, 37, 47, and 54. Their federal income tax for the year 1978 amounted to 17 percent of their gross income. From this $4,179.00 they deducted the amount withheld by their employer (line 55). They found that their balance due was $1,180.72; this payment was required by April 16, 1979.[11] Tricia and Tom had one more form to complete.

DETERMINING ESTIMATED TAX

Tom and his wife learned from the instructions on the tax form that they must file a "Declaration of Estimated Tax for Individuals" (Form 1040-ES). The purpose of this filing was to ensure their paying taxes on income other than their salary, on which the taxes were

[10] In 1977, the term *zero bracket amounts* replaced the standard deduction. The 1978 tax tables and tax rate schedules do not tax the first $3,200 of income, if you are married filing a joint return or qualifying widow(er); the first $2,200 of income, if you are single or unmarried head of household; or the first $1,600 of income, if you are married filing separately.

[11] Payment is normally due by April 15, but if this date falls on a holiday or weekend, it can provide an extra day or two for payment. In 1979 April 15 was on a Sunday.

withheld by their employer. This declaration, they read, is required of every citizen of the United States[12] if the total estimated tax is $100 or more and the person:

1. Can reasonably expect to receive more than $500 from sources other than wages subject to withholding; or,
2. Can reasonably expect gross income to exceed–
    a. $20,000 for a single individual, a head of household, or a qualifying widow or widower;
    b. $20,000 for a married individual entitled to file a joint declaration with spouse, but only if the spouse has not received wages for the taxable year;
    c. $10,000 for a married individual entitled to file a joint declaration with his spouse, but only if both spouses received wages for the taxable year; or,
    d. $5,000 for a married individual not entitled to file a joint declaration with his spouse.

Tom and Tricia first filled out the estimated-tax worksheet (Figure 15-5). Tricia's employer had given her a $1,000 raise; so their combined salary would be $23,000 in 1979. They expected their additional investments in 1979 to increase their other income by $100. After taking their exemptions, they listed their estimated taxable income as $23,560.00. Next they found their tax due ($4,213.80). The Tamllits then checked their records to find the amount their employers would be withholding ($3,332.00).

Tom and Tricia knew that they must file their estimated-tax declaration on or before April 16, 1979. Their estimated tax could be paid in full with the declaration or in equal installments on or before April 16, 1979, June 15, 1979, September 17, 1979, and January 15, 1980. They decided to pay their estimated tax quarterly. "Why not keep our money working by drawing interest or dividends instead of paying in advance? We'll wait until the due date in each instance." The couple make their check for $220.45 payable to Internal Revenue Service and posted the amount on Voucher 1, Form 1040-ES, (Figure 15-5). They made sure their first installment was in the mail by April 16, 1979, as they realized that there is a penalty for failure to make estimated payments on time.

Tom and Tricia had now completed their federal tax returns. They agreed that it had not been as difficult as they had anticipated

---

[12] Also every resident of the United States, Puerto Rico, Virgin Islands, Guam, and American Samoa.

1979 Estimated Tax Worksheet (Keep for your records—Do Not File)

1 Enter amount of Adjusted Gross Income you expect in 1979 . . . . $\underline{25,560.^{00}}$

2 a If you plan to itemize deductions, enter the estimated total of your deductions. If you do not plan to itemize deductions, skip to line 2c and enter zero . . . .

    b Enter { $3,400 if married filing a joint return (or qualifying widow(er)) . . . . } { $2,300 if single (or head of household) . . . . } { $1,700 if married filing a separate return . . . . }

    c Subtract line 2b from line 2a (if zero or less, enter zero) . . . . $\underline{-0-}$

3 Subtract line 2c from line 1 . . . . $\underline{25,560.^{00}}$

4 Exemptions (multiply $1,000 times number of personal exemptions) . . . . $\underline{2,000.^{00}}$

5 Subtract line 4 from line 3 . . . . $\underline{23,560.^{00}}$

6 **Tax.** (Figure tax on the amount on line 5 by using Tax Rate Schedule X, Y or Z in the instructions) . . . . $\underline{4,213.80}$

7 Enter any additional taxes from instruction C . . . . $\underline{-0-}$

8 Add lines 6 and 7 . . . . $\underline{4,213.80}$

9 Credits (credit for the elderly, credit for child care expenses, investment credit, residential energy credit, etc.) .

10 Subtract line 9 from line 8 . . . . $\underline{4,213.80}$

11 Tax from recomputing a prior year investment credit and work incentive (WIN) credit . . . . $\underline{-0-}$

12 Estimate of 1979 self-employment income $.... .... ; if $22,900 or more, enter $1,854.90, if less, multiply the amount by .081 (see instruction C for additional information) . . . . $\underline{-0-}$

13 Tax on premature distributions from an IRA . . . . $\underline{-0-}$

14 Add lines 10 through 13 . . . . $\underline{4,213.80}$

15 (a) Earned income credit (see instruction C) . . . .

    (b) Estimated income tax withheld and to be withheld during 1979 . . . .

    (c) Credit for Federal tax on special fuels and oils (see Form 4136) . . . .

    (d) Refundable business energy credit (see Schedule B (Form 3468)) . . . . . .

16 Total (add lines 15(a), (b), (c) and (d)) . . . . $\underline{3,332.^{00}}$

17 Estimated tax (subtract line 16 from line 14). If $100 or more, fill out and file the declaration-voucher, if less, no declaration is required at this time . . . . $\underline{881.80}$

18 If the first declaration-voucher you are required to file is: { Number 1, due April 16, 1979, enter ¼ . . . } { Number 2, due June 15, 1979, enter ⅓ . . } { Number 3, due September 17, 1979, enter ½ . . } { Number 4, due January 15, 1980, enter amount . } of line 17 here and on line 1 of your declaration-voucher(s) . . . $\underline{220.45}$

Page 2

Tear-off here

- -

Form 1040-ES
Department of the Treasury
Internal Revenue Service

1979 Declaration-Voucher

A. Estimated tax for the year ending _12-79_ (month and year)

B. Overpayment from last year credited to estimated tax for this year

Number 1

(Calendar year—Due April 16, 1979)

$ _____ $ _____

Return this form with check or money order payable to the Internal Revenue Service.

1 Amount from line 18 on worksheet . ▶ $ _220.45_

2 Amount of overpayment credit from last year (all or part) to be applied . . ▶   _-0-_

3 Amount of this payment (subtract line 2 from line 1) . . . . . . ▶ $ _220.45_

File this form even if line 3 is zero.

Sign here ▶ _Tom T. Tamllits_
Your signature

Tricia T. Tamllits
Spouse's signature (if joint declaration)

Please type or print

Your social security number: _000-00-000_   Spouse's number, if joint declaration

First name and middle initial (of both spouses if joint declaration): _Tom T. and Tricia T._   Last name: _Tamllits_

Address (Number and street): _121 Richton Avenue_

City, State, and ZIP code: _New Orleans, La. 70122_

Figure 15-5. The Tamllitses' 1979 Estimated Tax Worksheet and Declaration-Voucher 1 (Form 1040-ES). Source: Internal Revenue Service, Department of the Treasury.

but realized that they had been greatly aided by their good record keeping. They vowed to keep their records up to date in order to help them file as rapidly next year.

STATE AND LOCAL INCOME TAX

Each state independently determines the tax load it will place on its residents. Some states have no state income tax at all while others impose a heavy burden on the wealthy. State taxes, like federal taxes, are progressive — that is, the higher your salary the larger the tax. Table 15-4 gives the rate charged a single person in Louisiana in 1979 based on net income.

Table 5-4. Louisiana State Tax Rate for Single Person.

Income	Rate
First $10,000	2%
Over $10,000 to $40,000	4%
Over $50,000	6%

In addition to the state tax, some taxpayers must also pay an income tax to their municipalities. Or perhaps the state may not have an income tax but the community might. This is the case in Ohio, where communities like Athens levy an income tax. Athens imposes an income tax of 1 percent on all salaries, wages, commissions, and other compensation earned or accrued each year. This tax applied to all residents of the city and nonresidents who received income from organizations in Athens. The purpose of the Athens tax was to provide funds for general municipal operations; maintenance of equipment; new equipment; extension, enlargement, and improvement of municipal services and facilities; and capital improvements.

New York is one state where taxpayers residing in certain cities must pay both state and local income taxes.

ACTIONS YOU CAN TAKE TO COPE WITH INFLATION
AND THE ENERGY SHORTAGE

1. Prepare your own income tax returns whenever it is feasible. Use the free services of the Internal Revenue Service when you need assistance.

2. Take advantage of energy tax credits when they are available and work to your benefit.

3. Avoid taxes. Consider actions like purchasing highest-quality municipals and using depreciations to your advantage in any real estate investments. Also, examine capital-gain possibilities and time the selling of your home to maximize profits after taxes.

SUMMARY

Prepare your own income tax returns whenever feasible. If you keep good records, this should be a relatively easy task. You can pay to have your income tax done by an "expert," but this can be self-defeating. No one knows your financial affairs as well as you do. The time spent in reading over the yearly federal income tax material can be most helpful. If you have trouble, write, call, or visit an IRS office. Begin your work early — in February, if possible — so you are not caught in a last-minute rush.

Work out the results from itemizing your deductions as against the standard deduction. If you itemize deductions, it is most important that you keep detailed records. The Internal Revenue Service will not accept approximations. Some people find that it is possible to save by using the standard deduction one year and itemizing the next. In the year they are using the standard deduction, they wait to pay their charitable contributions, medical costs, and so on, until the first of the following year.

When your income exceeds $15,000, you should begin seeking out long-term capital gains, since the money received from this source is taxed at a maximum rate of 28 percent. As you move into the higher tax brackets, take advantage of tax-exempt investments.

Read with care the information furnished each year with your federal income tax forms. Some modifications are made annually, either in the format or in specific provisions that affect the amount of payment due.

RETIREMENT, WILLS, AND TRUSTS

Before discussing retirement, wills, and trusts, let us see how these topics fit into your overall financial picture. Effective estate planning and determination of the financial aspects of retirement are much easier if you have included them from the beginning as two aspects of a sound personal finance program. In the first chapter (Figure 1-2), retirement and estate planning, along with taxes, was mentioned as one of 16 topics to be considered in the development of a successful financial portfolio. The other areas are financial health, a spending program, housing, an insurance program, and a wide variety of investments. In each instance, the managerial functions of planning, organizing, and controlling serve to assist you in arriving at sound financial decisions.

The subjects of retirement, wills, and trusts are presented in the concluding chapter of this book because they wrap up the entire package in regard to personal finance matters.

If you follow the approach I have put forth, you will probably achieve financial health at an early date. Then you would build up an investment program that contains cash reserves, bonds, stock, and perhaps other ventures such as real estate.

Concurrently, you would satisfy your insurance and housing

requirements, and over the years make every effort to minimize tax payments in accordance with existing state and federal laws.

During all this time you would be maintaining orderly financial records, including those involved in a long-range financial-health program such as that illustrated in Chapter 3. In these computations are your yearly net worth as well as the value of your estate — material you would find to be most helpful in your retirement and estate planning. And the utilization of management functions comes in handy in readying your affairs.

The planning aspect, in particular, is the essential ingredient in successfully passing on your worldly possessions in the manner you desire. You may not achieve immortality — at least in the flesh — but you can, to a degree, make your financial influence felt by your descendants. Thus, effective financial management requires your efforts while alive in order to make an impact in the future. Likewise, sound planning is essential if you are to make the correct decisions with respect to retirement.

RETIREMENT

Retirement may be defined as withdrawal from the active work force, normally owing to advancing years. The decision to retire should involve many factors. However, the scope of this book is limited to money management; therefore, in this chapter we shall discuss the financial aspects of retirement only.

In plans for your retirement, an important consideration should be: "Will I have sufficient yearly income to support my family once I stop working?" This question can be answered readily if you have given adequate attention to this matter in the development and maintenance of your lifetime personal finance program. Another look at Chapter 1 (Figure 1-2) indicates that retirement should be included in viewing the total responsibility of a successful money manager. As pointed out in Chapter 2, the ideal time to begin planning the financial aspects of your retirement is prior to accepting your initial job. From the first you should plan when you wish to retire and whether the company for whom you decide to work has a pension program that corresponds to your desires.

Income From Pensions

Retirement may be 40 to 45 years away for today's college graduate. However, some organizations provide pensions after 20 years. For example, the army has a program that could give a newly commissioned second lieutenant the promise of retirement at age 41, assuming that she (or he) entered the service upon graduation. Her pension would be 50 percent of her base pay. If she remained another ten years, the pension would rise to 75 percent. As pointed out in Chapter 2, a colonel retiring today after 30 years of service would receive $24,000 a year.

In contrast to the military, there are firms that require people to remain at work until 55 or 60 prior to receiving payments, and maximum benefits may not accrue until age 65 or 70. Payments may vary markedly from 10 to 80 percent of an employee's salary in the year prior to retirement. Factors that may be considered in determining the dollar amount include length of service, age, and average annual pay. Other things being equal, the higher the salary, the higher the retirement payment. One successful corporation published the following payments for its key executives:

Position	Current Annual Salary	Estimated Retirement Benefits
Chief executive officer	$120,000	$46,600
Executive vice-president	80,000	27,000
Group vice-president	65,000	20,000
Vice-president	59,000	12,000
Vice-president	50,000	10,000

The estimated benefits are based on mandatory retirement upon the sixty-fifth birthday. This would enable these officials to be immediately eligible for the maximum Social Security payments.

If you retire in your forties or fifties, you have the problem of not receiving Social Security until age 62.[1] Social Security, as you recall from Chapter 9, has an inflation-proof system — that is, the payments increase to recipients in consonance with a rise in the consumer price index (CPI).

A number of corporate and government pensions are also coordinated with the CPI, and in the years ahead it can be expected that many more pensions will be. Furthermore, the amount of the pension (combined with Social Security) should provide an adequate standard of living in some cases.

Rising inflation has been the primary impetus for the increasing demand for annual raises in retirement benefits. The move from a 2.3

[1] The Social Security payments are 20 percent less if taken at age 62 than the full benefits would be if one waited until age 65.

percent inflation rate in the 1960s to recent double-digit figures caused considerable hardship for many people on fixed incomes.

Mandatory Retirement

Many Americans now have the choice of deciding whether they wish to continue working until age 70 or retire earlier. President Carter, in 1978, signed into law the necessary legislation extending mandatory retirement to 70 with an effective date of January 1, 1979. There were some exceptions. For example, the law does not apply to tenured professors until July 1, 1982.

The impact of this new legislation on the nation will not be known for some time. But for the individual, it means another choice as to when is the appropriate time to retire — 50, 60, 65, 67, 70? Keep in mind that Social Security will pay higher benefits if you keep working until age 70, and by 1982 will pay those higher benefits whether or not you continue working after that age (see Chapter 9).

The five-year extension is an important option. As a business manager responsible for your financial affairs, it is desirable for you to examine the pros and cons in working beyond 65. By taking this approach, as it relates to your particular case, you can make a sound decision. My observation: People who like their work are normally happier remaining on the job for as long as their health permits.

Other Retirement Income

In addition to certain pensions, and all Social Security payments, there are other sources of income capable of keeping pace with rising costs. These sources include good real estate, profitable hobbies, quality common stock, and homeownership. The importance of acquiring growth investments during your working years has been pointed up in previous chapters. However, your preretirement portfolio should also include prime-quality fixed-income holdings, such as U.S. Treasury notes and bank savings accounts. In the event of a depression or major recession, these investments would continue paying their annual return, and the principal would remain intact. In contrast, the growth holdings may decline markedly and income therefrom shrink drastically.

Another advantage to building up substantial savings while you work is that you may be forced to retire prior to the time you anticipated. A TV program pointed out that the decision as to date of retirement may not rest with the employee.[2] Mike Wallace presented the case of a man who desired to retire at 65. However, his corporation decided to provide his pension five years earlier. The result: He had anticipated an $800-a-month check but received only $125. His stock savings program paid him $10,000, in lieu of the approximate $75,000 he had expected at 65. The lack of Social Security payments and low income forced him to enter the job market, and his age precluded finding a position. His unemployment compensation, meager pension, and minimal savings made life very difficult from a financial standpoint.

Cases such as this can be expected to occur in the future. Some companies retire people early in order to survive financially. Others have no pension program. A number of workers encounter health problems and are forced to quit before they are entitled to receive retirement benefits. Such situations point up the importance of having a sound personal finance program that offers a variety of protective measures, including adequate insurance (health, accident, life), appropriate savings accounts, and growth investments.

Determining Financial Aspects of Retirement

In order to determine whether you are in adequate financial position to retire, you can utilize the budgetary process presented in Chapter 3. First, prepare a balance sheet in a format similar to Table 16-1. Next, make up an income-and-expense statement (Table 16-2). In my opinion, the time to prepare this detailed information is five years prior to your earliest planned retirement date. This will give you adequate time to be ready financially for the new challenges facing the retiree. If these statistical data are set down in detail much earlier, there may be too many unforeseen changes in your retirement plans to make it a worthwhile venture.

Once the two statements have been prepared, you can proceed to analyze them. Table 16-1 points out that "I" should be in satisfactory shape financially on retirement. I have $150,200 in worldly possessions and only $20,000 in debts. Thus, my true worth amounts to $130,200. A review of estimated income and expenses in the first year of retirement (Table 16-2) indicates that savings of $300 are anticipated. I have been generous in my estimate of expenses and allowed for a 7 percent annual rate of inflation in the five-year period

[2] CBS-TV, "60 Minutes," with Mike Wallace and Morley Safer, March 24, 1974.

Table 16-1. Where I Will Stand at Retirement — December 31, 1985 (Age 55).

My worldly possessions:		
Cash on hand	$ 200	
Cash in checking account	2,000	
Cash in bank	10,000	
Cash in S&L association	10,000	
U.S. Treasury note	30,000	
Corporate stocks:		
Shares, ABC Co.	6,000	
Shares, DEF Co.	7,000	
Shares, GHI Co.	8,000	
Shares, JKL Co.	9,000	
Shares PQR Co.	10,000	
Car	3,000	
Furniture	10,000	
Clothing	5,000	
Home	40,000	
		$150,200
My debts:		
Notes payable	$ 5,000	
Car payments	1,000	
Furniture payments	2,000	
Home mortgage	12,000	
		20,000
My true worth		$130,200

prior to retirement. My budgeted expenses provide for my youngest son to enter the state university in 1985. Cost projections indicate that $4,000 should be adequate for the freshman year as my son can be expected to provide another $3,000 from summer employment and part-time work during the school year.

The pension that "I" will receive is from a major corporation that has an excellent funded program. It is also protected by a sound insurance policy, and payments will rise in accordance with the CPI. Both my growth and fixed-income securities are of prime quality. Accordingly, my yearly income can be depended upon unless a major disaster occurs.

Once "I" have determined that I will have sufficient financial resources to meet retirement expenses the first year, I can proceed to develop my long-range retirement plan (Table 16-3) — the third step in the budget process. Let us look at how I went about it. I decided to play it safe and go beyond the normal life expectancy for myself and my wife. My primary concern was whether sufficient funds would be available for us to maintain an adequate living standard for the next 25 years. An analysis of Table 16-3 indicates that not only

Table 16-2. My Estimated Income and Expenses in First Year of Retirement—January 1–December, 31, 1985.

Income:		
Pension	$10,000	
Social Security		
Veterans Administration benefits	600	
Earnings (part-time work)	1,000	
Annuity	600	
Interest	2,400	
Dividends	1,800	
Profitable hobby	500	
Real estate	2,400	
Total income, 1st year retirement		$19,300
Expenses:		
Home	$ 4,000	
Food	3,000	
Car	1,000	
College expenses	4,000	
Clothing	800	
Vacation and recreation	1,000	
Medical	1,200	
Taxes	4,000	
Total expenses, 1st year retirement		19,000
Savings		$ 300

can I meet all expenses each year from estimated income, but through 2010 my net worth will increase. Thus, the estate for my heirs and for charity will rise each passing year. Likewise, if I and/or my wife live well beyond 2010 we should have no financial problems.

ACTIONS YOU CAN TAKE TO COPE WITH INFLATION AND THE ENERGY SHORTAGE—RETIREMENT

1. Do your retirement planning well in advance of retirement. Ideally, it should begin prior to selecting your first job. Of utmost importance—decide if your retirement income will meet your basic needs.

2. Once you are retired, it is essential that you budget with care and take into account the impact of inflation and the energy shortage.

3. Develop skills so that you can do minor repairs yourself. Consider part-time work (see Chapter 2).

4. Make your money work hard for you by investing it wisely in highest-return savings (see Chapters 11 and 12) and by investing in growth-potential areas (see Chapters 13 and 14).

Table 16-3. My Long-Range Financial Retirement Program (as of December 31, Each Year).

	1st Year (55)	2nd Year (56)	5th Year (60)	10th Year (65)	15th Year (70)	20th Year (75)	25th Year (80)
My worldly possessions:							
Cash on hand	$ 200	$ 200	$ 200	$ 200	$ 200	$ 200	$ 200
Cash in checking account	2,000	2,000	2,000	2,000	2,000	2,000	2,000
Cash in bank	10,000	10,000	10,000	10,000	10,000	10,000	10,000
Cash in S&L association	10,000	10,000	10,000	10,000	10,000	10,000	10,000
U.S. Treasury notes	30,000	30,000	30,000	30,000	30,000	30,000	30,000
Corporate stocks:							
Shares, ABC Co.	6,000	6,300	7,296	9,306	11,880	15,162	19,320
Shares, DEF Co.	7,000	7,350	8,512	10,851	13,860	17,689	22,540
Shares, GHI Co.	8,000	8,400	9,728	12,408	15,840	20,202	25,760
Shares, JKL Co.	9,000	9,450	10,944	13,959	17,820	22,743	28,980
Shares, PQR Co.	10,000	10,500	12,160	15,510	19,800	25,270	32,200
Shares, STU Co.							8,853
Car	3,000	3,000	3,000	3,000	3,000	3,000	3,000
Furniture	10,000	10,000	10,000	10,000	10,000	10,000	10,000
Clothing	5,000	5,000	5,000	5,000	5,000	5,000	5,000
Home	40,000	40,000	40,000	40,000	40,000	40,000	40,000
Total	$150,200	$152,200	$158,840	$172,234	$189,400	$211,266	$247,853
My debts:							
Notes payable	5,000	5,000	5,000	5,000	—	—	—
Car payments	1,000	700	700	700	—	—	—
Furniture payments	2,000	2,000	2,000	2,000	—	—	—
Home mortgage	12,000	12,000	12,000	12,000	10,760	1,397	—
Total	$ 20,000	$ 19,700	$ 19,700	$ 19,700	$ 10,760	$ 1,397	$ —
My true worth	$130,200	$132,500	$139,140	$152,534	$178,640	$209,869	$247,853

My estate:							
Insurance	$ 30,000	$ 30,000	$ 30,000	$ 30,000	$ 30,000	$ 30,000	$ 30,000
Total estate	$160,200	$162,500	$169,140	$182,534	$208,640	$239,869	$277,853
My income:							
Pensions	$ 10,000	$ 10,500	$ 12,160	$ 15,510	$ 19,800	$ 25,270	$ 32,200
Social Security	—	—	—	8,000	9,728	12,408	15,840
Veterans Administration benefits	600	630	730	931	1,188	1,516	1,932
Earnings (part-time work)	1,000	1,000	1,000	1,000	1,000	1,000	1,000
Annuity	600	600	600	600	600	600	600
Interest	2,400	2,400	2,400	2,400	2,400	2,400	2,400
Dividends	1,800	1,890	2,189	2,792	3,564	4,549	5,796
Profitable hobby	500	500	500	500	500	500	500
Real estate	2,400	2,400	2,400	2,400	2,400	2,400	2,400
Total	$ 19,300	$ 19,920	$ 21,979	$ 34,133	$ 41,180	$ 50,643	$ 62,668
My expenses:							
Home	4,000	4,200	4,864	6,204	7,920	10,108	12,880
Food	3,000	3,150	3,648	4,653	5,940	7,581	9,660
Car	1,000	1,050	1,216	1,551	1,980	2,527	3,220
College expenses	4,000	4,200	4,864				
Clothing	800	840	973	1,241	1,584	2,022	2,576
Vacation and recreation	1,000	1,050	1,216	1,551	1,980	2,527	3,220
Medical	1,200	1,260	1,459	1,861	2,376	3,032	3,864
Taxes	4,000	4,186	4,059	8,132	10,037	12,596	15,810
Total	$ 19,000	$ 19,936	$ 22,299	$ 25,193	$ 31,817	$ 40,393	$ 51,230
My savings	$ 300	$ -16	$ -920	$ 8,940	$ 9,363	$ 10,250	$ 11,438

5. If items are too expensive, don't purchase them. If enough buyers follow this approach, prices will drop. It is a basic law of supply and demand.

6. Walk more and ride less. It is better for your health, conserves energy, and saves money.

SUMMARY: RETIREMENT

Financial aspects of retirement should be considered initially when you develop your lifetime personal finance program which ideally should begin upon graduation from college. At that time thought should be given to when you desire to retire and if the company you select has a pension program that corresponds with your wishes. It can be anticipated that in the next 30 years, a number of corporate pension programs will be inflation-proof. This may permit some persons the opportunity to coordinate their retirement with Social Security and thus to have a livable retirement income. However, for the majority, it will be necessary to develop a sound investment program early in life. This could provide the additional income needed at retirement, as well as a healthy estate.

Five years prior to anticipated retirement, it is helpful to determine from a financial viewpoint, precisely what you expect to receive when you retire. This requires preparing a balance sheet, a statement of income and expenses, and a long-range plan. These statements should be revised annually. Such information can be most useful in arriving at answers to the questions: Will I have sufficient income to support my family once I stop working? Will the annual income continue to be sufficient until our departure from this world?

WILLS AND TRUSTS

Dying is an unpleasant thing to think about. It may seem a million years away to the college student, but come it must. Life expectancy today averages 70 years for males and 78 for females. However, car accidents alone caused over 50,000 fatalities in 1978, and the Vietnam war killed almost 49,000 Americans

The preceding chapters have discussed means of accumulating worldly possessions, and many of you will work hard to achieve this goal; but no one has found a way to take it with him. There are, however, means of specifying how you would like your wealth distributed after your death. A number of people fail to take advantage of them, and these people not only make lawyers rich but place an unnecessary financial and mental burden on their families.

This section of the chapter will discuss wills, trusts—including living trusts—and other preparations in regard to your estate. In order for your assets to be distributed after your departure in accordance with your wishes, appropriate estate planning is required. Wills and trusts are vehicles for achieving this distribution.

WILLS

A lawyer recently told me, "I have been involved in wills for 22 years but can't get around to making my own will. Like many others, I keep thinking all men are mortal with one exception."

This refusal to contemplate death often hinders otherwise rational people from undertaking this important responsibility of making a will and doing appropriate estate planning. It is an ideal area for procrastination because there are no deadlines to meet— maybe. You may also take the attitude of a feisty financier—"Hell, let them squabble over it!" Squabble they must because the various states have no provisions for the efficient transfer of property from the deceased to their heirs. Thus, there are several valid reasons for drawing up your will.

Your worldly possessions, regardless of size, represent a lifetime of work; and most of us have a pretty good idea of whom we would like to enjoy the fruits of our efforts. A will is a legal document that stipulates the way in which your worldly possessions will be distributed when you die. Each state has established its own laws with respect to what standards a will must meet. You may make a will at age 18, disposing of your real and personal property. Unfortunately, the laws of the state may not be in agreement with the decedent's wishes if he or she has not expressed them in writing. If there is no will, the property must pass to the heirs in accordance with state formulas. These vary markedly from state to state. And since each state is jealous of its right to taxes on a deceased person's estate, you should also be clear as to the location of your domicile, so your fortune is not involved in a long court action concerning where you have truly established a residence.

Also, if you leave no will, the administration of your estate will be subject to frequent examination by the courts. This is a costly venture, paid for by the estate, which, in the case of a small one, can be virtually destroyed by it. There are lawyers' fees, court expenses, executors' fees, administrators' charges, and other costs, most of which can be reduced through preparation of a will. And the provisions of the will can also produce sizable tax savings. I wish to emphasize for married couples the importance of both *husband* and *wife* having separate wills. Wives also die; if they have not left wills, their heirs face the same legal problems described above.

Will Format

An example of a will and its format are presented in Figure 16-1. This will would be appropriate where there is no heir to be considered except the wife and when the estate is to be divided according to law if the wife dies first. This format is a sample only and should not be utilized without consulting an attorney.

Note that the will specifies who is to receive the testator's[3] property. In this case, it is Mrs. Lamllits who receives "all the property . . . of whatever nature, real, personal or mixed to be hers absolutely and in fee simple."[4]

The will also provides that "just debts and funeral expenses be paid." It is good to keep in mind that burial costs can be unduly high. Remember, do not let emotions dominate your thinking if you have the responsibility for funeral arrangements. Some people are specific in their wills as to the type of casket and other arrangements they desire, and may even state approximate costs, to provide a good idea of the expenses involved.

The will should also name an executor[5] or executors. If it does not, the court will make the selection. It could appoint an individual, a bank, or a trust company. In the example, Mrs. Lamllits was appointed the executrix, with explicit authority "to sell at private or public sale, at such price as she shall consider proper, the whole or any part of my real or personal estate, or both, and to execute good and sufficient deeds and other instruments necessary or proper to convey and transfer the same to the purchaser or purchasers thereof. . . ."

Mr. Lamllits could also have made a provision in his will for money to be left to charity, to institutions such as universities, or to other individuals. Instead of leaving all his possessions outright, the testator can leave some or all in trust, in which case he would

---

[3] The person who has made the will. A *testatrix* is a female testator.

[4] *Fee simple* is giving the ownership of the property with unrestricted rights to dispose of it.

[5] Someone designated to carry out the provisions of a will. An *executrix* is a female executor.

LAST WILL AND TESTAMENT
OF
LARCO LABERTO LAMLLITS

Know all men by these presents that I, Larco Laberto Lamllits, a legal resident of the state of Michigan, being of full legal age and sound and disposing mind and memory, do hereby make, publish, and declare this instrument as my last Will and Testament.

1. I hereby revoke all wills or parts of wills heretofore made by me.

2. I direct that my just debts and funeral expenses be paid.

3. I give, devise, and bequeath to my wife, Lora Lazellia Lamllits and her heirs, all the property of which I may die possessed, of whatsoever nature, real, personal or mixed to be hers absolutely and in fee simple.

4. I hereby appoint my wife, Lora Lazellia Lamllits, as my Executrix, and I direct that she be permitted to serve without bond and that no proceedings be had with reference to my estate except such as may be legally essential.

5. I authorize and empower my Executrix, if and whenever in the settlement of my estate she shall deem such action advisable, to sell at private or public sale, at such price as she shall consider proper, the whole or any part of my real or personal estate, or both, and to execute good and sufficient deeds and other instruments necessary or proper to convey and transfer the same to the purchaser or purchasers thereof, and such purchaser or purchasers shall not be bound to see to the application of the purchase money.

In testimony whereof, witness my hand at Pine Lake, Michigan, this First day of January, 1978.

Signature of Testator

The foregoing instrument was signed, published and declared by the testator therein named, Larco Laberto Lamllits, as and for his Last Will and Testament, in our presence, and we, in his presence, and in the presence of each other, and at his request, have hereunto subscribed our names as attesting witnesses at Pine Lake, Michigan, this First day of January, 1978.

Signature of Witnesses   Address   Phone

Figure 16-1. Last Will and Testament of Larco Lamllits.

designate a company or individual to perform this function. Trusts will be discussed later.

No mention was made of life insurance in the sample will. This is correct, because insurance proceeds are usually paid directly to the person designated as beneficiary in the policy, either in a lump sum or over a period of time. This saves both administrative and tax expenses. If the benefits from an insurance policy are payable to an estate, the funds become part of the net worth, to be distributed with the other possessions in the will.

The format lists three witnesses, but some states require only two. It is desirable to have youthful persons as witnesses; they are more likely to be around at the time the will is probated. Changes in their addresses should be kept readily available with other important documents.

If Mr. Lamllits later desired to make a minor change in his will, he would make a *codicil* — an addition or alteration. It could explain current provisions or add new ones. In the event that important changes are necessary, it is better to write a new will.

Although the Lamllits will provided no unusual provisions, some people do include interesting stipulations. Heinrich Heine, the German poet, left a will giving his property to his wife on one condition — that she remarry. "Because," he stated in his will, "then there will be at least one man to regret my death."[6] John D. Morgan bequeathed $2 million to his two daughters but required that a test be made to determine if they "understand the principles of sound investments."[7]

Availability of Documents

In addition to your will, there are other papers and documents that should be available to your survivors. Some of the following may be essential in order for them to obtain the benefits to which they are entitled:

1. Birth certificate for yourself and each dependent in your family
2. Marriage certificate
3. Social Security number
4. Titles, deeds, and mortgage documents on your home, car, and other property
5. Insurance policies — health, life, accident, property, and others
6. Appropriate proof of military service
7. Financial records, including a list of company benefits

The best place to keep a will and other important documents is in your safe-deposit vault with copies given to your attorney. And *most important*, inform your spouse, attorney or some other responsible person where these documents are located.

[6] Robert S. Menchin, *The Last Caprice* (New York: Simon & Schuster, Inc., 1963), p. 71.
[7] Ibid., p. 71.

Executor/Administrator

In your will you may name a trust company or bank, instead of an individual, as your executor. Upon your death the bank would have the will admitted to probate, collect and inventory all assets, pay the debts, manage the property, submit a final account to the court, and effect the distribution.

Of course, a bank does not always have a personal interest in conserving your money, and some may give limited care to maximizing assets. Also remember that there is a cost involved. The charge for this executor function, in one state, is 2½ percent of the value of the inventory.[8]

You may reduce this fee in your estate by naming your wife, as Lamllits did, or a relative or friend to perform this function. You may also exempt your executor from posting a surety bond, which will otherwise be required.

If you die without a will, or if the executor you have named is unwilling to act, a bank may be named administrator by the probate court upon the request of one of the relatives or beneficiaries. The duties and functions are the same as for an executor.

TRUSTS

The Living Trust

Once you have acquired a sizable nest egg, you may wish to consider an area that has received increased attention in recent years. It is referred to as the *living trust* and is created during a person's lifetime, in contrast to the *testamentary trust*, which is created by one's will and becomes operative only after death. The living trust is designed to provide investment income to a person during his or her lifetime and then offer an economical means of passing property on to those who are to receive it ultimately. Under a living trust a bank or trust company assumes the administrative functions, and the owner may retain any amount of control over the investments that he or she desires.

A living trust may be either revocable or irrevocable; it is up to you to make the decision. The irrevocable trust is committed irrevocably and offers income and estate tax advantages. The drawback is that once you have made the commitment, you cannot, of your own will, recover the trust property. The revocable trust leaves you with the latitude to change or cancel it if you so desire.

---

[8] Established by Article 3351 of the Louisiana Code of Civil Procedure.

287

You may wish to establish a living trust for either your own or another's benefit. After you have acquired property, it may take too much of your time to manage it. The constant record keeping, estimating of taxes, and other responsibilities can be shifted to a trustee. By means of a living trust, you can receive current benefits and also provide appropriate protection for your beneficiaries after death. A prime advantage of the revocable living trust is that you have a first-hand opportunity to observe the trustee. You should obtain a good idea of the trustee's investment management talents, and if he or she does not perform to your satisfaction, you should seek a replacement promptly.

Let us assume you acquire a financial fortune early in life. Thanks to your dear old grandmother and a good job, you accumulate $100,000 by age 29. Your work keeps you traveling, and you do not have time to give this money appropriate attention. Accordingly, you decide to establish a revocable living trust, making yourself the beneficiary. As an eligible bachelor with no serious intentions, you decide to make your widowed mother, age 52, the recipient of this trust in case of your demise. You also specify that your younger sister, age 18, should be the beneficiary on the passing of your mother. The trust would have to be terminated at a set date in the future, with the principal distributed in accordance with your wishes. In your trust agreement you may direct the trustee to manage your securities for you — invest principal, reinvest capital gains and income, and provide protection and custody of the securities. The trustee would take care of such duties as cashing in matured bonds, exercising stock rights, collecting income, and completing purchases and sales of bonds, stocks, and money-market instruments.

The beauty of this living trust is that it gives you the freedom to make any changes in the trust agreement at any time you desire — and even to revoke it.

Testamentary Trust

In addition to the living trust, there is the normal trust arrangement for after death. A trustee is appointed in a will to manage assets for the decedent's family or others. This is the testamentary trust and may involve the bank or trust company in many of the same functions performed for the living trust. It could also involve such trust services as probating the will, collecting and safeguarding assets, settling debts, and minimizing taxes.

Table 16-4. Selected Annual Charges for Trust Management.

Principal Charge	
First $300,000	$5.00 per $1,000
Next $700,000	$2.00 per $1,000
Over $1,000,000	$1.00 per $1,000
Income Charge	
5% of the first $25,000	
3% above $25,000	

Costs of Trust Management

Annual charges for trust management vary, and it is a good idea to shop around among banks and trust organizations. A check with four institutions found the average charges listed in Table 16-4.

Guardian/Conservator

Another function a bank or trust company may perform is to act as guardian for the estate of a minor or the conservator of the estate of a person adjudged to be mentally or physically incompetent. The bank's duty is to manage, under court supervision, the person's property as it would under any trust agreement.

The success of such an arrangement is dependent, as in other trust functions, upon the quality of the trustee. I know of a bank that put the bulk of a man's estate assets into real estate. The property was a bad investment, and income to the widow and her young son stopped. Only through court action was the bank forced to return money to the estate.

The fee for such administration may be a percentage of income received, and in such a case there may be an incentive to earn higher yields with possible risk to principal.

When there are minor children, it is important to designate a guardian in one's will. This permits the parent to select the person to act in this capacity in the event the parents die together.

Insurance Trust

Insurance trusts are created by life insurance policies payable to a designated trustee. Upon the death of the owner the policies form the bulk of the trust, to which other assets may be added. Life insurance trusts are a popular estate-planning device today. This type of trust has the advantage of concentrating an estate and managing its principal with discretion when life insurance forms a large part of the total assets. Insurance trusts escape probate costs and federal estate taxes, and, like trusts and wills, are an essential element in estate planning. In order for insurance policies to escape estate taxes, the insured must have no control over the policy.

In addition to the annual charges listed in Table 16-4, these institutions charged the following fees for services rendered in the initial probate of an estate:

3% of the first $500,000
2% of the next $2,000,000
1½% of the balance
Minimum fee $2,000

All of the banks pointed out that additional charges would be made for such items as complex tax settlements, large real estate holdings, and prolonged legal battles.

It is apparent that the larger the estate, the smaller the overall percentage of charges for its probate work and administration. Of course, management costs should be only one factor in arriving at your decision; most important is that the firm has acquired a good reputation over many years of successful trustee management.

PROBATE COSTS

The estate must pay the costs of probate[9] and this can be a sizable figure. For example, one Ohio court lists several attorney's fees as follows:

1. Four percent on all probate property. This is based upon total valuation of all probate property, without distinction as to real or personal property.
2. Two percent on decedent's interest in all nonprobate assets listed either in Ohio inheritance and/or the federal estate tax petitions.
3. Minimum fee for legal services rendered the fiduciary in the administration of an estate is $200.[10]

There has been discussion in recent years about avoiding probate. Stocks held jointly with right of survivorship, irrevocable living

[9] *Probate*, as defined in *Webster's New World Dictionary*, is "the action or process of proving before a competent judicial authority that a will and testament of a deceased person is genuine."

[10] Probate Court, Athens County, Ohio.

trusts, and insurance are means of escaping probate costs. Norman F. Dacey wrote a popular book on the subject, *How to Avoid Probate*,[11] whose publication brought sharp criticism from lawyers. The book raises interesting issues and I recommend it for your reading.

In 1973 Wisconsin became the first state to pass a do-it-yourself probate law. Since its passage many Wisconsin residents have done their own probate work at considerable savings in money and time. At present 11 states have adopted the Uniform Probate Code which makes it easier for individuals with no legal background to probate estates. However, in complex probate situations, it normally pays to consult a first-rate attorney who specializes in such matters.

A dentist I know returned from St. Louis the other day and told his friends about the problems he had encountered in settling the small estate of his father. He said, "Dad did not place his only piece of property in joint ownership, and as a result, it will have to be probated at an estimated cost of $800." The dentist also reported that it took his entire two-week vacation to run down the records — they were scattered throughout his father's house, office, and even the garage. In spite of all his efforts, there were still essential items missing. He summed it up by saying, "I sure intend to put my affairs in order and to avoid probate wherever possible."

ESTATE TAXES

I have indicated that some probate costs can be avoided. However, in computation of the taxes due Uncle Sam, all your property must be listed, including such items as life insurance policies; real estate; gifts in contemplation of death; mortgages, notes, and property in joint ownership; cash; stocks and bonds; annuities, and revocable trusts.

This gross amount may be reduced by the cost of burial, lawyers' fees, debts, mortgages and liens, losses during administration, and most important, a marital deduction.

The Tax Reform Act of 1976 made important changes in regard to estate taxes beginning in 1977. The smaller estates benefited from the new law with some larger estates paying more taxes. The previous law allowed half of an estate to go to the surviving spouse tax free. The 1976 act exempts the greater of $250,000 or 50 percent of the decedent's adjusted gross estate. The filing requirement for estates of decedents who are United States residents and citizens was modified, as in Table 16-5.

[11] New York: Crown Publishers, Inc., 1965.

Table 16-5. Estate Taxes.

Year of Death	Maximum Gross Estate Exempt from Taxes[a]
1978	$134,000
1979	147,000
1980	161,000
1981 or later	175,000

[a]These amounts are reduced by taxable gifts made after 1976, the amount allowed under the specific exemption for gifts made after September 6, 1976, and certain other lifetime transfers.

Other changes related to gifts, orphan's exclusion, certain valuation of real property, farms or closely held businesses, generation-skipping transfers, IRA and Keogh plans, and carryover basis of property.

Let us now turn to the importance of the marital deduction. Assume that a couple reaches the million-dollar objective discussed in Chapter 3. Table 16-6 shows how the federal estate tax would be computed if the husband, in 1977, left his widow half of his adjusted gross estate.

Table 16-7 shows the tax if the marital deduction is not used.

By using this deduction, the husband saved $169,000. And the dollar benefits increased with the size of the estate. However, the marital deduction may not be the best decision in every case. Keep in mind that the *excluded interest must be included in the estate of the surviving spouse* if she retains ownership until her death. The IRS puts it well:

> The desire to save taxes by maximum use of the marital deduction may conflict with particular needs in a given situation. For example, a widower remarrying might want to provide for his second wife's support and maintenance after his death but at the same time be certain that ultimately the property would go to his children and grandchildren. He could not assure himself of this second goal and still qualify the property for the marital deduction. The potential loss to his children could outweigh the tax benefit derived from the marital deduction.[12]

[12] *Tax Coordinator*, Internal Revenue Service, Department of the Treasury, March 10, 1977, p. 46, 306.

Table 16-6. Tax on the Estate of Husband With Marital Deduction.

Gross estate	$1,000,000	
Less: Burial, claims, legal costs,		
other debts and expenses	50,000	
Adjusted gross estate		$950,000
Maximum marital deduction	475,000	
University bequest	200,000	675,000
Taxable estate		$275,000
Estate tax before credits		$ 79,300
Unified credit (1977)[a]		30,000
Federal estate tax		$ 49,300

[a]By 1981 this will increase to $47,000.

In addition to the federal government, your state can be expected to take a piece of your fortune. However, it will be a much smaller portion than the amount taken by the U.S. government. The state may impose an estate or an inheritance tax. The latter is a tax levied on the property received by the beneficiary.

It is important to remember that the federal estate tax is *not* an inheritance tax that individual states may impose. The federal tax is imposed upon the transfer of the *entire* taxable estate and not upon the share received by a particular beneficiary.

The better your financial records are kept, the easier it will be for someone you designate to prepare the federal estate tax return upon your death. And this will reduce costs and speed up payment to your beneficiary.

Table 16-7. The Estate of Husband without Marital Deduction.

Gross estate	$1,000,000	
Less: Burial, claims, legal costs,		
other debts and expenses	50,000	
Adjusted gross estate		$950,000
University bequest	200,000	200,000
Taxable estate		$750,000
Estate tax before credits		$248,300
Unified credit (1977)[a]		30,000
Federal estate tax		$218,300

[a]By 1981 this will increase to $47,000.

1. Prepare a will and keep it up to date. Check in particular to see that your bequests meet the future needs of your family, based upon your inflation projections.

2. Keep death costs to a minimum by obtaining information on all funeral expenses and, in your will or a letter of instructions, specifying your wishes.

SUMMARY: WILLS AND TRUSTS

Chapter 1 recommended taking a managerial approach to personal finance, and one function of management—planning—has been emphasized throughout this book. In regard to your own will or testamentary trust, this planning must be at its best. After all, you probably will not be coming back to check on its validity.

I would suggest the following points for consideration:

1. Make a will early in life. If you die without one, your property will be divided according to the law of your state, and this may not be in your best interest.

2. Use an able lawyer to draw up your will. If you do not, it is possible that the necessary legal requirements will not be met, and the will could be invalidated.

3. Update your will as circumstances change in order to meet your current wishes.

4. If you decide on going for the million-dollar objective, or some other goal you deem appropriate, you should give its distribution serious thought. In addition to providing for your family, you can do much good with your money through contributions to worthy causes. Perhaps your own college may be in need of assistance.

5. Provide for flexibility in your will and trust arrangements. Be sure to select a competent lawyer for your legal matters, and if you go the trust route, select a company with a distinguished record. Over the years, institutions have failed and beautifully drawn trusts gone for naught because of inefficient estate management.

6. The purpose of estate planning is to see that the maximum amount of your assets will be transferred from you to the individuals and/or organizations you desire as recipients. This can best be accomplished by letting as

few people as possible get a cut of the estate melon. Keep your administrative costs within reason, and exploit every tax-savings aspect.

In conclusion and in summary, manage your personal finances so that they are a source of enjoyment in life and a source of benefit when you are gone.

INDEX

home purchase or rental and, 141
income tax and, 271, 272
insurance policies and, 159, 181
personal care and, 102
real estate and, 250
retirement and, 166, 275–76, 279, 282
stocks and, 236
Ingersoll, Robert C., 238
Insurance, 168–82
automobile, 118, 169–76
boat owner's, 178
comprehensive personal-liability, 178
farm owner's, 179
flood, 177–78
health and accident, 179–80
homeowner's, 176–77
inflation and, 181
life (*see* Life insurance)
Medicare, 180–81
personal-property, 178–79
Insurance trusts, 289–90
Inter-American Development Bank, 210
Interest:
insurance company, 149
loan, 52–55, 57, 59, 60–63, 119, 132, 135
mortgage, 240–41
reporting, 262–63, 264
savings account, 184, 187–89
U.S. government securities, 205–8
Internal Revenue Service, 258, 292
International Bank for Reconstruction and Development (World Bank), 209
Investment literature, 225–26
Itemizing deductions, 267, 268

Job opportunities, 16–32
earnings, factors influencing, 18–24
energy shortage and, 31
future, 28–31
inflation and, 31
information sources, 24–26
management approach, 17–18
two-career families, 26–27
Jolliffe, Norman, 101
Journals, professional, 25
Joy of Cooking (Rombauer and Becker), 87
"Jumping-junior" policy, 151

Kaufman and Broad, 247
Keogh plans, 158
Klein, Martin, 99–100

Lahey Clinic, Boston, 98
Land, 239–41
Lease-secured bonds, 211

Leverage, 243–44
Lewis, Sinclair, 127
Liabilities, 36–37
Librarians, 88
License fees, automobile, 116
Life Financial, 146
Life insurance, 144–45, 159
amount of, 144–45
borrowing from, 55–58
credit, 60, 145, 146
group, 145, 152–53
industrial, 145, 146
inflation and, 159
ordinary, 145–52
variable, 153–55
Life-insurance companies:
annuities, 155–57
life insurance (*see* Life insurance)
pension plans, 157–58
Life Insurance Fact Book, 146
Life Rates and Data Reports, 146
Limited-tax bonds, 211
Living trusts, 287–88
Loan Agreement, 57, 58
Loans (*see* Borrowing)
Loan sharks, 61
Local bonds, 210–11
Local income tax, 271
Long-range plan, 39–42
Low-Calorie Diet, The (Small), 87
Low-income property, 248–49

Maintenance of automobiles, 118, 120–21
Management approach (*see* Personal-finance management)
Mandatory retirement, 276
Marital deduction, 292–93
Marital status:
living accommodations and, 128
Social Security benefits and, 162
Marketable securities, 205–6, 208
Mayo Clinic, Minnesota, 98
Meat group, 77
Medical coverage, 171
Medicare, 180–81
Mental condition, 11
Merchant Marine, 210
Merrill Lynch, Pierce, Fenner, & Smith, 223
Milk group, 77
Mobile homes, 138–39
Modified Life 5-10 Policy, 148
Money flow chart, 16–17
Money market, 195–99
Monthly income and expenses statement, 41, 46
Moody's Investor Service, 211
Mortgages, 210, 243